W9-DJA-367

Collective Autonomy

A HISTORY OF
THE COUNCIL OF
ONTARIO UNIVERSITIES
1962–2000

Collective Autonomy

A HISTORY OF
THE COUNCIL OF
ONTARIO UNIVERSITIES
1962–2000

by Edward J. Monahan

Wilfrid Laurier University Press

This book has been published with the help of a grant from the Canadian Federation for the Humanities and Social Sciences, through the Aid to Scholarly Publications Programme, using funds provided by the Social Sciences and Humanities Research Council of Canada. We acknowledge the financial support of the Government of Canada through the Book Publishing Industry Development Program for our publishing activities. We acknowledge the Government of Ontario through the Ontario Media Development Corporation's Ontario Book Initiative.

National Library of Canada Cataloguing in Publication Data

Monahan, Edward J. (Edward Joseph), 1928–
    Collective autonomy : a history of the Council of Ontario Universities, 1962–2000 / by Edward J. Monahan.

Includes bibliographical references and index.
ISBN 0-88920-443-8

    1. Council of Ontario Universities—History. I. Title.

LB2301.M58 2004   378'.006'0713   C2004-902695-X

Cover design by Leslie Macredie. Text design by P. J. Woodland.

Printed in Canada

Contents

 Preface

AFTER A FORTY-YEAR PROFESSIONAL career in the university world, first as an academic professing the discipline of philosophy and then as a university administrator, the leisure afforded by retirement has provided me with an opportunity to write the history of an association with which I was involved for half of my professional career and for about half of the association's lifetime to date.

The Council of Ontario Universities (COU) is a voluntary association that represents the publicly funded universities of Ontario. Established in 1962 as the Committee of Presidents of the Universities of Ontario (CPOU), it has been (and continues to be) a major player on the Ontario university scene and beyond in Canada. My involvement began in 1971, when I served for a year as the executive assistant to John Deutsch, principal of Queen's University. Dr. Deutsch was a principal architect of the Ontario university system and at that time was serving as a member of the Wright Commission on Post-secondary Education in Ontario. My involvement continued during my six-year tenure as president of Laurentian University of Sudbury, when I served as a member of council representing that institution. In 1977, I accepted the position of executive director of COU and served in that capacity for almost fifteen years, until retirement in 1991.

This history, the first full-length account of COU to be written, is intended to supplement the growing body of literature on the history of higher education in Canada. An "insider's" account, it offers a picture of the activities on an association that, while seldom achieving a high profile, has acted continuously and quietly to serve the interests of the university community in this province and beyond. Other publications, including the growing number of excellent institutional histories, provide broader accounts of the development of higher education in a province or the country, comparative studies of universities in different provincial or national jurisdictions, analyses of public policy issues involving Canadian universities, or more detailed accounts of the history of particular universities. This history fills a niche. It tells the story of an independent agency, one created by the universities themselves, whose mission is to serve as the voice of the collectivity of Ontario's public universities in speaking both to government, which funds and regulates these essential institutions on behalf of society, and to the broader community in whose interests the universities are committed to act.

My research has been made possible through the generous co-operation of COU staff. Dr. Ian Clark, the current president of COU, graciously approved access to council archives; senior members of the secretariat staff, many of them my former colleagues, have provided additional valuable information and comments. My predecessor as executive director, Dr. John B. Macdonald, and Edward Desrosiers, who served as the council's director of research during my term of office, both of whom read an earlier draft, have provided many helpful comments and suggestions. Inaccuracies and imperfections that remain are my responsibility. As a former player, I do not claim to be a disinterested observer; and I accept that some of my analysis and conclusions are open to challenge. I have endeavoured, however, to provide a balanced, even-handed account.

This book has been published with the help of a grant from the Canadian Federation for the Humanities and Social Sciences, through its Aid to Scholarly Publications Programme, using funds provided by the Social Sciences and Humanities Research Council of Canada. I am pleased to record my gratitude for this assistance. And finally I express my thanks to Dr. Brian Henderson, the director of Wilfrid Laurier University Press, and his staff, who with grace, good humour, and quiet competence have successfully led an aging academic through the prolix process of having a monograph published.

Edward J. Monahan

Abbreviations

AAC	Academic Advisory Committee
AAU	Association of Atlantic Universities
ACAATO	Association of Colleges of Applied Arts and Technologies of Ontario
ACUA	Advisory Committee on University Affairs
ACAP	Advisory Committee on Academic Planning
APEO	Association of Professional Engineers of Ontario
AUCC	Association of Universities and Colleges of Canada
BILD	Board for Industrial Leadership and Development
BIU	Basic Income Unit
BOI	Basic Operating Income
CAAT	College of Applied Arts and Technologies
CAUT	Canadian Association of University Teachers
CFI	Canadian Foundation for Innovation
CHST	Canada Health and Social Transfer
CIAU	Canadian Interuniversity Athletic Union
CMEC	Council of Ministers of Education, Canada
CODE	Council of Ontario Deans of Engineering
CODOC	an automated cataloguing system for government documents
COFM	Council of Ontario Faculties of Medicine
COFO-UO	Committee of Finance Officers, Universities of Ontario
COU	Council of Ontario Universities
CPP	Canada Pension Plan
CPUO	Committee of Presidents of the Universities of Ontario
CREPUQ	Le Conférence des recteurs et des principaux des universités du Québec
CSAO	Council of Senior Academic Officers
CUA	Committee on University Affairs
CUCC	College–University Consortium Council
CUPA	Council on University Planning and Analysis

CUSS   Co-operative Union Serial System
EPF   Established Programmes Funding
EQAO   Education Quality and Accountability Office
ETV   educational television
FIGPLAN   Financial Implications of Graduate Planning
FTE   full-time equivalent
GNP   gross national product
ICLRP   income contingency loan repayment plan
IDEA   Innovative Development for Employment Advancement Corporation
MAPS   union library list of maps
MCU   Ministry of Colleges and Universities
MEDICAT   a library cataloguing system for medicine-related topics
METANET   a communications network
MPP   Member of Provincial Parliament
MRC   Medical Research Council of Canada
NABST   National Advisory Board on Science and Technology
NCCUC   National Conference of Canadian Universities and Colleges
NDP   New Democratic Party
NSERC   Natural Sciences and Engineering Research Council of Canada
OACS   Ontario Advanced Courses
OCAV   Ontario Council of Academic Vice-Presidents
OCGS   Ontario Council on Graduate Studies
OCUHS   Ontario Council of University Health Sciences
OCUA   Ontario Council on University Affairs
OCUFA   Ontario Confederation of University Faculty Associations
OCUL   Ontario Council of University Librarians
OCUR   Ontario Council on University Research
OFS   Ontario Federation of Students
OGS   Ontario Graduate Fellowship Program
OHIP   Ontario Health Insurance Plan
OISE   Ontario Institute for Studies in Education
OLC   Office of Library Co-ordination
OPAS   Office for Partnerships for Advanced Skills
ORDCF   Ontario Research and Development Challenge Fund
OSAP   Ontario Student Assistance Program
OSIS   Ontario Schools: Intermediate and Senior
OUAA   Ontario Universities' Athletic Association
OUAC   Ontario Universities' Application Centre
OUBCP   Ontario Universities' Bibliographic Centre Project
OUS   Ontario Union of Students

OWIAA	Ontario Women's Intercollegiate Athletic Association
PAM	Public Affairs Management
PC	Progressive Conservative
PLA	prior learning assessment
RAR	Resource Allocation Review
SERP	Secondary Education Review Project
SSHD	Secondary School Honours Diploma
SSHRC	Social Sciences and Humanities Research Council of Canada
TVO	TV Ontario
UI	Unemployment Insurance
UGC	University Grants Committee
UNICAT/ TELECAT	A central, computer-based cataloguing support system
URIF	University Research Incentive Fund
U of T	University of Toronto
UWO	University of Western Ontario

 Introduction

The voluntary association of Ontario universities that was to become the Council of Ontario Universities (COU) had its beginnings in 1962, when its predecessor, the Committee of Presidents of the Universities of Ontario (CPUO), was formed. Its members are the provincially assisted, i.e., the publicly funded, universities in the province. Its mandate is to promote co-operation among these universities, and between them and the Government of Ontario, and, generally, to work for the improvement of higher education in the province. The council itself was established in 1971. During the almost four decades of its existence, the association has been the main voice for the universities in Ontario and a major player in the development and maintenance of the provincial university system. No history of higher education in Ontario would be complete or even adequate without its inclusion.

This is a record of the association through which Ontario universities as a collectivity sought to influence the development of the province's system while at the same time preserving their institutional autonomy. It is a record of the determined and largely successful efforts of these universities to protect university autonomy, rightly regarded by each as an important bulwark of academic freedom and of the academic values that are protected by this freedom. It is also a record of the strengths and weaknesses of system planning based largely on co-operation and co-ordination among the universities themselves and led by a voluntary association of member institutions.

Today, Ontario universities enjoy a justifiably high reputation for academic excellence in research and teaching. At the same time, the province enjoys one of the highest university participation rates in the world. To these accomplishments, the Council of Ontario Universities has been a major contributor. COU, of course, was not the only force acting in support of these basic academic values. University governing bodies, faculty associations, student groups (at both the institutional

Notes to Introduction are on p. 213

1

and provincial levels), support staff, and other groups, and many individuals both within and outside the university community, including the government, have also contributed their share.

This account traces the evolution of Ontario universities from ivory towers to public utilities, to use the apt expression of J. A. (Alex) Corry, principal of Queen's University and second chair of CPOU. The title of this book, *Collective Autonomy*, employs the term that the association itself chose to describe its activities in support of institutional well-being and co-operative system planning. This account might be considered as a proxy for a history of Ontario universities during the period. In fact, it is not, although most of the issues, events, and controversies recorded here would form an essential part of such a history. This account is both more and less than a history of Ontario's institutions of higher learning. It is rather more because it focuses on the universities as they have acted as members of a collectivity. It is much less because it ignores the distinctiveness of the individual institutions and the essential part each has played in contributing to the strength of the province's contemporary system of higher education. A better shorthand description might be that it is an extended essay in university–government relations as they have evolved in one provincial jurisdiction in Canada. But again, although such relations constitute a major component of such a history, this account is more than that. It is a record of the activities of a voluntary association of autonomous universities in its efforts to serve both its member institutions and the well-being of Ontario's higher education system, a record that relates the association's strengths and weaknesses, its victories and failures.

During nearly four decades covered by this history, Ontario universities (like their counterparts everywhere) have undergone many changes. Although remaining universities in the traditional meaning of the term—institutions of higher learning dedicated to research and teaching—they were not the same institutions in the year 2000 that they had been some forty years earlier. At the turn of the twenty-first century, Ontario universities are much larger than they were forty years ago. The student body is much less homogeneous. Their academic programs, curricula and methods of instruction are much different. Terms and conditions of appointment are much improved, at least for full-time, permanent members of academic staff. Now, however, a clearer academic hierarchy exists. At the top are the academic "stars," with high salaries, substantial research support, and light teaching loads; at the bottom is an academic underclass of low-paid sessional appointees on short-term contracts who bear much of the burden of undergraduate teaching. New forms of institutional management and governance are in place. Important as these matters are for the future, they are not the focus of this history. It focuses on the changes in Ontario universities resulting from the advent of large-scale public funding in the early 1960s and the consequent impact on university–government relations.

What is noteworthy in Ontario is the limited degree (comparatively speaking) to which the government of the province has become involved directly in university affairs, a benefit to the universities for which the Council of Ontario Universities deserves considerable credit. For the greater part of the period recorded here, government has been willing to provide substantial funding to the universities while leaving them largely free. Since the 1960s, higher education was considered to be a public good, one deserving of generous financial support. In the mid-'90s, however, a sea change occurred. A new government was elected, pledged to a "common sense revolution" predicated on neo-conservative principles that emphasized lower taxes, reduced public spending, and the value of the individual. This government considered higher education to be primarily a private good. And in keeping with this political philosophy, it moved away from a publicly *supported* university system to a publicly *assisted* one. As a consequence, university funding was drastically reduced, while planning was left almost entirely in the hands of the individual institutions, which were encouraged to compete with one another. This new environment caused a significant change in role for COU, the results of which it is still too early to assess.

Except for the University of Toronto, established in 1842 as the "provincial" university, in law Ontario universities were established as and remain private institutions. Established independently of one another, each has its own charter granted by the government under which it possesses the power to offer academic programs and to award degrees. Under these charters, each institution has its own governing body, which holds property, receives funds, appoints staff, and is responsible for the overall well-being of the institution. In addition to its governing body, each has an academic senate (or equivalent counterpart) responsible for its academic activities. Since the early 1960s, Ontario universities have received a large proportion of their revenues in the form of grants from the public purse. In recent years, in particular since the election in 1995 of the Harris government committed to a "common sense revolution," provincial government support for Ontario universities has significantly declined. As a consequence, the universities have again become heavily dependent on revenues from the private sector through a combination of student fees and private donations. Revenue from student fees now represents about the same proportion of the operating revenues of Ontario universities that it did in the late 1950s, before the beginning of large-scale public funding. In the period covered here, however, Ontario universities have been the beneficiaries of large amounts of public funds coming mainly from the provincial government.

As recipients of large amounts of public funds for capital and operating purposes, like all publicly funded institutions, Ontario universities have become increasingly subject to government legislation and regulation. Still, as private, self-governing institutions, they enjoy a high degree of autonomy. Today, they continue to possess a greater degree of autonomy than do most universities that receive a large proportion of their revenues from the public purse. Ontario universities have always been fiercely protective of their autonomy, and the association they formed has always considered the defence of university autonomy to be one of its major responsibilities. The dominant theme that runs through this record—sometimes reaching a crescendo, at other times almost pianissimo but always playing continuously in the background—is the ongoing tension between university autonomy and public accountability. The three principal players are CPOU, later COU; the government; and, for most of the period, the intermediary advisory body, the Committee on University Affairs (CUA), later the Ontario Council on University Affairs (OCUA), the buffer body between the two major protagonists. To be sure, other players, both within the university community and outside it, have played a role. That large and complex galaxy of organizations with which the university community interfaces has in various ways all played a part: faculty associations and student federations, particularly as organized in the respective provincial associations—the Ontario Confederation of University Faculty Associations (OCUFA) and the Ontario Union of Students (OUS), later the Ontario Federation of Students (OFS); and the various professional associations—in engineering, law, medicine, and education.

The ongoing, ever-present determination of the universities to protect their autonomy and the tensions thereby generated is captured in the title of this book. At various times and in various circumstances, this tension affects relations between the collectivity of universities and government: when the universities are pressed to respond to government policy initiatives (or lack of same) and to government regulations. At other times, it involves relations between and among the universities themselves: when the good of the collectivity does not coincide with the good of all of the member universities. Any attempt at evaluating COU necessarily involves an assessment of council's effectiveness in balancing the demands of university autonomy, both individual and collective, and public accountability as defined by the government.

Prior to the massive expansion in university enrolment that began in the 1950s, Ontario universities were private but poor. During the '50s, the coincidence of two factors—a rapidly expanding population eager for more education and a growing realization among leaders in government and industry that the well-being of Canada depended on a better educated workforce and citizenry—generated a willingness on the part of governments and taxpayers to provide public financial support to Canada's universities on a large scale. In this respect, Canada and its wealthiest province, Ontario, were part of an unprecedented expansion of university-level education across the Western world and beyond, an expansion that has been aptly described as the movement from elite to mass to universal post-secondary education. Beginning in Canada in the 1950s, first with the federal government and later extending to the provincial governments, a paradigm shift in university funding occurred. By the early 1960s, the majority of the revenues of Canadian universities came from the public purse in the form of federal government grants. When in 1967 (bowing to pressures from provincial governments) the Government of Canada ceased to provide direct operating support to Canadian universities, it agreed to contribute 50 percent of the funding that each province was providing its universities by way of operating grants. The practical effect of this decision was to centre responsibility for the public funding of Canada's universities in each provincial government.[1]

At the beginning of the 1970s, Ontario's proportion of university revenues obtained from the public purse, including the contributions of the federal government, exceeded 70 percent. In addition, the government controlled tuition fees. By this time, an Ontario provincial university "system" was already largely in place. The system had developed rapidly as the result of an informal, although scarcely articulated, social contract between Ontario's private universities and the government. Under the terms of the contract, the government committed to provide the funding; the universities agreed to provide the places for the rapidly growing number of young Ontarians who wanted to obtain a university education. The stated policy of the government was that there would be a place in an Ontario university for every qualified student who wished to attend, a policy that the universities agreed to implement.

The Ontario university system that came into being developed because the government of the day agreed to provide the funds required by the universities to meet the demand for university places. Unlike in many state jurisdictions in the United States and in many European countries, when large sums of public funds were designated for higher education no master plan was developed for Ontario. Nor was any government-appointed body struck and given executive authority to manage the system. In Ontario, the expansion was driven by social demand and largely managed by the universities themselves. Although a "buffer body" was established to assist in the development of a university system, it was always a purely advisory body.

Nor did the government take any steps to alter the private juridical status of the universities. With one exception, it was willing to provide substantial sums of money to the province's private institutions of higher learning. The exception, based on government policy that antedated Confederation, involved the exclusion of church-related, degree-granting institutions from eligibility for provincial grants. Not insignificant (although the subject is not treated extensively here), the maintenance of this policy caused a number of religiously affiliated universities in the 1950s to disestablish themselves from their founding churches in order to become eligible for provincial grants. Its implication for this chronicle is simply that, when the provincial government undertook to provide large-scale financial support to Ontario's universities in the early '60s, the institutions that became the beneficiaries were all secular ones. These are the institutions that joined the Committee of Presidents of Ontario Universities and continued as members of the Council of Ontario Universities. This prerequisite for membership in COU—that the institution be publicly funded—continues to this day.

Because the government took no direct legal steps to create a provincial university system, choosing instead to provide public funds to private institutions, some juridical purists argue that Ontario does not have a university system, only a collection of private institutions of higher education. There is a place for such a view, and some of the practical implications of the resulting ambiguity will be found from time to time throughout this history. One of the more interesting examples, and one that bears directly on the issue of "institutional autonomy" occurred in the early '90s during the debates within COU on how to respond to the demands of the Rae government concerning the application of the social contract legislation to the universities. The government considered all Ontario universities to be parts of a provincial university system and undertook to deal with them as a group. As the association representing the universities, COU agreed to negotiate on their behalf. One member university, Wilfrid Laurier, argued that each institution was autonomous and should be permitted to negotiate on its own, an argument that was rejected. When in 1998 COU undertook the most recent of its many reviews of structure, the review was organized around this issue: Do Ontario universities constitute a system? This account takes the view that Ontario does have a university system (without any quotation marks). It is the view the association itself took when choosing the title of its first annual report, *System Emerging* (published in 1967), and one it has maintained ever since.

In the early 1950s, when the Government of Ontario first began to increase its funding to Ontario universities and realized that funding would likely be ongoing, it sought advice on how best to exercise its fiscal responsibilities. In 1951, R.C. Wallace, principal emeritus of Queen's

University, was retained as a part-time consultant to provide advice on the distribution of grants to the universities and on co-ordinating their activities. In 1958, this advisory role was transferred to a small committee of senior civil servants. In 1960, this committee was named the Committee on University Affairs. Enlarged by the addition of several community leaders, it was given a mandate to co-ordinate the development of higher education facilities in the province and to provide a clearinghouse for university problems. Two years later, at the urging of a former Ontario premier, Leslie Frost, who had recently become a member, CUA invited the presidents of Ontario universities to a meeting to discuss how to deal with the impending large expansion in university enrolment. Two significant decisions emerged from that meeting. The first was a decision by the presidents to produce a plan for the development of Ontario universities; the second was a decision to organize themselves into a group that would undertake to exercise leadership in the development and implementation of this plan. Thus was born the voluntary association of Ontario universities that a few years later would become the Council of Ontario Universities.

When the decision was made to form an organization, the presidents of Ontario universities were neither prepared nor organized for collective decision making. But they recognized the need. The decision to organize was an act of enlightened self-interest, motivated in part by their desire to maintain control over the future of their institutions and in part by their recognition of the need to plan the expansion of higher education in the province. These university leaders were confident of their ability to produce a sound plan; the government was prepared to allow them the opportunity. With the assistance of the advisory body, the Committee on University Affairs, which stood between the government and the universities, an informal social contract was quickly developed and agreed upon. Government policy on university education was simple and straightforward; it was demand driven. A place in an Ontario university would be provided for every resident of the province who wished to attend and had the requisite academic qualifications. The universities agreed to provide the places if the necessary funds were made available; the government agreed to provide the funds. While willing to expand to meet the needs so long as requisite funding was provided, the universities wanted to be left free to determine how the expansion was to be accomplished. Respectful of university autonomy, the government of Ontario was content to leave the planning of the provincial university system largely in their hands. As the university system grew in size and complexity, government became more involved in university affairs. It continued to respect university autonomy, though not always to the satisfaction of the universities. Government policy on accessibility remained in place, though fierce arguments would develop over the adequacy of funding required to enable the universities to fulfill it.

At the time of their decision to establish an association, Ontario university presidents had had little experience with collective decision-making and interinstitutional co-operation. Still, this decision was not taken in a vacuum. A national forum for discussion of university affairs, the National Conference of Canadian Universities and Colleges (NCCUC), had existed since 1911. Though originally little more than a presidents' club that met annually to exchange views, in the 1950s it served as the principal locus for the lobby that played a major role in persuading the government of Canada to institute regular operating grants to Canadian colleges and universities. As the expansion of higher education gathered force in other provinces across Canada and the respective provincial governments became involved, universities in other parts of the country also began to organize. In 1964, the Association of Atlantic Universities (AAU), with members from among the universities in Nova Scotia, New Brunswick, and Prince Edward Island (and later Newfoundland), was set up. That same year, *Le Conférence des recteurs et des principaux des universités du Québec* (CREPUQ) was established in that province. As the universities expanded elsewhere, similar types of university associations were being established. Across the Atlantic, there was the British Committee of Vice-Chancellors; elsewhere in the Commonwealth (Australia, New Zealand, Africa, and India) other associations of university vice-chancellors were formed. In the United States, groups of university presidents were being formed, at both the national and state levels.

The organization formed by the Ontario presidents, however, was unique in some respects. When academic colleagues were added, it became more than a presidents' club. This decision meant that COU was committed to representing both the administrative and academic estates within the universities in the task of system planning and co-ordination. This did not always provide for smooth sailing. Some presidents never felt fully comfortable in the presence of academic colleagues. And some academic colleagues always felt somewhat awkward in their presumed role as representatives of the academic estate, a feeling that would be complicated some years later by the growth of faculty power as represented in unionized faculty associations. When a strong research division was added to the secretariat, COU put itself in a position to provide the database and analytical capacity needed for system planning. Because of its high quality and ready availability, COU's research output quickly became recognized and accepted as an essential component of sound planning. Given this, neither the ministry nor the advisory body saw any need to develop their own research capabilities. With the exception of the *Conférence des recteurs*, none of the other university associations in Canada, including the Association of Universities and Colleges of Canada (as the NCCUC had become in 1961), ever developed any substantial research capacity. As a consequence, COU came to be looked to for research support for university planning activities not only in Ontario but also throughout all of Canada. In short, the Council of Ontario Universities came to play a leading role in higher education in this country. If one accepts the principle that knowledge is power, possession of such an important resource might have given the council an edge in dealing with planning issues. However, in keeping with the university tradition that research should be unbiased and its results made freely available, COU always took great care to ensure that this power was never abused.

In jurisdictions with many universities, where co-ordination and co-operation among the institutions are required for the well-being of the system, some kind of central authority is usual. In Western Europe, where typically the universities are state institutions, such authority is centralized in a government ministry. In the United States, most often this authority is located in a government agency that has been given a legal mandate to exercise planning power on behalf of the state system. During the '60s, many U.S. states created statewide co-ordinating and governing boards to plan the state university system. By 1970, only two U.S. states were without a co-ordinating body of some kind. The great majority of the American co-ordinating bodies were established by law and given executive authority to plan and manage the state system. The United Kingdom had its University Grants Committee (UGC). Established in 1918 as a buffer body between the universities and government and composed mainly of academics, by the mid-1960s this committee had assumed leadership in the planning of that country's higher education system and was exercising considerable control over the universities within its jurisdiction. In Canada, as public support for higher education expanded in the '60s, most provincial governments instituted structures for the management and control of this expensive and complex area of public policy. Nova Scotia established a university grants commission in 1963. By 1968, all but two Canadian provinces had established some kind intermediary body. The exceptions, Newfoundland and Saskatchewan, each had at the time only a single university.[2]

Ontario followed the United Kingdom's UCG model. However, the advisory body established in this province was never given the powers exercised by the UCG. Ontario's buffer body was never established by legislation (only by Order-in-Council) and was never granted any executive authority. In this province, the intermediary body always had only advisory powers. System planning in this province has remained largely in the hands of the universities themselves, exercised mainly through a voluntary association of member universities (COU) by means of "collective autonomy." This structure of university–government relations has produced good results.

As this history shows, however, such a system structure suffers from clear weaknesses. Without a clearly defined role for the intermediary body, the inevitable tensions between the universities, which are responsible for delivering the services, and the government, which is footing the bills, have no proper locus for resolution. This weakness is exacerbated when the body representing the collectivity of universities is a voluntary association dependent upon consensus. Such an association can speak on behalf of its member institutions when all members are agreed on a course of action. But it lacks the authority required to bring them together as members of a system when some members dissent. What is good for the system is seldom simply the sum total of what is good for its individual institutional components. When the needs of the system are in conflict with the legitimate self-interests of its institutional components, a mechanism for resolving the resulting conflict is required. In extreme cases, when institutional self-interests are involved, it cannot be expected that individual universities will voluntarily deny their self-interests in favour of the system. When the locus of system planning is placed with the universities themselves and there is with no effective system counterweight, and if the universities do not respond adequately to system needs, these needs likely will remain unmet. In the planning vacuum thereby created, sometimes the government will intervene to fill it; however, as we shall see, this seldom occurred in Ontario.

As a voluntary association of autonomous institutions, cou has always faced the difficult task of achieving consensus. Given that the objectives of institutional members, in particular their ambitions, are not always congruent with those of their sister universities nor always in the best interests of the system, a fundamental issue arises. It is a given that self-denial is never easy for an institution to accept. In a voluntary association of institutions, therefore, concessions from member institutions are often difficult to obtain. Consensus within the collectivity always remains elusive and is seldom achieved without great difficulty. When the collectivity moves, it moves convoy-like, at the pace of the slowest vessel. Without consensus, no convoy can be formed. When the weather is fair and resources plentiful, with good leadership progress is possible and significant progress can be made. However, when conditions are stormy and resources in short supply, consensus on major policy issues is very difficult to achieve. The good of the collectivity becomes submerged amid competing institutional self-interests. Not only is agreement on a common action impossible to obtain, it is sometimes difficult to hold the convoy together, even in port. When the convoy is threatened, the stronger members tend to band together and undertake to go their own way. As a result, the ability of the group to act in concert diminishes greatly; as a consequence, morale within the collectivity is substantially eroded.

In the early period, COU was very proactive. Its role in system planning, undertaken when ample financial resources were available, was central. Considerable success was achieved. Later, however, when resources diminished, Council's weaknesses emerged along with the weaknesses inherent in the structure of the university–government interface. As the realization grew that COU was inadequate to the task of system planning, council gradually gave up many of its efforts to expand institutional co-operation and co-ordination for system planning purposes. It became much more reactive, its role increasingly that of a special-interest lobby. Because the universities, the association that represents them, and the government proved unwilling or unable to overcome the structural defects that had been created and were allowed to remain in the system, system planning was largely abandoned.

COU continued, however, to maintain a large presence on the provincial university scene by reason of its "service" role. In the early years, during which council was very proactive, its system planning initiatives were matched by an equal enthusiasm for what may be called "service" activities: association activities directed to the member institutions themselves and from which they obtained a direct benefit. Both sets of COU activities contained strong planning elements and often overlapped. Still, the principal focus of the two was different. Policy matters affecting the system, such as the operating grants formula, tuition fees and the constant debates on the adequacy of funding, focused on issues across the university–government interface and often brought these two parties into contention. In addressing them, council had always to be conscious of the need to maintain support among the member institutions for the positions it advanced. When dealing with issues in the service area, the focus was different. When COU was involved in matters such as common procedures for application for admission to university, library co-ordination, university athletics, gender equity, and the like, developing and maintaining the requisite degree of support among the member institutions was much easier to achieve. Here the interests of member institutions were more likely to be congruent, and when some institutions did not benefit as much as others, the negative implications were less significant. It should be expected, therefore, that in an account of Council's successes and failures, the success column will contain fewer of the policy issues and more of the service ones. Through such manifold activities, for better and for worse, the Council of Ontario Universities has become imbedded in the fabric of university education in this province. The strong university system that exists today in Ontario owes much the efforts this voluntary association composed of the universities themselves.

CHAPTER 1

Establishing a Firm Foundation

IN 1962, WHEN THE PRESIDENTS OF the universities in Ontario decided to form an association to represent their interests and to assist in the planning and co-ordination of higher education in the province, they were making a bold move into uncharted waters. Until then, Ontario universities had operated in near total independence of one another, with little or no concern for the effect decisions made by one might have on a sister institution or on the collectivity of universities. Little attention was paid to planning at the provincial level; the term "university system" had yet to come into use. As the presidents themselves described the scene, "In 1962 a reasonably strong case could have been made that the Ontario university was a law unto itself. The relations between the individual universities were remarkably casual. The only formal contact, apart from the National Conference of Canadian Universities and Colleges, was through the University Matriculation Board, which normally met once a year and whose terms of reference were limited to matters bearing upon university admission."[1] Ontario universities were neither prepared nor organized for joint decision making or action; the status of the group of presidents was far from clear, even to themselves. Their decision to organize, essentially a pragmatic one, was to have major consequences.

The decision took place in the midst of an almost explosive expansion in university enrolment. To cover the costs of meeting the growing enrolment demand, government grants were increasing rapidly. So, too, was the recognition of the need for greater planning and co-ordination. Until then, the universities in Ontario, each with its own charter, had considered themselves to be independent, autonomous institutions, and they were so treated by government. When governments at both the federal and provincial levels began to increase by orders of magnitude their financial support to Canada's universities, they recognized the need for better planning, co-ordination and co-operation among the uni-

Notes to chapter 1 are on pp. 213–216

versities. For the most part, however, they were content to allow the universities to do this. This was particularly so in Ontario, at least at first.

As planning for the expanding provincial university system began to accelerate, Ontario universities accepted that recognition of the needs of the system was a valid consideration. They insisted, however, on respect for institutional autonomy. They accepted that government had a legitimate interest in planning for the system and that some control by government over the expenditure of public funds was required. However, Ontario universities opposed too-great government involvement in these matters for fear that institutional autonomy, which they considered a requirement for a sound university system, be compromised. For its part, the Ontario government accepted that a large degree of institutional autonomy was essential to the continued well-being of the universities and a necessary condition for a strong system. Because of its accountability to the electorate for public policy and as custodian of the public purse, however, the government insisted that it must be involved. Public accountability demanded no less. All parties agreed in principle on these matters.

The devil, however, was in the details. The issue to be addressed, a perennial one facing universities in a democratic state, was how best to maintain the delicate balance between university autonomy and government control. What limits should be placed on institutional autonomy in the interests of the system? What degree of government control is excessive? The success of this voluntary association can be measured by judging how well it has maintained this balance, in terms both of its defence of institutional autonomy and its support for a high-quality, publicly funded provincial system of higher education.

The enrolment crisis facing Ontario universities in the early 1960s was not the first the institutions had encountered since the end of World War II. This time, however, it was qualitatively different. Undergraduate enrolment had tripled between 1945 and 1963; it was now projected to triple again in less than a decade and to continue climbing steadily thereafter. The population of Ontario was growing rapidly as the result of the combination of an increased birth rate and immigration following the end of World War II. More significantly, the proportion of students continuing formal education beyond the age of compulsory schooling was increasing at an even faster rate. Between 1951 and 1971, the size of the Ontario eighteen-year-old cohort (already born) would nearly double. Moreover, an increasing proportion of students were now electing to continue their studies after completing secondary schooling, which translated into a six-fold increase in the numbers enrolling beyond secondary schooling. At the time, this was one of the largest increases among the industrialized nations.

Powerful economic, social, and cultural pressures, as well as demographic demands, were fuelling this expansion. These in turn generated political pressures. In Canada as a whole, and in particular in Ontario—the country's most populous province and its economic engine—there was both a growing need and a strong demand for a better educated populace, and for more research of all kinds. Urbanization, industrialization, higher technology, increased administrative complexity in both the private and public sectors, and increased wealth: all these propelled the country's leaders to recognize the growing need for a better-trained labour force and a better-educated citizenry. When Canadians considered such matters, comparisons, as usual, were made with the United States. When governments in Canada began to reflect seriously on the requirements of public educational policy, the friendly giant to the south provided the benchmark.

The principal economic argument was simple in outline. As measured by Canada's lower gross national product (GNP) and higher unemployment rate, the country lagged behind the United States. The pundits and opinion leaders explained that the gap was largely due to the country's lag in education. A disproportionately smaller number of Canadians (and Ontarians) completed secondary schooling; an even smaller number completed university. Of course, other arguments were used, particularly for higher education. Higher education and research are a means of social progress. A higher education provides its beneficiaries with a ladder to economic and social mobility, and is an avenue to increased self-fulfillment. It produces a better-educated citizenry, important in any democracy, and it provides a stronger base for an enlarged and strengthened Canadian culture. For this northern land to achieve greatness, more resources were required for education at all levels. By the mid-'50s, the expansion and improvement of Canada's university sector became the centrepiece of the Government of Canada's development strategy for the country, a strategy that would soon be adopted as well by the provinces.

Under the British North America Act, education at all levels is a provincial responsibility. In this period, however, provincial governments were focused on schooling at the primary and secondary levels. During the 1950s, the Government of Ontario made a heavy investment in its public schools. In 1939, some 500,000 pupils were enrolled in the province's elementary schools, some 120,000 in its secondary schools. An able and energetic minister of Education, John Robarts, strongly supported by Premier Leslie Frost (whom Robarts later succeeded), embarked on a major expansion of Ontario's public secondary schools. By 1960, enrolment stood at 1,200,000 and 330,000 respectively, and it continued to grow rapidly. A similar expansion took place in Ontario universities, though on a much smaller scale. This expansion, however, was financed largely by direct grants from the federal government. It was largely unorganized and involved little planning beyond the institutional level. Each Ontario university possessed its own charter granting it the right to award degrees, including the doctorate, and to offer academic programs leading to these degrees. All were proudly independent and fiercely defensive of their autonomy. In no sense did they constitute a provincial university system.

Until the advent of substantial amounts of federal funding in the 1950s, Ontario universities remained poor. None had any substantial endowment, and revenue from fees was insufficient to provide more than a bare minimum of what was required. There was some provincial funding, but the grants arrived sporadically and the amounts were usually meagre. Government policy antedating Confederation prohibited grants to institutions with a religious affiliation. No significant capital grants had been made since the 1920s. The Government of Ontario paid the universities little attention, an indifference reflected in the fact that, between 1917 and 1950, university matters were debated in the legislature only four times and on none of these occasions was a vote taken. In 1944, prior to the arrival of the veterans, there were some 11,000 undergraduates enrolled in Ontario universities. Increased enrolment due to the "veterans' bulge" during the second half of the decade tended to obscure the fact that, in the immediate post-war period, enrolment directly from secondary schools was also increasing. By 1950, undergraduate enrolment stood at 18,000; by 1955, it had increased to 20,000. This increase was accomplished on a largely ad hoc basis without any coordinated planning. Individual universities responded with a series of more or less ad hoc increases in enrolment to meet the needs each saw for itself.

Facing growing pressures to expand in the early 1950s, the universities called for increased public funding. They turned first to the Government of Canada, which they regarded as the most appropriate agency to support what in their minds was clearly in the national interest. They were not disappointed. Over the next decade, a series of federal initiatives provided significant financial support. In 1951, the Government of Canada instituted direct funding for the operation of Canadian universities. The grant, initially fifty cents per capita of the population in each province, was increased to $1 five years later. By 1965, it was $5. In 1956, the federal government established the Canada Council with a fund of $100 million, $50 million of which was earmarked for a University Capital Grants Fund. Each university was provided with a capital "entitlement" based on the same formula employed for the operating grant; these grants were used to cover 50 percent of the cost of approved capital projects. By 1961, the total amount had either been spent or allocated. In 1960, the Central Mortgage and Housing Corporation instituted a loans program to assist in the construction of university student housing. In 1963, the Canada Student Loan Program was put in place. By this time, the federal government was making major financial contributions in support of Canadian universities. Operating grants were based on university enrolment by province and given entirely without strings attached; capital grants were on a matching basis.

During this period, all provincial governments, including that of Ontario, were drawn ineluctably into financing the universities in their respective jurisdictions. At first, increased spending by the Government of Ontario was slow and cautious; also, it was ad hoc. In 1951, provincial operating grants to Ontario universities stood at $8 million per annum; by 1958, they had increased to $20 million. As more funding became available, existing universities increased enrolment and programming. Some church-related institutions agreed to give up their religious affiliation in return for eligibility for provincial grants—McMaster University (1957) and the University of Windsor (1963). Other institutions were granted university status—Carleton University (1956) and Lakehead University (1959). Three new universities were established: University of Waterloo (1959), York University (1959), and Laurentian University (1960). Emerging policy on higher education was clearly and succinctly summarized by the Provincial Treasurer in a statement made in the legislature in 1959: "Our objective is to ensure that no student who has the capacity will be deprived of the opportunity of attending university and developing his [sic] talents to the fullest possible extent."[2]

With increased provincial grants came a modest effort to co-ordinate university activities. In 1951, the government appointed R. C. Wallace, principal emeritus of Queen's University, as a part-time consultant to establish close liaison between it and the universities in order to improve co-ordination of their work and provide advice concerning the distribution of grants. In 1958, this advisory role was transferred to a small University Committee composed of senior civil servants. In 1960, this committee was enlarged by the inclusion of community leaders and renamed the Advisory Committee on University Affairs (ACUA). Chaired by the minister of Education, its mandate was "to co-ordinate the development of higher education facilities [and] to provide a clearinghouse for university problems."[3] When the committee was expanded in 1964 by the inclusion of academic members and established by Order-in-Council, it became the Committee on University Affairs (CUA). This was the beginning of a "buffer body," which with significant modifications in mandate but no increase in authority, would exist until 1995. When Leslie Frost retired as premier in 1961, he became a member. At his suggestion, the advisory body brought the university presidents together to discuss system planning.

At the time, each university met separately with the committee to present its needs for operating and capital support. The procedure, in effect, involved "deficit funding." At these annual meetings, each university president presented data showing his (at this time all were male) institution's operating revenues and costs, as well as projected capital requirements. After review, ACUA petitioned the government to provide funds to cover projected cost overruns. The recommendations from the advisory body were based on its (presumed independent) judgment of each institution's needs; the government's allocative decisions were based on its judgment of ability to fund. The allocation of both operating and capital grants to the universities was discretionary.

This was the situation at the beginning of 1962 when the Ontario university presidents were invited to meet with ACUA to discuss system planning. Facing unprecedented and unremitting pressures for places, the universities were urgently seeking larger grants from the government. Recognizing the need for increased financial support and prepared to provide it, the government was seeking better means of improving university planning and co-ordination. At the 1962 meeting, the presidents agreed to undertake a study of the needs of higher education in the province, and they struck a committee to do so.

● THE DEUTSCH REPORT

The committee struck by the presidents had a decisive effect. Chaired by John Deutsch, then vice-principal, Administration, at Queen's University, it worked with admirable vigour and dispatch. Meeting in May, the presidents received and discussed a draft report; a month later they presented the final report to the Committee on University Affairs. ACUA accepted the report's principal recommendations and in turn recommended them to the government. Although initially reluctant to give the report public recognition (it was not published until January 1963), the government immediately accepted its basic approach and began to implement some of its principal recommendations. The Deutsch Report thereby became the blueprint for the development of a university system for Ontario. The presidents' group, now organized as the Committee of Presidents of the Universities of Ontario (CPUO), became the principal instrument for its implementation.

An informal social contract between the universities and the government quickly developed. Ontario public policy on university education was simple and straightforward. There would be a place in an Ontario university for every resident of the province who wished to pursue higher education in the province and who qualified for admission. The universities would provide the places; the government, the funds. The necessary details were to be developed by the universities through CPUO in conjunction with the advisory committee (ACUA), which would make recommendations to the government. In practice, system planning and co-ordination became a joint effort of the Committee of Presidents and the Committee on University Affairs, with the presidents' group usually but not always taking the initiative. Despite many changes, this broad policy remains in place to this day. Simple in outline, its detailed meaning has often proved to be far from clear. As the circumstances of both the universities and government changed over time, the two partners came to interpret the policy rather differently. These differences, however, lay in the future.

In addressing the problem of how to provide post-secondary education for greatly increased numbers of students, the presidents proceeded on the assumption that, despite the enrolment projections on hand, it was not possible to foresee accurately the shape of the future. Their primary concern was for the maintenance of academic quality. They accepted that the emerging system should be economical. Moreover, given the time constraints governing implementation, they recognized that the desirable ideal needed to be flexible and subject to practical considerations.

Increased numbers of potential university students were already enrolled in secondary school—the first shock wave of enrolment was anticipated in 1965, to be followed by a further large increase in the next year. By 1966, it was projected that there would be as many first-year students in Ontario universities as constituted the total university enrolment in 1963. Thereafter, the report stated, "we face an unremitting expansion of spasmodic intensity, with no contraction in sight in the foreseeable future, and with major crises three or four years ahead."[4] Formidable pressures were seen as affecting two program areas: arts and science and graduate studies. In the professional fields, there appeared to be sufficient places in engineering and law; however, there was clear need for another faculty of medicine, of dentistry, and of pharmacy, as well as for more facilities in social work and in physical and health education. Given these projections, all of the universities were asked to provide more places and to estimate the maximum numbers they could accommodate by 1965 and by 1970. However, the presidents saw "no need to establish another multi-faculty university in Ontario in this decade."[5]

The presidents examined in some detail how best to provide expanded educational opportunities in the longer term. Several options were considered: (1) adding a fourteenth year to the Ontario public school system; (2) converting some of the existing provincial technical and vocational institutes into two-year technical colleges; (3) reducing the public school system to twelve years and establishing a system of two-year junior colleges based on the U.S. model; and (4) establishing several new three-year liberal arts colleges affiliated with one of the existing universities. While acknowledging the need for more study of the junior college model, the presidents selected option 4—the affiliated college model. They proposed the establishment of three new liberal arts colleges: one in the Welland-St. Catharines area to be affiliated with McMaster University, and two in the Metropolitan Toronto area (one in the west and one in the east) to be affiliated with the University of Toronto.

To deal with the pressing need to expand the pool of qualified university faculty, the presidents proposed a "crash program" in graduate studies to produce a doubling in enrolment. Emphasizing that a sizeable increase in graduate enrolment could not be achieved without a substantial increase in both the value and number of graduate fellowships, they proposed a special per capita grant to be allocated to those universities operating graduate programs. They regarded this recommendation as *"the first and most essential action of all those that must be taken to meet the approaching emergency"* [italics in original].[6] They also recommended that the universities co-ordinate the development of library and laboratory facilities for graduate work, avoid unnecessary duplication of graduate courses and facilities, and tighten up graduate programming to reduce the time needed for completion of a doctoral degree.

Nor did CPUO ignore organizational structure. Noting that the existing administrative arrangements were no longer adequate, the presidents examined several options. Placing all forms of post-secondary education under the current Department of Education or establishing a new Department of Higher Education was rejected as involving an unacceptable level of direct government control. The presidents preferred the intermediate, buffer-body approach. Two options were offered. ACUA's mandate might be expanded and that body given responsibility for the whole of post-secondary education (except for the training of teachers, which would remain with the Department of Education). Alternatively, ACUA might retain its existing mandate and a second advisory body be created to handle the non-university sector. Although preferring the former, the presidents stated that either would facilitate co-ordination without the imposition of excessive government control.

The government adopted the basic approach of the Deutsch Report and accepted many (but not all) of its recommendations. Erindale College and Scarborough College were established in affiliation with the University of Toronto. However, two new universities were created: Brock University in St. Catharines, and Trent University in Peterborough. Furthermore, a new multi-faculty university, the University of Guelph, was established in that city by adding Arts and Science faculties to the colleges of Agriculture and Veterinary Medicine in Guelph with colleges that were previously affiliated with the University of Toronto. In addition, ignoring the presidents' opposition, a new Department of University Affairs was created.

As a first step in dealing with the financial needs of the universities identified in the Deutsch Report, the government made $200,000 available immediately to assist in expanding graduate programs. Meeting in July 1962 (their third meeting in as many months), this time with their finance officers, the presidents determined criteria for operating and capital funding, and decided on the distribution of the new funds. This provided them their first opportunity to make decisions on the allocation of money among the member institutions. The decisions, after debate and with some dissent, allocated 35 percent of the grant to the University of Toronto; 55 percent among four other universities (Queen's, Western Ontario, McMaster, and Ottawa); and the remaining 10 percent among Assumption (now affiliated with the University of Windsor), Carleton, Waterloo, and York. At that meeting, it was also agreed to form a seven-member Executive Committee.[7]

In September 1962, Premier Robarts announced the establishment of an Ontario Graduate Fellowship Program for the following academic year, 1963-64. In a major policy statement on higher education delivered in the Ontario legislature in March 1963, Premier Robarts announced an additional $3-million grant for graduate studies and indicated that each university would receive capital grants for the two coming years, 1963-64 and 1964-65, amounting to not less than those received in the current year. While it was less than they had requested, the universities were pleased. More significantly, in that same statement the Premier declared that Ontario now possessed sufficient universities for the foreseeable future. With the addition of Brock, Trent and Guelph universities, there were now fourteen freestanding universities in the province. Although they had initially proposed something rather different, the presidents now stated that this policy constituted "the soundest and most economical way of making university education available to all with the desire and the ability to undertake it."[8] Subsequently, three new colleges were established in affiliation with Laurentian University: Algoma University College in Sault Ste. Marie; Nipissing College in North Bay; and University College of Hearst in Hearst.

By 1963, the publicly funded university system in Ontario was essentially complete. Apart from two small additions—Ryerson Polytechnical

Institute (later Ryerson Polytechnic University) given limited degree-granting powers and Waterloo Lutheran University granted a secular charter in 1972 to become Wilfrid Laurier University—no new university charters would be granted for another quarter century, and then only to previously existing institutions. With the leisure of hindsight, it appears today that the government made a significant policy mistake in rejecting CPUO advice concerning the establishment of new university-level institutions. The CPUO recommendation (argued on grounds of academic quality) that any new institutions be established as colleges affiliated with existing universities, i.e., institutions which (at least in the beginning) would not have the right to grant their own degrees, was intended, among other purposes, to limit the number of full degree-granting institutions to those then in existence. While agreeing to establish two new colleges affiliated with the University of Toronto (Scarborough and Erindale), the government decided to set up three more new universities (Brock, Trent, and Guelph), each with unlimited degree-granting powers. This decision was consistent with its earlier decisions to establish full-fledged universities in northern Ontario—Lakehead in the northwest and Laurentian in the northeast—decisions that reflected a desire to provide greater geographical equality of access to university across the province. Laudable from an accessibility perspective, the decision broadened and reinforced the understanding that all Ontario universities are equal. Later (when funding became tight), this view would make it politically very difficult to rationalize the university system by forcing institutional role differentiation, much less by closing an institution. Ontario citizens and their elected representatives quickly became proud of their local university and resisted mightily any attempt to reduce the scope of its operations. In an area-based legislature such Ontario's, every MPP in whose riding there was a university could be counted on to defend the right of this institution to be a "real" university. As a consequence, a "two-tier" university system would never become a serious option in Ontario.

A second major policy error was made by government in accepting the CPUO recommendation for dealing with the non-university sector of post-secondary education in Ontario. Upon the advice of the presidents, the government rejected the option of establishing a community college system based on the U.S. model, one that would provide community colleges with a university degree path as well as a number of non-degree paths. Instead, the government created a new system of colleges of applied arts and technology (CAATs) unique to the province of Ontario. Built upon the province's technical and vocational school system, these community colleges would not offer university-level programs. Admission requirements would be less; programs would be of shorter duration and lead to certificates and diplomas, not degrees. Agreed to in 1965, the new college system was formally established in 1967. Its establishment created a binary divide in Ontario post-secondary education. Bridging that divide would take many years and today remains incomplete.

● UNIVERSITY–GOVERNMENT RELATIONS

From the beginning, CPUO realized that the universities' need for greatly increased public funding would not be met without a substantial increase in government involvement in its affairs. Determined, however, to protect as much as possible the autonomy of their institutions, the presidents set out to create a system in which the right of the universities to run their own affairs would be protected and bolstered by a clear, agreed-upon understanding of the respective roles of the government and the universities, plus a set of rules and regulations that would define how these roles were to be fulfilled. From CPUO's perspective, adequate funding along with a high degree of institutional flexibility in determining the expenditure of these funds, was a prerequisite. A high priority, therefore, was given to developing a mechanism to determine the amount of the annual government grant for university operations and the method of its distribution. Achieving these twin objectives would require the creation of a structure within which university-government relations might function and the development of an appropriate funding mechanism. CPUO immediately began efforts to secure these two objectives.

Meeting the universities' financial requirements involved funding for both capital and operating costs. Given the level of continuing federal operating support, the more pressing need in Ontario was for substantial capital grants to expand the universities' physical facilities, including laboratories and libraries. For the newly organized presidents, this became a high priority. A report prepared by its Academic Sub-committee and submitted to CPUO in October 1964 (but never published) projected necessary capital expenditures covering the four-year period 1964–65 to 1967–68, as falling in the $60–$65-million range. Total university system capital requirements covering the period to 1970–71 were projected at some $450 million (in 1962–63 dollars). When this report was submitted to the advisory body, the Committee on University Affairs (as it had become), the response was not favourable. The universities were criticized for not seriously considering the use of temporary physical facilities, after the manner in which the "veterans' bulge" had been handled after the end of World War II. CUA announced its intention to convene a meeting of university boards of governors and finance committees to discuss university financing without CPUO. This decision tended to confirm the presidents' opinion that this advisory body was not what was required for the development of sound provincial policy on higher education.

Ever fearful of increased government control, the presidents were determined to keep any machinery for system planning largely in their own hands. They were ready to accept expanded central planning so long as they could maintain effective control. On the interface between the government and the universities, they saw the need for an intermediary body that enjoyed the confidence of the university community and could stand effectively between the two protagonists. At a two-day meeting in November 1963, a lively discussion on university-government relations took place, a topic that would consume considerable time and energy over the next several years. A memorandum from the CPUO Research Committee (the first of many on the subject) argued the case for the establishment of a university grants commission. Recognizing the crucial importance of having an intermediate body to stand between the universities and (to their eyes) an increasingly interventionist government, and unhappy with both the mandate and the composition of CUA—an advisory body with no academic representation—CPUO looked to the United Kingdom for a model. The presidents sought a semi-independent university grants commission with responsibility and authority to plan and co-ordinate the Ontario university system—a body with strong academic representation, a full-time chair with academic experience, and its own staff. At the conclusion of the meeting, a four-page memo signed by eleven presidents presenting the case for a university grants commission patterned after the U.K. model was forwarded to the premier.[9]

The government listened but was not fully persuaded. The January 1964 speech from the throne announced a decision to create a new Department of University Affairs and to establish a new Crown corporation to handle university capital financing. CPUO had opposed placing university affairs under a separate government ministry. Once the decision was announced, however, the CPUO accepted political reality without comment or criticism. The universities knew the minister, William G. Davis (already minister of Education, who now would hold two portfolios), as a strong minister fully committed to university expansion and known to be supportive of university autonomy.

The issue of a proper intermediate body, however, continued to preoccupy CPUO. Following their February 1964 meeting, they sent another memorandum to Premier Robarts and Minister Davis, again urging establishment of a university grants commission and requesting an opportunity to discuss the matter. In March, Claude Bissell, Chair of CPUO and president of the University of Toronto, reported that Premier Robarts had come round to supporting the proposal to add academic representation on CUA and was prepared to give the committee a strong role in recommending on policy and in dealing with fundamental academic questions. However, the premier was not prepared to give the advisory body responsibility for decisions on university funding. The presidents were not alone in pressing for the inclusion of a strong academic representation on the buffer body. Later that same month, CPUO and the newly formed Ontario Confederation of University Faculty Associations (OCUFA) agreed to forward to the premier a joint list of academics judged suitable for membership on CUA. During this early period, the two organizations held similar views on the type of buffer body needed for the system, and they worked together to achieve the common objective. Later, in the '70s, when OCUFA became more involved in faculty union activities, relations became more distant.

When the legislation establishing the new Department of University Affairs was tabled in the legislature on April 22, 1964, the presidents were far from pleased with the details of the new department's mandate. It was to have responsibility for the development of procedures and administrative details covering all provincial grants to universities, the development of sound plans for future university expansion, the review of all proposed legislation affecting universities, the administration of all major programs of student aid, plus other university matters. There was barely a mention of the advisory body. Deeply concerned, the presidents asked their chair to see the premier again as soon as possible to reiterate their concerns about the role of the advisory body.

This intervention had a positive effect. When the bill establishing the new department was debated in the legislature in early May, Premier Robarts spoke to the role of the advisory body and described its functions in terms that closely approximated the kind of university grants body that CPUO and OCUFA advocated. The Committee on University Affairs would sit as an independent body between the government and the universities. It would consult with the universities prior to recommending on the global amount and its allocation among the institutions; it would direct research projects and work out with the universities such matters as the location of a new medical or dental school. Heartened by these words, the presidents then forwarded a further memorandum suggesting that CUA establish a structure that included standing committees with both lay and academic representation, name a member with university experience as full-time vice-chair, and be given its own budget. When the membership of the enlarged committee was announced in September, several of the nominations proposed jointly by CPUO and OCUFA were included.

In 1967, the appointment of Douglas Wright, a former dean of Engineering at the University of Waterloo and one of the first academics named to the advisory body, as full-time chair of CUA greatly improved relations between the two bodies. Following a model developed the preceding year with the establishment of a joint committee on the operating grants formula, joint CPUO–CUA committees now were formed on capital studies and on computer services. Informal contacts between the respective sub-committees and staff of the two bodies became frequent. The practice was begun of inviting Chair Wright to attend a portion of each CPUO meeting.

Under the aegis of the Committee of Presidents of the Universities of Ontario, many important system initiatives were now undertaken. University admissions procedures were standardized and planning begun to establish a central application centre. An interuniversity library transit system linking all of the universities was established, and planning was begun for a provincial research library. A formula for the calculation and distribution of government operating grants was developed and implemented. The presidents described the period as a one of "participatory planning." Although the initiative lay with the universities through CPUO, much of the planning was undertaken jointly with CUA. Relations between the two bodies were cordial and close; agreement between them was usually achieved. When disagreements arose—usually over money, when the advisory body did not accept the universities' calculations about the amount of funding required to meet expanding commitments—they were of minor significance.

Satisfied with the way in which the university system was developing, the government was generally content to leave matters alone. While declaring an interest, it preferred continuation of the emerging voluntary system in which the initiative rested with the universities. Minister Davis articulated this view in a public lecture at York University in 1966. In his view, "the degree of autonomy enjoyed by the provincially assisted universities of Ontario is equivalent to, if not greater than, that known by publicly supported universities anywhere—including the United Kingdom ... [And this is the preferred way.] There is ... much evidence to indicate that provided the universities can meet the responsibilities of our times we should undoubtedly be better off if they were allowed to continue to operate with such autonomy."[10] The government, however, would be vigilant. Davis went on the say, "On the other hand, if they cannot or will not accept those responsibilities, and if, for example, large numbers of able students must be turned away because the university is not prepared to accept them, or if, as another example, some of the less glamorous disciplines are ignored, despite pressing demands for graduates in those areas, or if, costly duplication of effort is evident, I cannot imagine any society, especially one bearing large expense for higher education, will stand idly by. For there will inevitably be a demand—there have been indications of this in other jurisdictions—that government move in and take over."[11]

At this juncture, the presidents judged that the balance achieved between their organization and the intermediary body represented the unique strength of the Ontario university system. CUA viewed the development of the system from the perspective of the public interest. While not insensitive to this interest, CPUO focused on the development of the institutions. Sometimes the views of the two bodies differed. Contact between the two was dynamic, and on occasion this produced sparks; nonetheless, it was productive. The working relationship, which involved frequent and friendly informal communications, as well as joint committee and staff work, reflected both sensitivity to academic values and concern for the public interest. While subject to further refinement and improvement, the presidents considered this structure to be "an advanced model of the new kind of government-university machinery, which is rapidly becoming the design of the future."[12]

Although great strides were being made and relations on the university-government interface generally good, CPUO was alert to the need to keep on top of a rapidly evolving scene. Among the developments that lay outside the direct orbit of the universities was the decision of the government to create a province-wide system of colleges of applied arts and technology (CAATs) to provide non-university post-secondary education and training, something they themselves had proposed. Once this decision had been made, however, province-wide planning for post-secondary education took on a new dimension. Recognizing the pace and breadth of the developments now taking place, and conscious of its limited ability to evaluate objectively university involvement in them, in 1966 CPUO recommended to the government the establishment of a commission to examine the whole of post-secondary education. The presidents were looking for the development of a blueprint for a post-secondary system in the province. This blueprint would provide a prominent place for the universities alongside the newly created colleges of applied arts and technology in a structure of university-government relations that maintained maximum autonomy for the universities, both institutional and collective. It would also give an appropriate place to a reformed and strengthened intermediate body with adequate representation from the university sector.

In June 1967, the minister of University Affairs responded, announcing in the legislature the establishment of a commission to study post-secondary education in Ontario. The commission was asked "to consider in the light of present provisions for university and other postsecondary education in Ontario the pattern necessary to ensure the further effective development of post-secondary education in the Province during the period to 1980, and in general terms to 1990, and to make recommendations thereon."[13] Owing to the difficulty in finding a suitable chair, it was some time before the commission began its work. Suggestions were solicited. Both CPUO and OCUFA proposed names (each rejecting some nominated by the other), but no one judged acceptable by both organizations was found who was willing to take on the assignment.

After more than a year, in September 1968 CPUO gave up and withdrew its recommendation for a commission. The association was in the process of transforming itself from a presidents' club into a universities' council with broader powers and an increased research capacity. Instead of pursuing efforts to find a chair for the proposed commission, the strengthened association offered its services in conducting research on system issues and its participation in carrying forward the results. The offer was not accepted. In April 1969, a twelve-member commission was finally appointed, with Douglas Wright (who continued as chair of CUA) named as chair. By the time the final report of the Commission was released in December 1972, much had changed on the university scene in Ontario.

● GRADUATE PLANNING

The history of graduate planning in Ontario, in which COU has been involved continuously, provides an excellent example of the strengths and weaknesses of planning based on interinstitutional co-operation among a group of autonomous universities led by a voluntary association. Recognizing the crucial importance of this program area and the need for substantial investment here, from the beginning the presidents accorded it high priority.

For starters, a large number of additional faculty would be needed to handle the projected enrolment growth. As the 1960s began, about 10 percent of Ontario university enrolment was at the graduate level, and the numbers were increasing slowly. Only a handful of doctorates were being awarded each year. The University of Toronto and McGill University together accounted for the bulk of doctorates awarded in English-language universities in Canada; the number, however, had never been sufficient to meet the needs of Canada's universities. Like their colleagues in other Canadian universities, most Ontario university faculty had done their graduate work abroad, mainly in the U.K. and the U.S. Some of the faculty needed to staff the expanding Ontario universities would continue to be recruited from abroad. However, with universities in most of the western world also growing, it was clear that Ontario universities would have to train many of the additional faculty required to staff their rapidly expanding institutions. In addition, there were the needs for an expanded commitment to research outside the universities in both the public and private sectors. The presidents saw themselves "grappling with a triple headed monster—the research needs of the country, for teachers, for pure scientists, and for an almost limitless number of applied scientists in business, industry and government."[14]

CPUO recognized that the high cost of graduate programming placed heavy responsibilities on the universities to plan carefully and to co-ordinate their efforts. In April 1964, the presidents authorized the appointment of an Advisory Committee on Graduate Studies, composed of the deans of graduate studies of those universities engaged in graduate work, and requested it to report from time to time on matters pertaining to graduate studies. Chaired by Ernest Sirluck, dean of Graduate Studies at the University of Toronto, it operated as a largely autonomous body. Later it evolved into the Ontario Council on Graduate Studies (OCGS) and in 1967 became an affiliate of CPUO.

Early in 1965, CPUO decided to undertake a province-wide study of graduate programming. After discussions with CUA, it was agreed that the two bodies would undertake jointly a comprehensive review of graduate studies in Ontario, to be conducted by three external commissioners. The Department of University Affairs agreed to provide financial support. G. A. Arlt, president of the American Association of Graduate Schools, Kenneth Hare, professor at King's College, University of London, and John W. T. Spinks, president of the University of Saskatchewan, were appointed and President Spinks was named chair. This group, The Commission to Study the Development of Graduate Programmes in Ontario Universities, was asked: (1) to examine post-graduate education in the Province of Ontario with reference to quality, need, and resources; and (2) to make recommendations concerning the development of work in this area during the next decade, with particular reference to the introduction or expansion of graduate programs in various universities and to financial support, including student aid. It was asked to report by September 1966.[15]

The report of the commission, the first major initiative in Ontario system planning, was keenly anticipated. When it came, it produced a shock. Nothing if not forthright, it described a province with fourteen fully chartered, autonomous universities free to declare their own objectives and to develop their own programs without regard or reference to their neighbours or to the needs of the province. These institutions competed with one other for their share of annual appropriations. The commissioners stated that the direction and rate of institutional development were determined not by rational and unified planning but by the institutions' ingenuity in securing funds. "The most striking characteristic of higher—not only graduate—education in Ontario," the commissioners noted, "is the complete absence of a master plan, of an educational policy and of a co-ordinating authority for the provincially supported institutions." The conclusion: there was "a pressing and immediate urgency for the establishment of a strong co-ordinating agency to plan and oversee the orderly development of graduate work in the province, for the purpose of arriving not only at a rational fiscal policy but, equally importantly, at a sound academic policy." This was a necessary part of the solution to a larger problem: "that of ensuring co-operation between, and co-ordination of, the efforts of the fourteen provincially supported universities in the development of an overall master plan to meet the needs of the Province ... to convert unrestricted competition into harmonious co-operation."[16]

The commission's proposed solution: the establishment of a provincial University of Ontario, an Ontario Universities' Research Council, a greatly strengthened co-ordinating agency, implementation of funding by formula for government grants, a centralized approach to library planning, and a number of other actions. Having received pre-publication copies of the report on a confidential basis, the presidents devoted a large portion of their September 1966 meeting to a discussion of its principal recommendations. Three major concerns were expressed: the general over-centralizing approach, the proposal to establish a Provincial Research Council, and, in particular, the proposal for the establishment of a University of Ontario. There was unanimous agreement that "the proposal for a University of Ontario was not acceptable, indeed unsuitable for the Ontario scene."[17]

At this meeting, CPUO chair Alex Corry, principal of Queen's University, reported to his colleagues that Minister Davis had already been dissuaded from supporting the proposal for the establishment of a University of Ontario but that Davis would be anxious to offer some alternative when commenting on the report when it was released. His colleagues urged Chair Corry to become involved in the planning of a press conference to be held in connection with the release of the report. At the same time, the presidents referred the report to their Advisory Committee on Graduate Studies for detailed comment. At its November meeting, it was reported that CUA was also opposed to the proposal for a University of Ontario. At his appearance before CPUO at the same meeting, Minister Davis stated his firm opposition. Having already been leaked to the press, the Spinks Report was officially released at a press conference on December 29, 1966. The minister, Chair Corry (representing CPUO), and Dr. Arthur Bourns (one of the academic members of

CUA), attended this conference. None of the three commissioners was present. It was later explained that, as a result of a "miscommunication" involving the minister's office during the holiday period, the commissioners had not been invited. In the sequel, the universities received some bad press, but the impact was minimal and quickly passed.

Anxious to be seen as conscious of the need for greater planning and co-ordination in graduate planning (as indeed they were), the presidents moved quickly to address the other recommendations in the report, many of which they supported. The new Ontario Council on Graduate Studies (OCGS) agreed with the view of the Spinks Commission that all Ontario universities should move toward the development of honours and master's programs in the central academic disciplines (though not necessarily in all of them) and that doctoral programs ought to be restricted to a smaller list of institutions where adequate funds and facilities are available. It also agreed that the Province should equip itself with an authorization procedure for doctoral programs. So, too, did CPUO. OCGS then developed a procedure for the peer evaluation of graduate programs—the appraisals process.

Endorsed by the presidents, this procedure became the accepted method for the academic assessment of graduate programs at both the doctoral and master's level in all Ontario universities. Administration of the program was in the hands of OCGS. Appraisals were conducted by committees of consultants—three for doctoral programs, almost always two for master's—all recognized scholars in the given subject field with recent experience in graduate teaching and thesis supervision, and familiarity with administration. Only one consultant per committee could come from within the province. Appraisal of a doctoral program was to be valid initially for a period of five years; for master's programs, there was no time limit. Universities applying to have graduate programs appraised would pay CPUO (COU) a fee: $2,500 for a doctoral program and $1,500 for a master's program.

It was acknowledged that this procedure would require some sacrifice on the part of the co-operating universities. Criticism of the initial requirements produced an amendment to the procedures that, in the case of a program initially failing appraisal, the appraisals committee might grant approval at a specified future date once all the requirements had been met. A suggestion that universities be allowed to seek "advice" from OCGS without putting a program up for formal appraisal, however, was rejected. The university had a choice: it could elect either to have the program appraised or not. Objections from the Ontario Confederation of University Faculty Associations that the process stripped individual universities of their right to determine which academic programs a university would offer were overcome through discussion. By the end of 1969, all Ontario universities had formally agreed to submit new graduate programs to the Appraisals Committee of OCGS for an academic-quality assessment. At first, appraisals were entirely voluntary. In 1968, however, upon recommendation from the Committee on University Affairs, the government made passing a OCGS appraisal a condition for funding. Only students enrolled in a graduate program that had undergone successful appraisal were eligible to be included in the enrolment count for funding under the operating grants formula. Thereafter, all Ontario universities submitted all of their new graduate programs for appraisal.

Appraisal became the standard method for the academic assessment of new graduate programs in Ontario universities. In the first three years, seventy-two programs were appraised; only a handful failed to be approved. The small number of negative decisions on appraisal (as continued to be the case) reflected the strength of the process, not its weakness. Unless they were confident of a positive result, universities were not prepared to submit a program for appraisal. In a report on the first three years of operation, M. A. (Mel) Preston, Chair of the Appraisals Committee, noted that "the Appraisals Committee performs two rather different roles ... it assures the academic communities—provincial, national and international—in a very visible way that the graduate programmes in Ontario universities are able to meet the standards of a rigorous [academic] appraisal [and] ... its existence and procedures ensure that all important questions of standards, of research emphasis, of curricular development and of educational philosophy are raised and are carefully considered by those involved in graduate work."[18]

In the early 1980s, a system of periodic appraisals was introduced under which all graduate programs, both new and old, were required to undergo appraisal on a seven-year cycle. An external assessment of the appraisals process undertaken in 1986 for the Ontario Council on University Affairs concluded that "the Appraisals Process which is currently in place produces reliable and credible judgements of the academic quality of existing and proposed graduate programs in Ontario."[19] A 1999 COU review of OCGS examined a number of concerns and criticisms, and has offered a number of recommendations calculated to "further ensure the dependability and utility of the process."[20] Developed, administered, and paid for by the universities themselves, the appraisal process is one of the big success stories of COU. In place now for more than thirty years, the appraisals process represents a major contribution to the development and maintenance of high-quality graduate programs in the Ontario university system.

Although indirectly reducing duplication through the elimination of substandard academic programs, the appraisals process was not developed to serve the purposes of system planning and co-ordination. A second process—discipline assessment—was developed to address this more complex and contentious issue. This process evolved more slowly and would ultimately prove unsuccessful. In addressing this issue, the Ontario Council on Graduate Studies initially proposed a scheme for province-wide interuniversity consultation within individual academic disciplines and professions to produce a provincial inventory of existing resources in each discipline, and thereby to lay the basis of planning for the development of a comprehensive plan for graduate programming. Endorsed by the presidents, it took more than a year before a meeting of university representatives of all the major academic discipline groups was convened to explore ways in which to begin interuniversity co-operation in graduate studies and to avoid unnecessary program duplication. In his opening address at the May 1968 meeting of the discipline representatives, Principal Corry, chair of CPUO, stated that "this may well be the most important business the universities have attempted together," while acknowledging that "the process of co-operation would not be painless and would require all universities to pass self-denying ordinances and curb their aspirations in some directions."[21]

Progress was slow. A year later, twenty-eight discipline groups had been formed and a proposal developed that OCGS establish an Advisory Committee on Academic Planning (ACAP) to assist the discipline groups, and to provide advice to OCGS and CPUO on how best to proceed. It was proposed that ACAP take under its purview both undergraduate and graduate program development, particularly the latter, and conduct assessments in specific disciplines on request from CPUO. However, the details remained to be worked out, and approval from all of the universities had yet to be obtained. Some concern continued to be expressed over the lack of data on manpower requirements in some disciplines, data judged an essential requirement for discipline planning at the system level. While the universities debated these matters, both the government and CUA were concerned over lack of progress in addressing the issue of system planning for graduate studies.

The Spinks Commission's proposal that an Ontario Universities' Research Council be established was rejected by CPUO. The presidents preferred to see research remain with the graduate enterprise and be based in the individual universities. For similar reasons, they preferred to see the development of needed library resources based in the institutions. Other recommendations from the Spinks Report, however, were dealt with in a more positive way. The presidents moved quickly to undertake the co-ordination of library expansion. Noting that the long-term division of responsibility among the universities would depend on the eventual division among them of responsibility for graduate programming, CPUO nevertheless approved the creation of a provincial library system to include a province-wide reader service in which all universities would share facilities for moving library materials from one university to another, as well as the establishment of a bibliographic centre in the proposed new Humanities and Social Sciences Research Library at the University of Toronto. In addition, while struggling to develop a system approach to graduate planning, on recommendation from an affiliate, the Committee of Ontario Deans of Engineering (CODE), in 1969 the presidents decided to undertake a comprehensive review of engineering education in the province. The objective was to create a master plan to guide the growth of engineering education in Ontario during the '70s. The outcome of this study would have a significant effect on the future of interuniversity program planning in Ontario.

● THE "DE-CANADIANIZATION" ISSUE

An unanticipated by-product of the rapid increase in enrolment and the hiring of new faculty to teach the increased numbers of students was criticism that Canadian universities were being taken over by foreign academics, mostly Americans, who understood little and cared less about Canadian affairs and culture. Initiated by two members of the English Department at Carleton University, Robin Mathews and James Steele, a vigorous public debate developed, one that found the universities quickly on the defensive, as reporters, editorialists, TV hosts and (later) politicians joined in a chorus of criticism against them. The criticism focused on two issues: employment and curriculum. The universities were criticized for their alleged failure to offer appointments to qualified Canadian academics, for appointing too many non-Canadians, especially Americans, to faculty, and for admitting too many non-Canadians to graduate programs. Not only were these non-Canadians said to be taking employment from Canadians, their lack of knowledge about Canadian culture and their insensitivy to it were said to reduce the quality of education being provided in the universities. Since large sums of public money were going to universities (the critics argued), the universities should be giving preference to Canadian academics and graduate students, and should ensure that the curricula took Canadian culture and values adequately into account.

The attention of CPUO was first drawn formally to the issue in the fall of 1968 when the chair of CUA suggested that a quota be placed on the number of non-Canadians admitted to Ontario graduate schools. Uncomfortable at the prospect of quotas, the initial response of the presidents was to request that no action be taken pending a study. OCGS was asked to conduct a survey, and the results were published in the spring of 1969. The survey showed that that some 66 percent of all Ontario university graduate students were Canadian citizens and a further 13 percent were landed immigrants. It was conceded, however, that such data were not very meaningful unless accompanied by further data showing how many of the graduates of Ontario universities remained in Canada after the completion of their programs. At about the same time, Professor Mathews published data that showed a sharp increase in the number of non-Canadians appointed to faculty at Canadian universities, including some showing that in one Ontario university a majority of faculty in some departments were now non-Canadians. He called for an immediate imposition of hiring quotas.[22]

Arguing that scholarship is universal and that citizenship is not a meaningful criterion for faculty hiring, CPUO rejected the call for quotas. They agreed, however, that the extent of the problem should be examined in a more systematic fashion. The new research division was asked to work with the Dominion Bureau of Statistics to undertake a more comprehensive collection of data. Further, since the critics were suggesting that qualified Canadians were being bypassed in the largely informal appointments procedures then employed by many universities, the presidents proposed that openings for faculty should be more widely advertised. In September 1969, CPUO issued a policy statement in which it was recommended that all Ontario universities make a commitment to advertising all positions.

The results of the faculty survey were published in the spring of 1970. They showed that in the year 1969–70, Ontario universities employed some 8,000 full-time faculty. Of these, 61 percent were Canadians, 15 percent Americans, and 12 percent British. By discipline, the proportion of Canadians ranged from 47 to 81 percent. Given that the universities had added some 5,000 new faculty during the five-year period 1964–65 to 1969–70, while awarding only some 2,000 new doctorates, these results were viewed as unsurprising. Moreover, the report added, if appropriate hiring practices were to be followed, from then on all qualified Canadians should be able to find an appointment in a Canadian university.[23] Regarding this response as self-serving, the critics remained unpersuaded. Their anger was raised when a related issue arose: graduate school enrolment continued to rise at a time when the increase in undergraduate enrolment was slowing and university budgets were coming under increasing pressure. As a consequence, the number of new faculty appointments was declining at the same time that graduate school production was increasing. This dilemma would haunt that scene as the debate continued into the '70s.

● FINANCING THE SYSTEM

As public funding of the system increased, the practice of providing essentially ad hoc discretionary grants was more and more called into question. On the government side, pressure was growing to undertake more detailed examination of the financial affairs of the universities. Ever jealous of their autonomy, the universities were becoming apprehensive that the government would move to a line-by-line examination of institutional budgets. For the presidents, a mechanism to determine clearly and objectively how public funds would be disbursed to the universities was a high priority—they wanted a formula for the distribution of government grants among the participating institutions. Such a formula would eliminate any need for either the government or CUA to undertake detailed examination of university expenditures. In addition to providing added protection for institutional autonomy, a formula would provide other advantages. Based on objective criteria, it would provide equity among the participating institutions, thereby avoiding any suggestion of unfairness and favouritism—a benefit both to the universities and to government. It would also provide the universities with greater financial stability and thereby assist them in planning. In short, a grants formula would achieve three important objectives shared by both the universities and the government: autonomy, equity, and stability.

Funding by formula was far from unknown. It was already employed in a number of leading U.S. state jurisdictions and had been introduced in New Brunswick in 1963 following a recommendation in the report of a Royal Commission headed by John Deutsch of Queen's University, the same John Deutsch who had spearheaded the development of the basic blueprint for the Ontario university system. In 1965, both CPUO and the minister accepted the principle of a formula for the distribution of operating grants to the universities. Formula funding for universities was also strongly supported by the Bladen Report, an influential report on financing higher education in Canada published that same year.[24] CPUO and CUA each had a committee studying the issue; now they joined forces. The formula introduced in 1967 was the product of a joint CPUO–CUA subcommittee, one of the first fruits of the collaborative efforts undertaken by the two bodies after Dr. Wright became chair of CUA.

In contrast with the almost incomprehensible complexity that developed later, the original formula for operating grants was simple. Entitlements under the formula were provided to each institution as a block grant. The university was left entirely free to spend the allocation as it saw fit. The amount of the institution's grant was based on enrolment, weighted by program. This amount was determined by a basic building block, the Basic Income Unit (BIU), estimated to be the rough equivalent of the average cost of a student registered for a general baccalaureate in arts. Students enrolled in other more costly programs—honours, professional, and graduate programs—were accorded higher weights. Although referenced to a program cost analysis undertaken at the University of Toronto, the value of the BIU and the formula weights were not derived from any actual cost studies. Tuition fees were taken into account, since a standard tuition fee (along with the program weights) was included in the calculation of a university's Basic Operating Income (BOI). The formula, however, did not consider other sources of university revenue such as endowment income, gifts, and earned interest.

It was recognized that the formula did not adequately meet the needs of the four newer, "emerging" universities (Brock, Trent, Lakehead, and Laurentian), where the institutional infrastructure was still being constructed and where, owing to their small size, economies of scale were not possible. Because of this inherent defect, provision was made for these universities to receive an additional grant based on an examination of their actual needs. Similarly, additional non-formula grants were provided to the two bilingual universities (Ottawa and Laurentian), which offered academic programs in both the English and French languages.

The decision to introduce the formula was proudly announced by the minister as "an outstanding example of what can be obtained through the co-operative approach to university problems.... Not only has the principle of the formula been widely endorsed, but the particular approach advocated has been accepted as probably the most advanced method for the distribution of government funds that has yet been devised in the Western World."[25] In the first year of the formula's operation, 1967–68, on recommendation from CUA the government set the value of the Basic Income Unit at $1,320, an amount that fell short of CPUO's expectations. To prepare its case for the coming 1968–69 academic year, the presidents agreed to have their universities pool financial data to prepare a consolidated submission to CUA on the needed value of the BIU. (This was the beginning of the development of standardized financial reporting under the direction of COU's Committee of Finance Officers [COFO]). At the same time, the necessity of providing improved means for calculating the costs of operation of the emergent universities was recognized and a Sub-committee on the Financing of Emergent Universities, which had been established the preceding year, was asked on an urgent basis to prepare a brief.

When the operating grants for 1968–69 were announced, CPUO was again disappointed. Although the value of the BIU was increased by 10 percent, the presidents had recommended 15 percent. To deal with the funding problems of the four small emerging universities, CPUO had also recommended a formula that involved "a point of emergence" based on size, with the amount of the special grant decreasing as each university approached "emergence." While discussions with CUA on this issue were continuing, the government announced that the emergent grant would now be "time-based." This grant would be provided for only a limited period of time, after which it would be discontinued regardless of enrolment in the university at that time. CPUO was critical of this decision.

During the first two years, several ambiguities and technical problems affecting the application of the formula were identified and rectified through the joint efforts of the universities working through CPUO and the staff of the Department of University Affairs. Enrolment counting was improved, differentiation between general and honours students was achieved, and the counting of graduate students on a three-term-per-year basis was introduced. Standardized audit procedures were also developed and implemented. A review of formula weights based on data related to costs was undertaken. As a result, in 1969 the formula weight for medicine was substantially increased. The presidents, however, received the news "without enthusiasm" since it was not accompanied by any increase in the global operating grant, and therefore it "rewarded" those universities with faculties of medicine at the expense of those with none. Despite many studies, apart from minor modifications, the formula weights developed in the late 1960s have remained unchanged.

In the early '70s, faced with the need to expand university research activities at a time when enrolment was stabilizing at both the undergraduate and graduate levels, a proposal emerged to modify the operating grants formula by dividing the global sum into two categories: an instructional funding unit and a research funding unit. Employing this division (its supporters argued), funding for university research could be "de-coupled" from an enrolment-based funding unit for instruction, thereby protecting research funding from declines in enrolment. The Commission on Post-Secondary Education in Ontario (Wright Commission) took this approach, recommending that operating funds be divided into instructional and research envelopes.[26] COU and the universities vigorously opposed such a division. Citing the sacrosanct principle of university autonomy, they argued that the institutions should be left entirely free to determine how the global operating grant was to be allocated internally. Given the strength of the opposition, the proposal was never seriously considered by the government. The suggestion that in Ontario universities the funding of research should be separated from the funding of teaching would be back on the table more than twenty years later when it was proposed by OCUA as a means of reducing the proportion of university operating funds going to the support of research at a time when enrolment was again climbing and overall funding was severely constrained. That second time, the proposal was intended to protect funding for instruction from inroads being made to increase financial support for research—the reverse of the earlier rationale. Again, the proposal was strongly criticized by the universities and nothing came of it.[27]

When, in 1967, the federal government discontinued its direct funding of Canadian universities and colleges, the policy of the Government of Ontario not to provide funding to church-related post-secondary institutions threatened the existence of those Ontario institutions that continued to maintain affiliation with a church body. These included several federated and affiliated colleges and one freestanding university, Waterloo Lutheran. When the minister asked CPUO for suggestions on how to address the problem, the presidents first declined comment. After reflection, however, Minister Davis was informed that, should the government decide to provide funding to these institutions, CPUO would be willing to act as a conduit through which grants might flow to church-related colleges affiliated or federated with CPUO member universities. Since the new federal–provincial arrangements provided that the federal government would match fifty-fifty provincial operating grants to universities, the government decided to fund church-related institutions at 50 percent of the amount planned for under the formula. It also accepted CPOU's offer to have the "constituent" universities serve as a conduit through which funding to the affiliated and federated colleges was flowed. Waterloo Lutheran University received its grant directly.

The capital needs of Ontario universities remained high on the CPOU agenda; it argued for a formula approach to capital funding as well. In 1960, the federal government made loans available to universities through the Central Mortgage and Housing Corporation for the construction of student housing; in 1966, its provincial counterpart, the Ontario Student Housing Corporation, was formed. The Ontario Capital Aid Corporation, set up in 1964, provided funds for capital construction, which eligible institutions, including universities, could access by the sale of debentures. Under the regulations, to be eligible for funding, universities were required to raise 15 percent of the capital cost of academic facilities and 50 percent of the cost of all other capital projects. In addition, all university submissions for capital grants had to be examined by CUA, and the recommendations of that body were made on a discretionary basis. The presidents wanted a formulaic approach to capital funding analogous to that adopted for the operating grants.

In 1966, the Sub-Committee on Capital Financing was formed; a year later, the Joint CUA/CPUO was struck. Its objective was to examine the enrolment projections, create a space inventory for Ontario universities on a standardized basis, and develop a set of university space standards. Responding to the pressures, in 1968, the government announced a new interim policy on capital grants. The distinction between academic and non-academic capital projects was abolished, and the government now agreed to pay 80 percent of the cost of all approved projects to the value of $10 million, and 95 percent of the cost above $10 million. In addition, CUA was to review the universities' capital plans as a whole and set priorities under a set of new procedures. These changes were welcomed by CPUO. However, when the advisory body began to exercise its new role, it held up approvals for new facilities in engineering and geology, and for libraries pending more complete justification of need. This was not so welcome. Nor were the presidents pleased by a government announcement that same year (1968) that the total sum available for capital grants to universities in 1968–69 was $125 million, an amount considerably less than the total of the universities' capital plans. With the restricted sum now available, the interim capital formula, which had been agreed to with some misgivings by the universities, became an instrument for the distribution of scarcity.

The search for an acceptable capital formula continued. A Physical Resources Survey commissioned by the Joint CPUO/CUA Capital Studies Committee and funded by the ministry raised concerns among some members of the university community, who questioned the uses to which the data might be put. There was general support in principle for the development of province-wide space standards to determine university capital requirements. However, some universities were concerned that these standards might be used against them to "level down" capital spending. The universities accepted the need to develop realistic space standards; however, consensus on what these constituted was proving difficult to achieve. The universities were confounded by their inability to achieve consensus.

As the '60s neared an end, the four emerging universities experienced financial difficulties that threatened their viability. Both operating and capital support were inadequate. The government had placed them on notice that the special Emergent Grant, now time-based, would be discontinued. The interim capital formula failed to take into account their special needs, and the resulting shortfall in capital funding prevented them from constructing the facilities they required in order to grow. These universities were in a Catch-22 situation. CPUO undertook a study of the situation as a matter of urgency.

● ESTABLISHING A STRUCTURE

At the December 1962 meeting, their sixth in ten months, the presidents agreed to form "a continuing organization consisting of the heads of all the universities and colleges in Ontario," and to hold regular meetings at least three times a year. Three officers were named: Claude Bissell, president of the University of Toronto, chair; Edward. E. Hall, president of the University of Western Ontario, vice-chair; and William Small, secretary of the York University Board of Governors. Membership included the fourteen provincially assisted universities in Ontario. At their next meeting, in February 1963, the presidents voted themselves a name: "Presidents of the Provincially Assisted Universities and Colleges of Ontario." (To correct an oversight in the original motion, "The Committee of" was added at the following meeting in June.) By the time, almost four years later, the organization adopted a constitution the name had become the Committee of Presidents of the Universities of Ontario (CPUO). The 1966 constitution formalized the principal purposes that had governed the Committee of Presidents from its beginnings: "to promote co-operation among the provincially-assisted universities of Ontario, and between them and the government of the province; and, generally, to work for the improvement of higher education for the people of Ontario."[28]

The Committee of Presidents was designed to be decentralized. Membership was restricted to the executive heads of the member institutions, though the term "executive head" was not employed at the time. It was understood that the Committee would call on the services of personnel with relevant expertise from the member universities on a needs basis. In February 1963, the Deutsch Committee became the Academic Sub-Committee; later that same year, the name was changed to the Sub-Committee on Research. A large number of committees and affiliated groups were soon established. Affiliates were discipline groups; for example, the Committee of Ontario Deans of Engineering (CODE) and the Committee of Ontario Faculties of Medicine (COFM), or groups established by the presidents for special purposes; for example, the Council on Admissions and the Ontario Universities' Television Council. By October 1967, these groups totalled twenty, including nine subcommittees and eleven affiliates.

At the outset, there were no membership fees. When the issue was first raised in late 1963, it was decided not to establish a membership fee because of the committee's informal nature. However, it was agreed to levy a $50 fee on each institution to establish a Publication Fund to meet the costs of publicity. A year later it was agreed that, for the year 1964–65, each institution would contribute 10 cents per student enrolled to a central fund to cover operating expenses. This established the principle that membership fees would be based on enrolment in the member institutions. When the operating grants formula was introduced, the basis for calculating association fees was changed to weighted enrolment, derived from the institution's Basic Income Units, a practice that has been followed ever since. Out-of-pocket expenses for attendance at meetings, whether those of CPUO or its subcommittees and affiliates, were borne by the member institutions. Once the secretariat was established, the cost of the meetings was covered through the central budget. Member institutions, however, continued to be responsible for meeting the travel and accommodation costs of those attending. Except for secretarial support, borne in part through the central budget, affiliates covered their own expenses.

During the early years, the issue of composition was raised on several occasions. It would not be finally resolved until 1970, when an amendment to the constitution formalized the practice of having a second representative from each member institution, the academic colleague, participate fully in the work of the association. At this time, the Committee of Presidents became the Council of Ontario Universities (COU). The issue of composition, however, was never put permanently to rest. It would arise again from time to time and complicate the ability of the association to address effectively more pressing system issues.

Before settling on a council composed of two members from each institution, various options were explored. At the March 1964 meeting, the question was raised: Should the group be enlarged to include others in addition to the executive heads? Discussion was postponed pending the results of the presidents' efforts to secure academic representation on the advisory Committee on University Affairs. In keeping with their newfound concern for the involvement of academics in the development of the emerging system, however, the presidents appointed two members of teaching staff to the research committee. At the same meeting, H. F. Legaré, rector of the University of Ottawa, proposed that the presidents sponsor an annual meeting to which university registrars, business officers, and information officers would be invited. Such a meeting was held in the fall of 1964, the first of several such "conferences" sponsored by CPUO over the next few years. That same fall, J. G. Hagey, president of the University of Waterloo, proposed the establishment of an Ontario Universities' Council to be composed of representatives of various sectors of the university community, but then withdrew his proposition.

When, also in late 1964, the question was raised whether it was time for CPUO to establish a permanent secretariat, the initial response was: Let's wait to see how the recently announced Department of University

Affairs develops. In June 1965, however, the presidents asked the research committee to study the overall needs of the organization and to recommend an administrative structure that would most effectively serve the interests of the universities of Ontario. Reporting in October, the committee recommended establishment at an early date of a central office with a full-time executive vice-chair. Accepting this recommendation, the presidents also approved an increase in membership dues for the coming year (1966–67) to $1 per student to cover the necessary costs and named a search committee to recommend on the appointment of an executive vice-chair as soon as possible. At the February 1966 meeting, the chair reported that Edward Sheffield, former director of Research at the Association of Universities and Colleges of Canada (AUCC), had agreed to accept the role of vice-chair of CPUO for an initial period of two years beginning on July 1, 1966. An operating budget for the coming 1966–67 year, presented by Dr. Sheffield, was approved at this meeting. It projected a total expenditure of $47,000, including $26,300 for staff and $1,500 for office accommodation (300 square feet at $5 per square foot). Quarters for CPUO were secured at Massey College, University of Toronto.

With a secretariat now established, it was agreed that a formal constitution should be drafted. After a busy four years at the helm, President Bissell resigned as chair and was succeeded by Alex Corry, principal of Queen's University. During a discussion of CPUO affairs at its June 1966 meeting, T. H. B. (Tom) Symons, president of Trent University, suggested the need for a procedure to record differences of opinion among members in documents distributed on behalf of the association. "Note was made of the extra-ordinary difficulty of bringing together the old and new universities due to the disparity in the magnitude and nature of the problems encountered. Under these circumstances, it was not surprising to find a variety of interests and the assertion of individual (institutional) concern rather than complete and continued unanimity on the part of the presidents of all universities. The important fact remains that the regular meetings of the Committee of Presidents provided opportunity for constructive criticism and self-criticism."[29]

The issue of how to determine whether the concerns of specific member institutions had system implications that ought appropriately to engage the concern of the collectivity soon arose to test the young association. Two incidents in 1967 illustrate the point. Following the publication of the Duff-Berdahl Report,[30] many Canadian universities undertook reform of their structures of internal governance, including the addition of academic representation on governing boards. Concurrently, university student leaders began to press for student membership on governing boards. After a review of its governance structure, the University of Western Ontario (UWO) proposed amendments to its Act, and a private member's bill was introduced in the legislature to effect the changes. This provided an occasion for public debate concerning the role of students in university government. During examination in the legislature's Private Bills Committee, the students succeeded in persuading the committee to propose amendments to permit the students to elect one of their own number to sit on the university's board of governors, in substitution for the university's proposed representation for the students by an individual who was not a student.

Considering university autonomy to be at stake, the presidents moved. At its March 1967 meeting, CPUO took strong objection to the action of the legislative committee, describing it as an unwarranted intrusion into the university's internal affairs. As CPUO saw it, universities must be free to determine for themselves the composition of their governing boards. The chair of CPUO wrote Premier Robarts expressing the committee's grave concern that the amendments to the UWO Act approved in the "Private Bills Committee" violated the principle of university autonomy, and expressed the hope that no legislative action would be taken unless the clauses dealing with the composition of the board of governors were passed as originally approved by the University of Western Ontario. The presidents were at pains to state that this did not involve taking a position for or against the desirability of having student representation on university governing boards. The CPUO position was that the university should be free to determine such a matter for itself. The government agreed. At third reading, it introduced its own amendments to the bill, revisions that had the effect of restoring the original text. In a subsequent letter to the chair of CPUO, Minister Davis agreed that the universities should be left to settle matters of governance for themselves, but he expressed the hope that CPUO would address as quickly as possible the question of student participation in university governance. His hope proved forlorn. When almost a quarter-century later the Rae government set out regulations covering the composition of governing boards, there was no criticism from COU or the universities. The boundaries defining university autonomy had obviously moved.

The decision of CPOU to enter the lists on this matter had other consequences. The presidents had invited the chairs of the university governing bodies to attend the meeting. (In earlier times, the chairs of university governing boards had frequently been directly involved in negotiations with the government, often meeting informally with the premier to argue their institution's case.) Energized by the threat to university autonomy, the chair of the board at the University of Guelph proposed that board chairs should form their own organization, noting that university presidents could not always be expected to speak on behalf of the chairs. This did not go down very well with the presidents. Although they accepted that board chairs should be involved from time to time to argue on behalf of the universities, the presidents were of the view that it would be a mistake for board chairs to meet together without them in attendance. The chair of CPUO was asked to convey this view to the chair of the board of the University of Guelph, and he did so.

When the issue did not directly affect university autonomy, however, CPUO was less inclined to become directly involved. Meeting a month earlier, immediately after the announcement of the operating grants for the coming 1967–68 year, the presidents discussed how they might protest what all judged to be an unacceptably low level of increase. In addition to concern over the level of the increase in the global grant, the presidents of the four emerging universities were particularly upset over the inadequate amount provided as a supplementary grant to their institutions. They sought to have their criticism included in the CPUO response. While CPUO Chair Corry encouraged the four to make common cause, he expressed the view that it would be inappropriate for the committee as a whole to become involved. Although he thought that the complaint was unlikely to produce any increase in funding, President Bissell argued that the universities should stand together on such a matter. His view did not prevail. Later, CPUO agreed to study the need to develop a formula for the Emergent Grant.

In June 1967, the presidents again reviewed the structure of their organization. There was general agreement that some changes were needed but no consensus on what these changes should be. A decision was made that CPUO should continue in its present form as a presidents' organization, but that, for the purpose of improving communications with the academic legislative bodies of the member institutions, members might bring an academic colleague to some (but not all) meetings. Member institutions were given discretion as to how the academic colleague was chosen; in practice, most were chosen by the senate or analogous senior academic body of the university. Academic colleagues began to attend CPUO meetings in September 1967.

The early years saw some experimentation with ways of improving communication among the various university constituencies. In June 1966, CPUO and the Ontario Confederation of University Faculty Associations (OCUFA) jointly sponsored a conference on university affairs. A year later, the Ontario Union of Students (OUS) was included in a tripartite conference. Inclusion of students in these conferences was partly the result of a realization that students had a legitimate role to play, and partly a response to the growing militancy of the student leaders, who were making increasingly strident demands for a voice in university affairs. The experiment was not a success. In the post-conference review, Francis Leddy, president of the University of Windsor, who was responsible for its organization, reported that the conference had left the students "puzzled." Dissatisfied with the original agenda, the invited student leaders had demanded the addition of a session on university governance. The session was added but the topic did not interest many presidents; the students were then annoyed at how few of them attended. At the review, CPUO agreed that some other form of communication with the students should be attempted, perhaps by meeting with them separately. But this suggestion was not followed up.

CPUO never succeeded in engaging Ontario university student leaders in its activities. In this period, student leaders tended to be very militant and confrontational, as much interested in using the universities as instruments of social and economic reform as in improving the lot of the students on campus. On the issue of the role of students in university governance, a major student issue, the presidents took the position that this was a matter for each university to determine for itself. Despite this, the CPUO Sub-Committee on Research and Planning (Planning had been recently added to its mandate) produced a paper on the subject. Presented to CPUO at its November 1967 meeting, a meeting also attended by representatives of university boards of governors, it was later published as a "study paper."[31] The paper, which took a somewhat conservative position on the role of students in institutional governance, was immediately dubbed the "Grey Flannel Report" by the student leaders and severely criticized for its tokenism. It had little impact on the debate. The presidents subsequently conceded that they had made a mistake in not consulting the students during the preparation of the paper. Thereafter, CPUO declined to be drawn into this contentious issue. Relations between CPUO and the Ontario Union of Students continued to be cool, particularly on policy issues affecting the role of student organizations in both local institutional and provincial university affairs.

Disengagement from the issue of student involvement in university governance, however, did not mean that CPUO ceased to be involved in some major issues affecting students. Its involvement had begun in 1962, when the presidents lobbied successfully for the Ontario Graduate Fellowship Program. Thereafter, the Ontario Council on Graduate Studies was assigned responsibility for monitoring this program and recommending improvements. During the '60s, both the number and value of these fellowships increased, though never to the complete satisfaction of the universities. A Sub-Committee on Student Aid was established early, as was an Association of Student Awards Officers, which became an affiliate of CPUO. In 1966, when the government established an awards program to provide financial assistance to undergraduate students, CPUO representatives, as well as representatives from OCUFA and OUS, were named to the advisory Committee on Student Awards. That same year, the government established the Ontario Student Housing Corporation to provide funding for the construction of student residences. CPUO immediately struck a Sub-Committee on Student Housing to assist member institutions in dealing with this corporation.

A few years later, the Ontario Union of Students, like its national counterpart, the Canadian Union of Students, self-destructed. Both unions voted themselves out of existence. A much less radical group, the Ontario Federation of Students, succeeded the OUS. Essentially a creature of participating local student councils, OFS needed broad approval for any policy statements it developed and for the activities it undertook. This guaranteed that it would adopt a much less confrontational approach and narrow its focus to issues of direct concern to students: such as tuition fees, student assistance, and student housing. During the '70s, when student aid and housing continued to be issues in which the government was heavily involved, particularly student aid during the period when Harry Parrott was minister, COU worked along with OFS on a number of joint committees. Relations between the two groups, however, were never close. And when in the '80s, the pressures to expand revenue caused COU to support increases in tuition fees, something to which OFS was unalterably opposed, contacts became infrequent and more acrimonious.

In January 1968, the presidents discussed a proposal for the creation of a General Assembly of Universities of Ontario. To include university administrators, faculty, students, and board members, the assembly would serve as a vehicle for the regular dissemination of information on issues of importance to the universities, and would provide an opportunity for the exchange of opinions among the various university groups, "while the CPUO retained the central role." Adoption of this proposal implied a return to the original composition of the committee as a presidents' club without academic colleagues. When a majority opposed the proposal, it was abandoned. The committee then agreed to continue to experiment with the inclusion of academic colleagues, but not to formalize this arrangement. During the debate, the role of board chairs was again raised. "The consensus appeared to be that it should not be necessary to meet regularly with board chairmen since presidents should have the confidence of their boards."[32] It would be another decade before the board chairs became formally organized. The relationship between the board chairmen and the successor to CPUO (COU) would never be very active or effective.

In December 1967, two more institutions, Waterloo Lutheran University and the Royal Military College of Canada, were invited to join CPUO with observer status. The matter had come up two years earlier, when the president of Waterloo Lutheran University enquired about joining the club, but a decision had been deferred. This time the Department of University Affairs was consulted. When the deputy minister made it clear that Waterloo Lutheran was not a provincially assisted university, the presidents agreed that it would not be appropriate to extend full membership. It was recognized, however, that Waterloo Lutheran had a legitimate interest in CPUO affairs and was affected by many of its activities, and that the decision of the government to provide half-funding to church-related institutions gave it quasi-publicly funded status. The Royal Military College, although a federal institution, was judged to be in a similar situation; it was also invited to join as an observer. Both institutions accepted. Since observer institutions were declared eligible to attend a part of most CPUO meetings and to receive copies of the minutes of full meetings, and because they were invited on appropriate occasions to attend meetings of CPUO sub-committees and affiliates, this form of second-class status carried little negative implication. In 1971, the Ontario Institute for Studies in Education (OISE), an affiliate of the University of Toronto, also was granted observer status. The reasons for this decision are not recorded. By 1975 (as a result of a mutation whose cause remains unrecorded), observer institutions had become associate members of COU. This raised the number of council members to seventeen, a number exceeded only when more institutions were accorded degree-granting status: Ryerson Polytechnical Institute in 1978 and Nipissing University (previously Nipissing College of Laurentian University) in 1993. Waterloo Lutheran was accorded full membership in 1973, when it divested itself of its religious affiliation and reinvented itself as Wilfrid Laurier University. When OISE was fully integrated into the University of Toronto in 1995, it ceased to be a member.

In the summer of 1968, John B. Macdonald, president of the National Science Council and former president of the University of British Columbia, succeeded Dr. Sheffield as executive vice-chair of CPUO. Upon appointment, he was asked to recommend on a suitable structure for the association. His subsequent report described the existing structure as complex, the result of an accumulation of tasks rather than a conscious attempt to design a satisfactory structure. In principle, he argued, structure should follow form. The objectives of the organization should determine its structure. The basic problem facing the association involved a paradox: how to maintain institutional autonomy and at the same time develop system planning.

Dr. Macdonald presented two options. One, conventional and adopted in many jurisdictions, involved development of a clear definition of the role of a central planning body vis-à-vis the individual universities. Adoption of this approach would require provincial legislation to give the central body the necessary executive authority to make binding collective decisions. Were such legislation to be imposed by the government, it would result in the creation of the University of Ontario by another name, an option that had already been firmly rejected. If the universities themselves were to adopt this approach and undertake to establish their own body with executive authority, it would be necessary to amend all of the individual university acts, which was bound to be a rocky road. An alternative approach, the one Macdonald favoured, would be to develop a system embodying meaningful "collective autonomy." This option, he argued, offered better prospects. Based on the aphorism that knowledge is power, this approach would emphasize the development of a joint capacity to examine issues on the basis of careful and competent research and analysis; one that would present a clear exposition of the alternatives and seek to obtain consensus on the most reasonable one. It would encourage the universities to develop a consensus on planning that would diminish the need for legislative intervention. The only coercion would be that of logic. Individual universities would find it difficult, although not impossible, to reject the collective judgment. At the same time, the area of debate would be greatly narrowed and the ability of the universities to speak effectively to government would be increased.

The kind of structure required, Macdonald argued, was one that would provide the Ontario university community with an acceptable and persuasive voice, both to its constituent members—governors, administration, faculty and students—and to the public and the government. At the same time, the structure he proposed would possess capability for sophisticated and efficient analyses, followed by the ability to reach agreed-upon collective policies expeditiously. Such a structure, he argued, could protect institutional autonomy at the same time the needs of the system were met. Dr. Macdonald recommended that the Committee of Presidents be transformed into a collectivity of university representatives with a more functional arrangement of responsibilities—a council of universities of Ontario, composed of two members from each institution, the executive head and an academic colleague, with a full-time executive director and an expanded secretariat staff capable of undertaking research on behalf of the system.[33]

By September 1969, this proposal had been accepted in principle by a majority of the member universities, and plans were proceeding for its implementation. In the interim, given the pressing need to expand CPUO's capacity to collect and analyze data on the operations of the universities, a research division had been established within the secretariat and a full-time director of research appointed. Over the next several years, the association's research capacity grew to exceed that of both the ministry and CUA, and became the primary source for system data collection and analysis. To provide the required additional space, the secretariat was moved from Massey College to larger quarters at 230 Bloor Street West in Toronto. The formal change in designation, from "Committee of Presidents" to "Council of Ontario Universities," took place when the CPUO constitution was amended in March 1970. Although brought under a microscope by COU several times in the ensuing decades, this structure remains essentially unchanged.

● OTHER SYSTEM PLANNING ACTIVITIES

From its beginnings, CPUO was significantly involved in the development of a structure in which university–government relations might be managed, in planning for graduate studies and in work on university financing. In addition, it was engaged in a number of system planning exercises in which various components of member institutions were directly involved. Some of these planning exercises were seen from the beginning as time-limited; when the project was completed, the agency established to oversee the project would be disbanded. Initially, others were seen as ongoing. However, in some cases, changed circumstances or unforeseen developments (including failure) caused a later decision to terminate the activity. The most successful and most enduring of the activities in which CPUO initially became involved are those that can be classified as falling within the category of "service" activities: those activities that pose no threat to institutional autonomy and carry little political freight.

UNIVERSITY TELEVISION

Efforts to develop a co-ordinated approach to the development of educational television (ETV) began early. Two factors—one quantitative, the other qualitative—persuaded the presidents to take a strong interest in the development of this instructional medium: the crisis of student numbers prompted them to explore its use for mass teaching, and a growing awareness that some instructional material can be better taught by means of television. A Sub-Committee on Television was struck in 1964; a year later, a major report was published—the third and last of the reports emanating from the Deutsch Committee.[34] This led to the establishment of the Ontario Universities' Television Council as an affiliate of CPUO. In June 1966, before CPUO itself had a secretariat, the Television Council established an office staffed by a part-time executive officer and a full-time assistant to serve as a centre for information and advice on closed-circuit (and later broadcast) educational television.

This council worked to develop standards for equipment and to establish guidelines covering the rights and responsibilities of university academic staff using ETV (in collaboration with the Canadian Association of University Teachers). The council also collaborated with the Ontario Department of Education on its proposed development of an educational television network. Under the council's aegis, the presidents urged the government to appoint a broadly representative commission on educational television. These efforts were rewarded in 1968, when the minister announced the government's decision to establish the Ontario Educational Broadcasting Authority (later TVO), to be responsible for the production of educational television in the province.

With the establishment of this agency, the direct involvement of CPUO in educational television was gradually reduced. In 1973, the council and the sub-committee were disbanded. The medium had failed to live up to its early promise as a cost-effective way of delivering instructional services across a broad spectrum. As a result, though they continued to develop specialized programs, by this time most universities had abandoned plans for large-scale academic programming via ETV. It was now time for collective activity in this area to cease.

UNIVERSITY COMPUTING

CPUO's parallel interest in the development of university computing led in 1967 to the establishment of a Sub-Committee on Computing, with a mandate to study and make recommendations to the presidents on problems related to the development, co-ordination, and financing of university computing services in Ontario. The sub-committee recommended the establishment of a network of regional computer centres. The Committee on University Affairs, also studying the area, supported the idea of regional university computing centres, but preferred that they be established outside the universities and funded directly by the Department of University Affairs. In 1969, to keep pace with rapidly moving events, CPUO established a Computer Co-ordination Group headed by a full-time director to serve as a clearing house for information related to computer technology. That year, the government committed $5.2 million in earmarked funding for the expansion of university computing facilities, to be distributed among the universities in the same proportion as the operating grants. It would be a one-time grant. Thereafter, the announcement said, university expenditures on computing would be funded through the operating grants. In 1971, the presidents' involvement in computer matters was refocused and expanded with the establishment of an Office of Computer Co-ordination. The activities of this office are examined in the next chapter.

LIBRARY CO-ORDINATION

After the Spinks Commission had drawn attention to the weak state of most Ontario university libraries, the presidents moved quickly to develop a co-operative approach to sharing existing resources and to initiate planning for expansion. In 1966, the Ontario New University Library Project, funded by the government and administered by the University of Toronto (U of T), provided 35,000 volumes to support undergraduate programs in arts and science at Guelph, Brock, and Trent universities, and at U of T's Erindale and Scarborough colleges. That same year, CPUO approved in principle the creation of a provincial university library system to include province-wide reader services, an interlibrary transit service, and a provincial bibliographic centre to be established at the University of Toronto. The Ontario Council of University Librarians (OCUL), made up of the chief librarians of member institutions, was formed in 1967 and became an affiliate of CPUO.

The first practical fruit of these collaborative efforts came in 1967, when the interlibrary transit service was inaugurated. Operating out of York University, it provided daily service by truck to the twelve universities in southern Ontario and by air to the two northern universities, Lakehead and Laurentian. In 1969, Quebec universities were added. The service was an immediate success and demonstrated the value of co-operative activity from which both the participating institutions and the system as a whole derive benefit. It continues to this day.

Province-wide planning for library collections proved more difficult to effect. In 1967, the presidents accepted an offer by the University of Toronto to make space available in the university's new Humanities and Social Sciences Research Library (later renamed the Robarts Library), then in the planning stage to house the provincial bibliographic centre. Two special sub-committees were struck to develop standards for the assessment of university library needs in the province, one for undergraduate programming and the other for graduate programming and research. Both groups retained consultants to undertake the preliminary work. In the fall of 1968, the undergraduate sub-committee reported failure. It had concluded that, given all of the variables, no single set of quantitative standards was sufficient. Dismissing the committee with thanks, CPUO decided that the task of developing such standards was too time consuming and laborious to warrant further pursuit.

That same year, agreement was reached with CUA on a set of guidelines for the development of an Ontario universities' library system, and all of the universities committed themselves to it. These guidelines embodied two basic propositions: (1) each university would become essentially self-sufficient in the provision of library services for undergraduate programs and be effectively interdependent in the provision of library services for graduate programs and research; and (2) the provincial system would involve appropriate co-ordination and centralization of technical processes, including automation where necessary, and appropriate centralized storage of less frequently used materials. The universities recognized that, while extensive duplication of library collections was necessary in the basic undergraduate program fields, they could not afford to duplicate strong research collections in all fields. Working out how to prevent duplication, however, was to prove very difficult. Existing collections and their use would first have to be assessed, then the library collections within each university would have to be rationalized. Ultimately, a system of co-operative planning would have to be developed to identify those discipline areas in which library holdings required expansion. This latter would need to be done in conjunction with the expansion of graduate programming then being undertaken through OCGS and ACAP. Much effort would be expended on this task; in the end, the results were meagre.

At the outset, no university had sufficient information on the library holdings of its sister institutions, and no practical mechanism existed for gaining access to these holdings. At the same time, many universities had plans for library expansion and were requesting capital grants for this purpose. Faced with these multiple requests for library funding, CUA was pressing for greater rationalization in this expensive area. At a joint meeting of CPUO and CUA in the summer of 1968, a sharp exchange took place over library space requirements for the system. The Committee on University Affairs supported the proposed new research library at the University of Toronto, including the provincial bibliographic centre; however, it considered that, in total, the capital requests of the universities for library expansion were excessive and showed lack of system planning. As a consequence, CUA withheld approval of all university requests for capital grants for libraries pending further justification of space requirements. To resolve the impasse, the presidents asked the Ontario Council of University Librarians to undertake an assessment of Ontario universities' library needs to 1976.

A preliminary report from OCUL, presented to CPUO in April 1969, was judged to be incomplete and was handed to the CPUO research division for further development. A year later, a revised report was accepted by CPUO and forwarded to CUA. Based on projected levels of enrolment to 1975–76 and involving extrapolation from existing university library policies—although admittedly not taking into account the longer-term development of new technologies—the report concluded that by 1975, the system would need an additional 1.0 to 1.4 million square feet of library space, at an estimated cost of $40 million. CUA remained unconvinced. In the meantime, CPUO launched the Ontario Universities' Bibliographic Centre Project. In addition to improving communication and co-operation among Ontario university libraries and establishing liaison with similar provincial and regional groups, one of the project's principal aims was a standardization of bibliographic records among the university libraries in order to provide a basis for the development of a system union catalogue. As the decade ended, much remained to be done.[35]

UNIVERSITY ADMISSIONS

Before CPUO was established, university admissions was the one area in which Ontario universities already co-operated, through the University Matriculation Board. An expanded co-operative approach to admissions was quickly developed. In October 1964, a meeting of university registrars was convened to examine the issue of multiple admissions. It produced ready agreement to pool information on unfilled places in a central clearing house, for weekly distribution among the universities during the annual admissions cycle. A 1965 report, *Ontario Universities' Application Centre,*[36] developed a comprehensive scheme for collective action on admissions, but no action was taken on implementation. In 1966, the Ontario Universities' Council on Admissions was established as an affiliate of CPUO. A set of common admissions procedures was agreed upon for the 1967–68 admissions cycle. The year 1968 saw the adoption of a common application form and common dates on which offers of admission would go out from the universities to applicants.

Serious planning for a provincial applications centre began in 1969. Some problems continued over multiple applications and acceptances, and there was some nagging public concern (occasionally exacerbated by questions asked of the minister in the legislature) about qualified students failing to find a place. As well, the recently released Hall-Dennis Report recommended extensive changes in the secondary school system, recommendations that called for improved liaison between the universities and the secondary schools in matters affecting curriculum and testing.[37] This combination of factors persuaded both the presidents and the government that the time had come to centralize university admissions. It would be three years, however, before the Ontario Universities' Application Centre (OUAC) opened. An immediate and major success, OUAC has served the Ontario university system well ever since. The Application Centre is an enduring example of a COU service activity of proven value to both the students and the universities. When direct service is the primary objective, political considerations and institutional ambitions can be accorded second place. Voluntary agreement on collective action can be more easily reached and maintained.

In 1968, the Council on Admissions was asked to examine the issues surrounding admission to university of students from the colleges of applied arts and technology. This presented a complex set of problems. Preoccupied with other more pressing matters, the universities were not very interested; as a result, the study went nowhere. It would be almost 20 years, in vastly changed circumstances, before these issues were effectively addressed and resolved. The negative effects of the government's decision to create a binary post-secondary system that dealt with universities and colleges of applied arts and technology (CAATs) separately had begun.

TEACHER EDUCATION

In 1966, the MacLeod Commission on the Training of Elementary School Teachers recommended that the then current one-year program beyond grade twelve for the training and certification of elementary school teachers in Ontario be replaced by a full university course, including professional training in either a concurrent or a consecutive mode.[38] With strong support from the minister, moves to implement the recommendation began immediately. CPUO became involved straightaway. A Sub-Committee on Teacher Education, chaired by James Gibson, president of Brock University, was struck to recommend policy and procedures to be followed in the establishment of new programs in teacher education, and to act as a continuing advisory committee on the matter. In 1968, a statement of principles embodying the essential conditions under which the universities would assume responsibility for teacher training in the province, especially those covering financing, was approved for use by member institutions in working out individual agreements with the Department of Education.

A year later, CPUO and the Department of University Affairs agreed on a set of common principles. In March 1969, these principles were set out in a memorandum of understanding released jointly by the minister, CUA and CPUO. This memorandum noted that the costs of providing teacher training in the province should eventually be financed through the university formula grants system. Its work done, the Gibson Committee was discharged with thanks. Later that same year, a Joint CUA-CPUO Sub-Committee was struck to work out the details. Its work, published in March 1971, became the basis for inclusion of teacher education in the Ontario operating grants formula.[39] CPUO efforts represented a substantial contribution to the development of improved academic and professional education for elementary teachers in the province. A decade later, when the Ministry of Education undertook what proved to be a long-running exercise in the reform of secondary school education, COU established machinery to assist.

CHAPTER 2

The Winds Shift: Dark Clouds Begin to Form

DESPITE THE HOST OF ISSUES confronting their institutions, as the decade began the mood among the leaders of the Ontario university community was one of quiet confidence. When the collectivity was established in 1962, these leaders had been sometimes suspicious of one another, and cautious. The presidents were hesitant, their initial joint decisions sometimes halting. Co-operation among Ontario universities was a new concept, one that seemed to contradict the cherished principle of institutional autonomy. The presidents, however, had recognized their mutual interest in facing collectively the problems generated by the projected unprecedented expansion in enrolment and the prospect of increased pressure from the government—pressure that inevitably would arrive conjointly with the large increases in public funding that all of them considered essential to fuel the expansion of their institutions. They realized that, unless checked and balanced, at the extreme such pressures could lead to a loss of autonomy and ultimately to government control—an unwanted and feared prospect.

By 1970, much had changed. Ontario now had an interdependent system of universities. University revenues, largely derived from government grants, had increased to match enrolment growth; an operating grants formula was in place; graduate planning had begun; and a buffer body containing academic representation was in place. The Committee of Presidents of the Universities of Ontario (CPUO) was a strong, vibrant organization composed of two representatives from each member institution—the executive head and an academic colleague, a fact shortly to be officially recognized by a constitutional amendment that changed the name of the organization to the Council of Ontario Universities (COU). Council was assisted by a large number of committees and affiliated groups: in 1970, twenty-four committees and councils, and thirteen affiliates. With an annual budget of some one million dollars, three-quarters of which was contributed by the member institutions, its activities were supported by a secretariat staffed by some thirty-five persons.

Notes to chapter 2 are on pp. 216–220

A number of co-operative enterprises had been undertaken; co-ordination of university activities was increasing. The recent establishment within the secretariat of a research division had significantly improved the analytical and planning capacity of the collectivity. In the year 1970, a total of forty-three studies either had been completed or were in progress. This included *Ring of Iron*, whose publication marked the first major exercise in province-wide academic discipline planning.

A positive relationship had been established between the Committee of Presidents, representing the collectivity of universities, and the Committee on University Affairs, the buffer body standing between the universities and the government. This structure was said to constitute "the unique strength of the Ontario system." CUA, advisory to the government, was balanced by CPUO, which represented the interests of the universities. Together these bodies served to maintain the "delicate balance" between institutional autonomy and the well-being of the system, a necessary condition (it was judged) for the creation of confidence in the system by the university community, the government and the public. The interface was dynamic, although sparks could and sometimes did fly. The resulting decisions, however, usually reflected both sensitivity to essential academic considerations and genuine concern for sound public policy. This unique pattern of system co-ordination, while subject to further refinement and improvement, was said to represent "an advanced model of the new kind of government-university machinery which is rapidly becoming the design of the future."[1]

Still, this was not a time for complacency. More needed to be done to improve quality and to expand system planning, particularly in the area of graduate studies, where the universities were under pressure from both CUA and the Department of University Affairs to rationalize this expensive area of academic programming. Uncertainties existed over enrolment, and adjustments would need to be made to deal with slower growth. There were indications of coming reductions in government grants, and some issues affecting the structure of the system remained unresolved. The draft report of the Commission on Post-Secondary Education in Ontario (Wright Commission), which would address many of these issues, was expected soon.

This mood of quiet optimism soon proved misplaced. The universities were not as strong or as popular as their leaders thought. The ground was beginning to shift under them. The period of rapid enrolment growth, which some still thought would continue intermittently for a protracted period, was coming to an end. Those universities that had achieved their enrolment objectives and were planning to cap enrolment would be relatively unaffected. Those still in an expansion mode, mainly the newer and smaller institutions, were much more exposed to the negative financial impact of a failure to meet their enrolment targets. System enrolment continued to rise slowly, but the effects were felt differentially. In some universities, enrolment declined. These perturbations would have an effect on the system and on the voluntary association of universities that served them.

In terms of system planning, three factors were at work: (1) the changing economic environment and, as a consequence, (2) the changing view of the government toward further investment in higher education, and (3) changing public opinion about the value of universities. The Ontario university system, now large, complex, and still growing, was proving expensive. To the members of the university community, this was as it should be. Economists, politicians, and the paying public, however, began to see it differently. During the 1960s, encouraged and supported by academic experts, opinion leaders, and (above all) by the government in power, higher education had been a major growth industry in Ontario. At the beginning of the '70s, a dramatic shift occurred. The economy faltered. Reduced government revenues produced a concern over the extent of public spending on higher education. The downturn in the economy resulted in shrinking employment opportunities for university graduates. The universities were no longer seen as major engines for the production of economic growth. A public that a decade earlier had enthusiastically supported increased spending on universities now grew more critical. Reduced faith in the ability of the universities to generate jobs was accompanied by a growing sense that they were not very responsive to the needs of a changing society. Their reputations were further damaged by media accounts of the excesses of the student radicals and faculty militants, and the controversy over their "de-Canadianization."

As late as 1968, the Ontario treasurer could stand in his place in the legislature (as his predecessor had done a decade earlier) and state: "Education is our principal tool for increasing the productive capacity of our economy, for creating a better society, and for providing the opportunity for every citizen to develop his [sic] fullest potential."[2] A year later, his cabinet colleague, the minister of University Affairs, would stand in that same place to announce: "we have reached the end of the line; ... we cannot afford to increase by any significant degree the amounts (of funding) being directed to universities in future years."[3] As overall economic conditions forced governments to introduce constraints on public expenditure, the university sector now found itself in competition with other areas for funds at the same time that its claims to public funding were taken less seriously. Government efforts to control spending began to affect university revenues; they also began to intrude on university autonomy.

As the '70s began, those economists who earlier had confidently asserted that greater investment in higher education would improve the economy and would even show "measurable profits" both for the individual and for society as a whole were replaced by a more conservative breed. These "rate-of-return" theorists challenged the conventional economic wisdom that heavy investment in higher education would yield profitable social returns. David Dodge, an economist then on the faculty at Queen's University, argued that too little attention had been paid to non-educational factors such as native ability, family background, class origins, and ability to learn on the job. These factors, he argued, played a greater role in determining a worker's productivity than did his or her level of formal education. His analysis of the social rate of return in three highly paid professions—accountancy, engineering, and science— led him to conclude that these returns were "negative at a rate of five percent or better."[4]

Given this shift in the wind among economists, declining government revenues and concern that the Canadian labour market would be unable to absorb the increasing numbers of university graduates caused a spending break to be applied. New budgetary tools now came into use. As the new decade began, with a view to improving the province's ability to undertake long-term financial planning, the Treasury Board introduced "program budgeting." This approach was designed to limit expenditures and reduce deficits without raising taxes. Under program budgeting, the Treasury Board Secretariat determined centrally overall spending projections for each ministry/department and the ministry was then asked to prepare a five-year budget forecast within the spending constraints it was given.

The university sector immediately felt the effects of this new approach. Early in 1970, Treasury Board advised both the Ministry (as it had become) of University Affairs and CUA that the increase in the value of the BIU for the coming year, 1970–71, should not exceed 6 percent ($1,640), slightly less than the $1,650 recommended by CUA. The letter, however, went further. In the light of the need for general constraint, CUA was advised to revise downwards its recommendation on increases in capital funding for universities, to raise the loan ceiling on the Student Awards Program, to consider eliminating of the Ontario Graduate Fellowship Program (OGS) and the Ontario scholarship program for Grade thirteen graduates, and to introduce tuition fees in colleges of education equivalent to those in arts and science.

Both the ministry and CUA raised strenuous objections. Minister Davis did not object to Treasury Board setting a total spending limit. But he did object to "the style of approach employed," one that entered into details about how the global grants to the universities should be allocated. This approach, he said, called into question CUA's integrity. "For if the Treasury Board is to make these kinds of decisions,... then there is reason to ask why we need an advisory body at all."[5] In January 1972, this "interference" of Treasury Board in university affairs provoked a public outcry. It also ruptured "with a vengeance" the spirit of co-operation that until then had existed between COU and CUA. Shortly before the advisory body was scheduled to submit its recommendations on funding for the coming year, a document from Treasury Board was circulated to the CUA members. Again, several alternatives were proposed. The memorandum concluded by stating that decisions would need to be made among these alternatives in order to guide the ministry when preparing its 1972–73 estimates in order to meet the required limitations on overall spending. Presented with this document, one of the academic members of CUA, Professor Phyllis Grosskurth of the University of Toronto, took the position that such a document limited the advisory body's autonomy. It permitted the committee a choice only among a restricted set of alternatives that were already before the cabinet. She resigned and went public.[6]

The fears of COU and the universities were realized when a short while later, the minister announced several changes in policy. These changes included items from the now infamous Treasury Board memorandum: an increase of $100 in undergraduate tuition fees, an increase in the loan ceiling in the Ontario Student Awards Program from $600 to $800, and the imposition of a third-term fee for graduate students. CUA had, it turned out, reluctantly agreed to the first two, but had not been consulted on the third. Relations between COU and CUA soured.

● RING OF IRON

The first major effort at academic planning for the Ontario university system took place in the professional discipline of engineering, undertaken by CPUO with the co-operation of the Committee of Ontario Deans of Engineering (CODE). In 1969, the presidents decided to undertake a comprehensive review of engineering education in the province and asked CODE, a CPUO affiliate, to draw up plans. The objective was to develop a master plan that might be used as a guide for the growth of engineering education during the '70s—one that would provide high-quality programs and make best use of resources and opportunities for innovation while maintaining maximum freedom of choice for the students. Funded by the Department of University Affairs, the study was undertaken by a three-member independent commission composed of a full-time chair, Philip Lapp, an engineer from private industry, and two part-time members, John Hodgins, former dean of Engineering at McMaster University, and Colin Mackay, former president of the University of New Brunswick. The commission began work in October 1969. Its report, *Ring of Iron*, along with three accompanying research reports, was released in December 1971.[7]

The report was both comprehensive and contentious. Its defining concept was the need for the development of an integrated system of engineering education in Ontario, one in which each school would play a distinctive role, with the group of schools together providing a variety of programs and approaches to engineering education in the province. The report addressed three basic questions: Are there too many engineering schools in Ontario? Can adequate provisions be made for anticipated enrolment to 1980? What should be the enrolment pattern and distribution? Addressed in the light of two major criteria—academic quality and cost—the answers to these questions were employed to establish a basis for determining the size of each engineering school in the province. The commission concluded: "If Ontario is to achieve a rational pattern of engineering education, it will be necessary to establish enrolment quotas at the bachelor's, master's and doctorate levels. Individual institutions cannot continue to act independently in such matters; each must operate as a component of the system."[8]

The enrolment plan for the system developed by the commission assigned specific roles to each university based on its judgment of what was consistent with regional, provincial and national requirements for engineers. It then assigned both system and individual institution enrolment targets for all undergraduate and graduate programs. Although convinced that too little attention had been paid to such matters as efficiency and productivity, the commission rejected cost-benefit analysis as inappropriate. Instead, it developed a method for computing unit costs (that is, cost per student) based on average class size: the average number of full-time students per full-time equivalent member of teaching faculty. Employing a simple (what most today would consider simplistic) analysis, it judged that to be viable academically and economically, a school of engineering should have at least ten full-time equivalent (FTE) faculty and offer a minimum of three programs with an enrolment of 200 to 275 students in each. From this basis, the commission argued that the minimum undergraduate enrolment in any school should be between 600 and 1,300 students. To ensure "a reasonable balance" between undergraduate and graduate programs, it proposed that the total number of graduate students should be equal to the number of bachelor's degrees in engineering awarded in the previous year. At the same time, it urged that enrolment above 2,000 students in any school be discouraged to overcome "dehumanizing tendencies." Based on these criteria, in 1969–70 only two universities (Toronto and Waterloo) had enrolments above the minimum. Three others (Carleton, Queen's and Guelph) had enrolments near the minimum; enrolment in each of the other six was well below the minimum. The commission's conclusion: "Ontario has more engineering programs than can be justified by any criterion other than the need for geographical distribution."[9] Yet new programs continued to be introduced.

Even taking into account projected increases in enrolment, the commission concluded that system enrolment capacity in engineering would be excessive until 1975 at least. Unless enrolment in the smaller schools increased, cost inefficiencies would continue to be higher than necessary and academic quality would vary. It recommended a reduction in first-year student intake at both the University of Toronto and the University of Waterloo, establishment of an upper limit on enrolment intake in the other faculties of engineering, development of a new program at Lakehead University to include graduates from the local CAAT technology program, and elimination of the two-year program at Laurentian University. Based on a projection of the number of baccalaureate degrees awarded in 1971, it also recommended that system graduate enrolment be limited to 450 in 1973–74. Furthermore, the commission recommended that no new school of engineering be established in Ontario before 1980, and then only if it could be introduced as part of the total provincial system. Addressing these recommendations would test the ambitions of individual universities; above all, it would test the will of the collectivity (COU) to engage in participatory planning for the system.

Debate in council over the recommendations in *Ring of Iron* (known as the Lapp Report) took place in the context of increased financial pressures on the universities resulting from overall enrolments that were no longer meeting projections, resultant reductions in government funding, and the release of the report of the Commission on Post-Secondary Education in Ontario (Wright Report). The first objection to the report was registered at the council meeting at which *Ring of Iron* was tabled. It came from Laurentian University, which voiced strong opposition to the recommendation that the university's two-year program in engineering be closed and no new students admitted in 1972. Laurentian requested support from COU for a request that the Ministry agree to continue funding for the program. (Earlier the same day, council met with John White, the new minister of Colleges and Universities, who had succeeded William Davis, now the premier. The minister, soon to become well known for his motto "More scholar for the dollar," informed council of growing public antipathy toward the universities, in particular with respect to their overemphasis on expansion, a message that was not well received.) The executive director of COU advised council that he had spoken to Dr. Lapp, who declined to revise the commission's recommendation. The president of the University of Guelph, William Winegard, while expressing sympathy toward the regional considerations put forward by Laurentian University (located in the heart of the province's hardrock mining industry), noted that all seven four-year engineering programs were operating at 25 percent capacity, and that current needs for engineers could readily be met without the Laurentian program. (Winegard would later become chair of COU, and subsequently, chair of OCUA and a member of the Fisher Committee.)

Several members of council supported this view. After lengthy discussion, it was agreed that council "was not in a position to give encouragement to Laurentian University as requested in the [University's] Brief and would not be in a position to take any official action on the Lapp Report until it had conducted its own review."[10] However, council did agree to write the minister, asking the government not to take any action on the report pending the formulation of a COU position. A year later, when council formally addressed the recommendations in the Lapp Report, no position was taken on its recommendation regarding the Laurentian program. After noting that arguments for and against closing the program had substance, council simply suggested that Laurentian deal directly with the government before deciding whether to close the program. The program stayed. Several years later, it was expanded to four years, with specialization in mining engineering.

Several of the report's other recommendations concerning individual institutions were rejected. The Lapp Report recommended that the faculty of engineering at the University of Waterloo become a separate technical university with its own board and senate and be affiliated with Waterloo, a recommendation supported by the faculty of engineering but opposed by the university. This recommendation was rejected on the grounds that it would not be proper for COU to comment on a matter that essentially involved internal institutional organization. The recommendation that the University of Ottawa establish a common core undergraduate curriculum similar to that already in place at Carleton University was rejected on the grounds of Ottawa's bilingual and bicultural character. Other recommendations, such as the one that Lakehead University terminate its present program and establish a two-year degree program specifically designed to accommodate technology graduates, were simply ignored.

Recognizing the desirability of drawing engineers from a wider spectrum of secondary-school students, the Lapp Report recommended that credits in chemistry and physics no longer be required for admission to undergraduate engineering programs. This recommendation was rejected by COU. Recommendations that greater emphasis be placed on laboratory experience, including the implementation of policies to ensure the availability of state-of-the-art equipment and that curricula be continuously monitored, were accepted. The recommendation that undergraduate enrolment by program be controlled to maintain a steady state in the system, with first-year student intake by institution to serve as the basic controlling factor, was accepted, although not without some misgivings.

The Lapp Report recommendations concerning graduate planning proved to be the most controversial. Concluding that the universities were on track to overproduce the numbers needed to meet the demands of the profession, the report recommended an overall reduction amounting to 17 percent, and assigned maximum enrolment numbers to each of the existing programs. Several universities, at various stages in the development of their programs in engineering, objected to the enrolment assigned them. The report also recommended a quality assessment of all graduate programs based on an U.S. model that would provide rankings, and the exploration of ways to facilitate part-time graduate studies. COU eventually agreed to the recommended 17 percent reduction in system graduate enrolment, but decided that it should be done pro rata by institution based on enrolment projections for 1971–72. At the same time, council requested the Advisory Committee on Academic Planning (ACAP) of OCGS to undertake discipline assessments in all areas of graduate programming in engineering, the results of which would be used to provide recommendations for future system PhD enrolment and for the division of this enrolment among the specialities and universities. CODE was also asked to undertake a qualitative appraisal of new undergraduate programs and to include in these appraisals an assessment of need in terms of both academic and cost considerations. These actions had the effect of postponing some of the tough decisions recommended in *Ring of Iron*. The proposal on part-time graduate studies was ignored.

Putting on its best face, COU concluded that *Ring of Iron* had produced positive effects. Council, it was said, had gained valuable experience in system planning, experience that would be useful for future planning activities. The exercise had provided concrete evidence of the universities' collective capability of undertaking critical self-evaluation. Others were less sanguine in their assessment. Members recognized, however, that subsequent steps taken by the collectivity to implement council decisions would be watched closely by the ministry and CUA as a test of the determination and ability of the universities to manage their affairs and to work together on behalf of the system. Events would show this to be the case. As the decade proceeded, the problems of effectively managing the complex process of system graduate discipline assessment, including those in engineering, were to draw increasing criticism from both the buffer body and the Ministry.

●THE WRIGHT REPORT

The search for an improved structure bridging the university-government interface continued. When the Commission on Post-Secondary Education in Ontario was established in 1969, CPUO moved immediately to have its Committee on Research and Planning prepare a brief. Transmitted to the commission in March 1971 and later given wide distribution, the brief entitled *Towards 2000: The Future of Post-Secondary Education in Ontario* covered a wide range of topics.[11] Future oriented, critical, provocative, and intended to generate debate (which it did), this document could not, and did not, command in its entirety the support of all COU member institutions, a point that was made clear when it was issued.

Towards 2000 adopted accessibility to post-secondary education as the major principle that should govern future developments. It suggested ways of broadening the student base and of opening up the routes to post-secondary education so that no student would be blocked from further progress by rigidities in the system. It argued for a progressive development of student aid, with more reliance on grants than loans, even suggesting that financial credits toward post-secondary education might be accumulated while students were still in secondary school. Considering learning to be a lifelong matter, it urged increased interpenetration between the worlds of education and work, suggesting that credits be granted for work experience as well as for academic courses and that a system of "citizens' sabbaticals" be instituted.

Towards 2000 stressed the importance of post-secondary education to Canada as a nation, both as a unifying force in a bilingual country across the English-French divide of civilization and culture, and as a contribution the country could make abroad. It dealt with the role of the federal government in post-secondary education, including constitutional issues and Canadian science policy. From the provincial perspective, the brief argued that the post-secondary system in Ontario would be better integrated by bringing the colleges of applied arts and technology (CAATs) into a better-defined relationship with the universities through the University of Ontario model. As a corollary, it argued for a single Department of Post-Secondary Affairs and possibly a single advisory body for both the universities and the CAATs. At the same time, it urged a decentralized system of institutions characterized by flexibility and with vertical mobility for students, organized regionally where appropriate.

Visionary in thrust, few of the ideas promoted in this brief were ever translated into firm plans. CPUO, while playing lip service to a number of the ideas, actively promoted very few. The hard realities of institutional self-interest and the growing concern over the inadequacy of government funding prevented the association from seizing an opportunity to exercise the kind of leadership role that had marked the efforts of the presidents a decade earlier.

The association was more concerned with maintaining its prominence in the structure of the university system while continuing to avoid the hard decisions concerning its own internal management. The decision to change the name of the universities' association from the Committee of Presidents of the Universities of Ontario to the Council of Ontario Universities came as a result of another special committee to review the structure of the system. Early in 1970, CPUO set up a Special Sub-Committee on the Structure of the Ontario University System, chaired by Tom Symons, president of Trent University, with a mandate to make recommendations on a variety of issues regarding the effectiveness of the system. These included the respective roles of member institutions, the collective organization (CPUO), CUA, and the government. Apart from some minor modifications, all of the committee's recommendations were accepted.

Judging that the collectivity needed to improve its capacity to reach decisions in the common interest and to do so expeditiously, the Symons Report recommended that the Executive Committee assume a larger role in the handling of routine business and in directing the approach to be taken on major issues. It also recommended greater reliance on interuniversity groups related to the parent organization, and proposed a new category of committee, a management board, to be responsible for the routine management of co-operative programs sponsored by the association and for recommending on policies and budgets for these programs. Consensus, not voting, was proposed as the preferred way of arriving at collective decisions. Finally, the report also recommended that the association, which for several years had included a second representative from each member institution (the "academic colleague"), now formally recognize this fact by changing its name. The recommendations affecting the association were implemented; those addressed to the other system players fell, for the most part, on barren ground. The most visible result: on May 1, 1971, the Committee of Presidents became the Council of Ontario Universities.[12]

The Symons Committee noted with concern a recent development toward an adversarial relationship between COU and CUA. In addition to tensions resulting from CUA advice on the operating grant, problems had developed as a result of requests from the advisory body for more data from the universities and from differences of opinion over the role of certain joint CPUO/CUA committees. At one point, the chair of CUA rejected a proposal from CPUO that the Joint CPUO Capital Studies Committee deal with the vexing issue of capital funding, and the chair declined to meet with the CPUO executive to discuss the matter. The presidents then refused CUA requests for data on capital matters pending a meeting with the advisory body to clarify the reasons for the request and the usefulness of the data being requested.[13] This brief contretemps was resolved at a joint meeting. Tempers, however, remained somewhat frayed. After a joint COU/CUA meeting in December 1971, one in which ministry officials also participated, one university participant expressed concern over the "tasteless remarks" made by CUA and ministry officials that had marked the meeting's conclusion, and stressed the importance of "improving civility" at future meetings. The executive director promised to discuss this with Reva Gerstein, the new chair of CUA.[14]

The Symons Committee paid special attention to the role of the advisory body, reaffirming the universities' conviction that a strong and independent Committee on University Affairs was vital to the effective functioning of university-government relations. A series of recommendations were made: the advisory committee should be kept at full strength; members should be appointed for three-year terms, renewable for another two years; membership from the humanities should be increased; the deputy minister should be a full member; as a matter of regular procedure, COU should submit nominees for membership; and the CUA secretariat should be strengthened. Adopted and forwarded to the minister, these COU recommendations produced some changes. The minister agreed to have COU submit nominations on an annual basis. (A similar provision was made for OCUFA.) Thereafter, the advisory body was kept up to full strength and representation from the humanities increased.

The *Draft Report of the Commission on Post-Secondary Education in Ontario* was released late in 1971, more than four years after the commission's establishment and after nearly two years of deliberations.[15] Intended as a discussion piece, the *Draft Report* produced a chorus of criticism. The views expressed on the nature of university-government relations and on the structure that should govern these relations caused consternation in the university community. To COU, the report "appeared to have been hastily written [and] contained a conglomeration of principles, opinions and recommendations [but little by way of evidence]."[16] Acknowledging that the province had been well served by its post-secondary education system, and expressing a preference for effecting improvements through evolutionary means, the commission expressed its concern that the centre of power was shifting too far in the direction of the government. To arrest this drift, it proposed the creation of three co-ordinating boards to be established by law, each with executive powers. Each of these boards would have responsibility for one of the three post-secondary sectors defined by the commission: the universities, the colleges of applied arts and technology, and the Open Sector (containing a miscellaneous group of teaching and cultural institutions). In addition to these three sectoral boards, there was to be a fourth, a senior advisory committee, an Ontario committee on post-secondary education similarly composed, whose responsibility would be to provide advice to the minister on the allocation of funds among the three sectors. The University Co-ordinating Board was to have twelve members appointed by the Lieutenant-Governor-in-Council on advice from the minister of Colleges and Universities, six chosen from within the university community, and six representing industry, labour and other lay groups.

What really upset COU and the universities was the sweeping powers to be accorded the proposed Universities Co-ordinating Board. It would be authorized to establish new faculties and programs and to discontinue existing ones, to establish general university admissions policy, and to distribute capital and operating funds to the universities. Regarded as a major intrusion into university autonomy, this proposal galvanized COU into a flurry of activity. Council conceded that the universities ought not to be left entirely on their own to operate in a vacuum, and that some decisions affecting the provincial university system should be made collectively. But, council argued, after consulting widely and having due regard for public policy, the university community itself should remain responsible for making decisions on how best to discharge the universities' responsibilities. In a fit of hyperbole, COU asserted that, if implemented, the proposals in the *Draft Report* would "remove from the universities all the freedoms essential to the idea of a university."[17]

How best to achieve a proper balance between the requirements of institutional autonomy and collective decision making had been a long-standing dilemma. Resolving this issue was now seen by COU as urgent. The starting point of the debate within council was a consideration of the basic responsibility of government for the development of public policy for a large, publicly funded university system. Council accepted that decisions on what in general should be paid for by public funds, and the amount of these funds, must rest with the government. Beyond these "global" decisions, however, lay a host of issues related to co-ordination and rationalization. COU argued that in this area, the collectivity of universities should continue to play the central role.

From the outset, it was clear that no member of council supported the commission's proposals (Principal Deutsch, a member of both the council and the commission, did not participate in the debate, except to state that the commission had yet to make a final decision.) It was also accepted, although grudgingly by some COU members, that the existing machinery for central decision making on behalf of the system was inadequate and required change, and that, if the system were to operate effectively, individual universities would have to give up some of their traditional autonomy.

Carried out over four meetings, two of them special meetings devoted exclusively to the issues, the debate in council proved long and difficult. Four alternative models were examined. The first, and most extreme, postulated the centralization of power in the ministry, with no buffer body. Judged to be totally foreign to the traditions and values of the universities, and seen as likely to turn the universities into arms of the civil service, this option was rejected out of hand. A second model was that proposed in the *Draft Report*—a buffer body with executive authority in specified areas. This was seen to have the same disadvantages as the first model, though not to the same degree: to buffer the government from the universities by the interposition of an intermediary body. A variant—the University of Ontario with a central board of regents and a central administration—was subject to the same defects. A third model would establish a single buffer body through an integration of COU and CUA, with members appointed by both the government and the universities. Although superficially attractive, this model, it was argued, would rob the universities of an independent voice and create the illusion of partnership while shifting the locus of power to the government—since, when the interests of university and government appointees on the buffer body diverged and could not be reconciled, the government would make decisions by default.

A fourth model consisted of a "double buffer": one body that would advise the government and whose members would be chosen by the government, and a second body representing the universities, with a specific mandate to co-ordinate and rationalize the university system to the minimum considered necessary. The first would be a reformed CUA, the second a reformed COU. This model, it was argued, would have a number of advantages. Direct government control would be limited to funding levels and major policy matters. Accountability would be provided through the trustee function given to CUA. Central bureaucracy would be minimized by use of the universities' resources already in place at COU. Responsibility for system planning and co-ordination would rest with the university collectivity (COU), thereby preserving the fundamental autonomy of the universities. The major difficulty would involve the capacity of even a reformed COU, as a voluntary association of member universities, to make difficult decisions against the institutional interests of some of its members.

After lengthy debate, the fourth model was adopted by COU and recommended in Council's *Response to the Draft Report*. However, there was no consensus. Described as "a conclusion reached after long reflection and one that demonstrated Council's confidence in the ability of the university community to accept collectively a new set of obligations consistent with the enlarged dimensions of university education in Ontario," the proposal provided an outline, the details of which remained undeveloped.[18] The bland, self-serving description of this model masked the inability of council members to unite behind a structural proposal that might strengthen system planning. In the end, it made no difference.

The final report, published in December 1972 under the title *The Learning Society*, showed that the commission had changed its mind.[19] The earlier proposal on structure was revised in favour of a recommendation that a single body for the university sector be established by legislation and given executive authority over specified areas. The intermediary body that the commission now recommended would have less authority than what had been suggested earlier. Direct control of the institutions by the ministry was rejected as incompatible with university autonomy. But the commission considered the existing Committee on University Affairs to be inadequate. It was not a neutral buffer body balanced equally between the universities and the government. The current structure, created largely without foresight, purported to do one thing but in fact did another. "The harsh reality of growing government control was obscured by the legal fiction of institutional autonomy and the imputed protective role of the Committee on University Affairs."[20] The commission rejected both direct control of universities by the ministry and the University of Ontario model. It also rejected COU's proposed "double buffer," which it described as posing insuperable difficulties, and, in terms of public policy, as representing a step backward.

What was required, the Wright Commission concluded, was a buffer body established by law, with some clearly defined executive powers. "Both government and the universities should be prepared," it argued, "to delegate part of their jurisdiction to a third body—the buffer—to be used in accomplishing those tasks that no government body, university, or college can perform alone or in concert and that would satisfy public authority that system-wide planning and co-ordination were orderly and effective." To function as a satisfactory buffer, the body would require more than advisory powers. "If a body is to initiate as well as mediate, insulate and protect, it must by definition be able to exercise authority within its area of jurisdiction."[21]

COU now did an about-face and accepted what only a short time before it had rejected out of hand. If greater control were to be exercised over the universities, it would be better exercised by an intermediate body than by the government. In its response to the commission's final report, council "strongly supported" the Wright Commission's recommendation for a buffer body with limited executive powers, "on the understanding that the [new] council would seek systematic planning advice from COU and would work closely with COU on the implementation of plans."[22] So, too, did the Ontario Confederation of University Faculty Associations (OCUFA), the Ontario Federation of Students (OFS), and most individual universities. The government, now led by Premier Davis, was not persuaded. Having an intermediate body whose advice it could accept or reject remained the preferred option. The government was not interested in giving executive authority to a buffer body, however much this authority might be limited.[23]

Few of the Wright Commission's recommendations were ever adopted. The universities regarded them for the most part as too radical; the government considered them too costly and was not displeased to discover lack of support for them in the university sector. Developed within the mindset (no longer current) that large-scale public funding for post-secondary education was a high priority, many of its recommendations were rejected on the grounds that they could no longer be afforded. (The commission failed to "cost" its proposals.) Its proposals for a strengthened provincial university planning structure fell afoul the government's unwillingness to grant any executive authority to an intermediate body. Its proposals for establishing better articulation between the university and community college sectors also were lost.

Two years were to pass before the government addressed the issue of system structure. In 1974, a bill was introduced into the legislature to establish an Ontario Council on University Affairs (OCUA) to advise the minister and the lieutenant-governor-in-council on university affairs. The bill also provided authority to the minister or the council to collect and publish such information and statistics on the universities as were considered necessary or advisable. The universities immediately objected strongly to this provision. They argued, once again, that it infringed on institutional autonomy. At second reading of the bill, the government withdrew the objected-to clause—a decision that immediately drew fire from the opposition parties, who supported it. The legislation was then abandoned. Shortly afterward, the new council was created by Order-in-Council. (Ironically, under the Audit Act, the government already possessed the authority to collect and publish university data.)[24]

The new body, OCUA, was established by Order-in-Council, not by legislation. It was to be an advisory body with no executive authority, little different from its predecessor. COU, OCUFA, OFS, and their respective constituencies had expended much energy and no little anguish for nought. The tripartite structure of the provincial university system was ameliorated somewhat by the creation of this new advisory body; however, its basic weaknesses remained.

The new chair of OCUA, Stefan Dupré, a dynamic academic well respected in the university community and well connected to the government, moved quickly to distance the new advisory body from the government and to establish good relations on both sides of the buffer. Some changes, largely cosmetic, were made in the way the new advisory body operated: its quarters were moved outside the building that housed the ministry; the deputy minister ceased to serve as council secretary. A more organized approach was taken to the conduct of business. Council now met regularly, both with the universities and representative associations (OCUFA, OFS, et al.); these meetings were open. OCUA advisory memoranda to the government were published, though only after the government had made a decision on the recommendations they contained. From its beginning, OCUA exhibited a strong interest in two major system issues: graduate planning and system funding. Gradually, it came to assume a leadership role in both, a role previously played by COU.

●GRADUATE PROGRAM PLANNING

The evolution of graduate planning in Ontario universities during the 1960s and 1970s is one of the most interesting and significant aspects of the recent history of higher education in the province, and of the respective roles of COU, the advisory buffer body, CUA (later OCUA), and the government. Because the graduate enterprise involves the allocation of such a large proportion of university resources, including time and energy expended in debate, decisions and policies in this area inevitably affect developments in other areas, particularly undergraduate programming. "In no other area of university activity [in Ontario] are the strengths and weaknesses of co-operative planning and voluntary association among a group of fifteen [as they were then] universities more apparent or more real."[25] The way in which graduate system planning developed in Ontario also served to define, in part, the way in which the government elected to deal with the complex and increasingly contentious issues affecting the provincial system.

Given the slow pace of progress that CPUO and the universities were making in the co-ordination and rationalization of graduate studies, at the beginning of the 1970s the government placed an embargo on the funding of new programs. As noted above, it also raised the formula fee for graduate students and introduced some restrictions on their financial support. The funding embargo was introduced on advice from the Committee on University Affairs. The decisions on fees and student support were taken unilaterally. Both sets of decisions upset COU and the universities. At the time, the Advisory Committee on Academic Planning (ACAP), charged by COU with developing a comprehensive program of discipline-planning assessments, had yet to inaugurate an effective program. Eight discipline assessments were planned for the first year of the program, six for the second. The first assessments were not scheduled for completion until spring 1973.

The universities considered the funding embargo on new graduate programs to be unfair and likely to inhibit the orderly development of graduate studies. The government had acted because it was dissatisfied with the rate of progress in system planning in this important sector. Some concessions, however, were soon agreed upon. In negotiations with CUA, COU succeeded in having two important changes made. First, an embargo list was established covering disciplines judged to be in danger of over-expansion; disciplines on this list were given priority for assessment. It was agreed that programs in disciplines not on this list would revert to their pre-embargo position—that is, new programs in these disciplines would be funded if they passed appraisal. Secondly, it was agreed that the four emergent universities—Brock, Trent, Lakehead, and Laurentian—should be able to offer master's-level programs in the central academic disciplines. The rationale was that all universities should be involved in graduate programming and such minimal involvement did not require justification based on an accepted overall provincial discipline plan. At the same time, all universities were asked to place more emphasis on program planning. Beginning in 1972-73, the four smaller universities were asked to submit five-year plans for approval, and they were permitted to offer only those new graduate programs included in an approved five-year plan. The larger universities were asked to submit three-year plans. With these concessions, discipline assessment proceeded.

By now, it was evident that the design and implementation of a planning process for the orderly development of graduate programs in Ontario universities was proving a considerable challenge. The impetus for system planning and co-ordination stemmed from the Spinks Commission. When its proposal for the establishment of a graduate University of Ontario was rejected, the universities themselves undertook to develop a voluntary, collective approach to system planning. In 1968, the Advisory Committee on Academic Planning (ACAP) was formed to guide the development of academic discipline groups and to co-ordinate the work of rationalizing graduate studies in the province. Initial progress was very slow. It took more than two years for the assessment process to be approved by the universities. Some academic discipline groups opposed the process in principle. This attitude stemmed from a genuine concern felt by faculty that any restrictions would interfere with their legitimate ambitions to develop graduate programs and plans for research involving the use of graduate students. ACAP acknowledged this problem and endeavoured to find ways to address it. But no acceptable solution was ever found.

When eventually implemented, the discipline assessment process proved to be complicated, time-consuming, and controversial. Under the peer-review model adopted, planning began with the appointment of an academic discipline group composed of representatives from each participating university. Working with ACAP, the discipline group defined the boundaries of the assessment, determined the procedures and the terms of reference for the external consultants, and recommended a list of possible consultants. ACAP named the consultant teams. After receiving a briefing on the nature and objectives of the planning exercise and provided with relevant data from each of the participating universities, the consultants undertook site visits. These involved broad consultation with faculty, students, and administration. A draft report was then prepared and circulated for comment to both ACAP and the discipline group. This was followed by a final report, which was circulated for comment to ACAP, the discipline group, and the participating universities. ACAP then prepared its own report. This report, along with the consultants' report and the universities' comments, was then submitted to COU. After approval by COU, the discipline assessment was submitted to OCUA, with a recommendation that the embargo on funding for new programs in that discipline be lifted. A positive recommendation by OCUA to the ministry opened the door to funding, and the discipline assessment report was published. Once funding was provided, COU monitored the universities' continuing compliance.

Such a complex process was time consuming. It also provided considerable room for slippage. Problems arose when a department whose program was being assessed did not like the consultants' report or when (as happened frequently) ACAP's recommendations differed from those of the consultants. Controversy arose as soon as the first discipline assessments came before COU in 1973. Questions were raised immediately over how much emphasis should be given to the consideration of manpower requirements, a matter affecting total system enrolment. Given that manpower forecasting was far from an exact science, many academics took the position that graduate enrolment should not be closely tied to such requirements. It was argued that estimates of future manpower requirements for doctorates, which would have to be projected out for at least five to ten years, could never be very reliable. Moreover, given the high degree of interchangeability in employment for the graduates, even the best estimates would be of doubtful validity. Some conceded the need to limit enrolment in high-cost doctoral programs when the employment prospects for graduates were seen to be limited or declining, and when the number of qualified Canadian students entering graduate work was also declining. These arguments among academics were never satisfactorily resolved. More concerned about the proliferation of costly graduate programs at a time when overall funding was being constrained, government officials were restive at the universities' failure to resolve the issue.

Another major bone of contention among COU member institutions involved the issue of "critical program size." A question was raised: What is the minimum enrolment required to maintain a doctoral program of acceptably high academic quality? Many academic departments were anxious to move into doctoral work. However, at a time when employment opportunities for graduates were diminishing and the supply of qualified Canadian doctoral candidates was also declining, some doctoral programs, particularly the newer ones, were likely to have small enrolments. In several disciplines it was clear that, for the foreseeable future, total system enrolment could be handled in a substantially smaller number of programs than already existed. In these circumstances, one option was to maintain only the highest-quality programs, with enrolment sufficient to meet student demand; close small programs and refuse approval to all new ones pending an upturn in both manpower requirements and student demand. Popular among government planners interested in reducing expenditures, this ran counter to the ambitions of many member institutions. This option was a non-starter in COU.

Many of the early planning assessments to come before COU sparked controversy. When the chemistry assessment arrived in March 1973, council was confronted with conflicting recommendations. The consultants found five programs to be academically substandard and recommended that they be discontinued. ACAP took a more lenient position. It recommended that the universities with programs judged substandard be permitted to reduce the scope of the program and submit the program for immediate appraisal. It made a similar recommendation for two other programs judged marginal by the consultants. After lengthy debate, COU accepted the ACAP recommendations. Seven graduate programs in chemistry that were judged on appraisal to be substandard would have to be revised and undergo immediate academic appraisal. In conducting their appraisals, however, the appraisals committees were instructed not to consider the unresolved issue of "critical size."

Debate on this issue in COU was joined several months later. Some members argued that the concept of critical size lacked any empirical basis. Most acknowledged that academic quality was at stake when enrolment in a program was small, but they remained uncertain about how to determine both the minimum threshold and the weight to be given such a factor when rendering an overall judgment on the program. Others saw any use of such a criterion as inappropriate for universities that held unlimited charters (as all Ontario universities did). Some argued that this approach reflected a U.S. attitude that placed undue emphasis on the relationship between size and quality. When ACAP (to which the matter had been referred) took the position that size was relevant, the COU chair, President Winegard of the University of Guelph, opined that, while ACAP had established the validity of the concept, determination of actual numbers would "be very hard to justify." The number would depend upon both the discipline and the number of programs in the discipline. The ACAP paper "was received by COU for information only" and the issue remained unresolved.[26]

The consultants in economics rejected one program as substandard. Subsequently, the university announced that the program would be restricted to a single field. Council then took a softer line and decided that the program should undergo another appraisal. At the October 1973 meeting of COU, Michael Oliver, president of Carleton University, whose university programs in chemistry and economics had been featured in the debates, urged council to postpone a final decision on both disciplines pending completion of planning assessments for the remaining programs in the physical and social sciences. The Council of Deans of Arts and Science supported this proposal. Given that it would be several years before discipline assessments in all of these program areas would be completed, COU (with one dissenting vote) stood firm and rejected this proposal. It was agreed, however, that in future planning assessments an additional principle be included—complementarity of programs.[27]

The sociology assessment created even larger problems. The consultants' report, which ACAP judged to be "vague and contradictory," recommended continuation of the five existing doctoral programs and the establishment of one more. Expressing concern over the academic quality of the five existing programs, ACAP recommended that no more than three programs be continued, and it proposed ranking them to provide a basis for recommendations on funding. ACAP then proposed that additional consultants be named to complete the assessment. The five involved universities were not pleased. A straw vote in council supported the ACAP position, but it would be another two years before the sociology assessment was completed.

More than three years after the publication of *Ring of Iron*, in 1973 an interim report on the discipline assessments in engineering came before COU as a matter of urgency. The urgency was related to the need to deal with council's earlier decision agreeing that doctoral enrolment should be reduced to 450 overall by December 1974. Despite an acknowledged small number of qualified Canadians and the growing number of foreign students in these doctoral programs, ACAP recommended that the cap be lifted. COU agreed. This decision passed without comment from either CUA or the ministry. However, the continuing inability of COU and its member universities to take decisive action in system planning had not gone unnoticed.[28] Eventually, six discipline reports on engineering, each covering a speciality, were received and dealt with by COU. By the end of the 1970s, twenty discipline assessment reports (including the six in engineering) had been completed. By this time, however, the importance of discipline assessments in the graduate planning process had substantially declined.

Graduate planning entered a new phase in 1975 when OCUA took up the matter. Its spring-1975 hearings focused on graduate planning. These hearings provided the basis for OCUA Advisory Memorandum 75-IV, submitted to the minister in June of that year. This memorandum provided a snapshot of the current graduate planning process. By employing comments from the universities themselves, OCUA offered a shrewd analysis of the strengths and weaknesses of the process. The universities were accorded full marks for their efforts to maintain and improve quality by means of program appraisal. The memorandum also acknowledged that the discipline assessment process had made solid contributions to system planning. However, it cited continuing criticism of the process from within the university community, and it registered concern that one essential dimension was missing from the planning process. In a period of fiscal restraint when overall enrolment in graduate studies was stable, new programs continued to be added. The process included no provision for examining any increased financial implications for the system.

In 1966, when the Spinks Commission had examined the orderly development of graduate studies as "a pressing and urgent necessity," total graduate enrolment in the province stood at 6,874 and was projected to reach 18,640 by 1975. For the remainder of the '60s, enrolment increases had matched the projections. In 1972, the Wright Report projected full-time graduate enrolment to reach 20,300 by 1975. However, in that year an embargo on funding for new graduate programs was introduced. Since then, overall system enrolment had stabilized. Increases had occurred in some discipline areas, mainly education and business, but these had been matched by declines in the core arts and sciences disciplines. In 1975, overall graduate enrolment in Ontario universities stood at 13,724, only marginally above what it had been in 1971. Moreover, in the core academic disciplines, where enrolment was holding steady, an increasing proportion of doctoral students was coming from offshore.

The universities, OCGS, and COU interpreted graduate planning as being geared to the orderly accommodation of growth. But this, the OCUA memorandum stated, was no longer in line with reality. The system was facing a future in which funding could be expected to be constrained. This meant that faculty complements in the universities would be held at current numbers. There would be fewer employment opportunities for newly minted PhDs. Moreover, as a greater proportion of faculty resources came to be allocated to undergraduate programs, less faculty time would be available for graduate supervision. Yet, as was noted in a brief from the University of Ottawa, "The question nobody seems to dare raise is the following: Is the existing enterprise in graduate studies in Ontario too large for the population or the economic capacity of the province?"[29] Posing another question, what should be the results of a graduate planning exercise geared to current realities? OCUA inserted an answer from the University of Waterloo's brief: "Weak programs will be trimmed back or perhaps in some cases eliminated, potentially strong programs will be strengthened ... [, and] already strong programs will be maintained."[30]

This was not what was occurring. Admittedly, the discipline assessment process had led the universities to undertake more careful self-evaluation and to expand interuniversity co-operation. The universities were making earnest efforts to establish a high-quality system without unnecessary duplication or redundancies, and progress was being made. However, this was not good enough. Considerable criticism of the assessment process was being heard from within the university community. It was considered too cumbersome and bureaucratic. Doubt was expressed that the long-term benefits would prove worth the large expenditures of time, energy, and money. Moreover, it was widely noted that the quality of the academic assessments varied; a number of universities pointed out that some of the consultants' reports had been very weak.

Despite its reservations, OCUA nonetheless recommended that the funding embargo be lifted on those disciplines that had successfully completed the assessment process, and that several new graduate programs in unembargoed disciplines be granted eligibility for funding. At the same time, the advisory body gave notice that henceforth it would review COU recommendations only once a year. Moreover, it specified that reports recommending funding for new programs should now include the financial implications of such funding. Minister of Colleges and Universities James Auld accepted these recommendations. In a four-page letter to OCUA, which was circulated among the universities (the intended primary audience), the minister expressed his views about the graduate planning process. He wrote that the government had agreed to fund half the cost of new graduate programs "in the expectation that graduate program offerings would be rationalized and unnecessary duplication would be eliminated while at the same time ensuring a spectrum of offerings across the system. This has not occurred. While pleased with the development of high quality graduate programming, it is apparent that in numerical terms the assessment process is not rationalizing graduate programs." Of the fifteen assessments completed to date, involving two hundred and thirty six existing programs and thirty new ones, only nine (three MAs and six PhDs) had been closed or might be closed. Another nine recommended for closure were likely to be retained as "specialized" doctorate programs, and current university three-year plans called for the addition of a further one hundred and three new programs. "By now, all universities should know that the provincial government faces a financial future which allows for little or no expansion and indeed requires difficult decisions and trade-offs between various academic goals and priorities.... As the third largest recipient of government grants, the universities must recognize this reality in their internal planning... [government's] concern is not with qualitative judgments on individual programs but rather with the range and distribution of programs within the system having regard to overall system size and existing program strengths and weaknesses, and with how many programs can be sustained and supported in any discipline."[31] He stated that account needed to be taken of the reality that judgments based solely on academic grounds might incur a financial burden that the province could not bear. Furthermore, assurance was needed that "the development of graduate programs does not occur at the expense of support for other university responsibilities." The universities needed to be encouraged to make the admittedly difficult decisions themselves and to ensure that efforts to rationalize the system continued. The universities were asked to submit new three-year program plans that reflected these revised terms. The objective, concluded the minister, was to provide "a spectrum of programs of the highest quality accomplished within the limits of the Province's resources." This, the minister stated, would require each university to identify those segments of graduate work in which it excelled so that institutional strengths could be co-ordinated into a collectively strong system.[32]

The minister's message was clear, but the universities and COU did not seem to be listening very attentively. They acknowledged that the emphasis of the graduate planning exercise was on quality; still, they argued, significant financial benefits (which were unstated) had undoubtedly accrued. Aware that there was seen to be an urgent need to re-examine the graduate process in order to develop the financial implications, COU struck a Special Committee on the Financial Implications of Graduate Planning to examine the matter. A second OCUA memorandum issued later the same year (also accepted by the minister) spelled out more clearly the new approach to graduate planning. The operating grants formula for the funding of graduate programs was suspended for a two-year period beginning in 1976–77. During this period, formula grants for graduate programs would be totally insensitive to enrolment changes. This action, it was argued, would foster an atmosphere in which planning could proceed free from short-term revenue considerations. To underline the point, OCUA expressed itself interested "not only in new program development, but in the possible reduction of established programs."[33]

Although not thrilled with these developments, the universities elected to put the best face on them. Based on the recommendations of its Special Committee on the Financial Implications of Graduate Planning, COU's spring-1976 brief to OCUA proposed a new and slightly different approach to graduate planning: the FIGPLAN. To emphasize improvement in academic quality, the appraisal process would be strengthened; to improve discipline planning, ACAP would become involved in the assessment process at an earlier point. The program appraisal process and the discipline planning process would be reinforced by the development of a clear statement of the basic goals and objectives for graduate study. Once these had been agreed upon, more specific attention could be given to designing a more suitable system planning process and a more appropriate funding mechanism. To allow more time to develop the necessary details, COU proposed extending the graduate funding freeze for a third year.

A game of give-and-take ensued. OCUA reacted favourably to the COU proposals. Then it proceeded to push the implications further. Since overall graduate enrolment had been relatively stable over the past five years, quality, not size, ought now to be the primary concern. To focus on this consideration, the advisory body made two further proposals. First, after the end of the three-year freeze, graduate planning should be conducted on a five-year basis, with the first quinquennium to begin in 1980–81. Secondly, a series of statistical "macro-indicators" should be established to obtain a general profile of graduate programming in the province in order to assist both the institutions and the collectivity in system planning. Planning for the first quinquennium should reflect the principal characteristic of the period—consolidation. It should also embody four objectives: protection and enhancement of quality, elimination or prevention of unnecessary duplication, adequate support of outstanding doctoral programs (despite declines in enrolment), and development of new fields of study where there was genuine need. To assist in acquiring the necessary statistical data, the advisory body requested that COU, through OCGS, provide data on five sets of macro-indicators for each doctoral program: the number of full- and part-time faculty, the number of full- and part-time students, the number of students holding competitive scholarships, the dollar value of peer-adjudicated research grants awarded faculty by the federal granting agencies, and the number of degrees awarded. To complete the package, in addition to meeting the new, more rigorous appraisal standards, OCUA added two new funding criteria. From then on, proposed new graduate programs would have to be (1) unique in the province and (2) intended to fill a plainly apparent manpower need.

The universities clearly supported the thrust to place greater emphasis on quality. They were much less enthusiastic about the other elements of the OCUA proposals. Despite their reservations, however, COU/OCGS undertook an extensive modification of relevant bylaws and procedures in order to strengthen the appraisal process and to institute ACAP involvement in the early stages of discipline planning assessments (FIGPLAN). It was agreed that the new procedures would go into effect in 1977-78 for a two-year trial period. In a retrospective comment, the then chair of OCGS noted that these new procedures increased rather than reduced the cumbersomeness of the process while failing to address effectively OCUA 's concern about costs.[34]

In its third advisory memorandum on graduate planning, issued in February 1978, OCUA further refined the objectives for graduate planning by including the need to maintain a satisfactory amount of scholarship and research—a bow in the direction of providing support for academics not engaged in doctoral programs—and reiterated the requirement that new programs should show evidence of need both in Ontario and in Canada. It then added a new funding criterion: that the programs already have admitted students. The universities protested vigorously that this additional criterion was unduly burdensome. An institution, it was argued, would be required to incur all of the major expenditures for a new program prior to its being assessed for eligibility for funding and without any guarantee that it would receive funding. Neither OCUA nor the minister was impressed by this argument. OCUA 's advice was accepted; the new funding criteria went into effect.

COU was dismayed. The universities, it said, were receiving mixed signals about the future of graduate planning. The principle of university autonomy was again invoked. OCUA was becoming increasingly centralist and interventionist. Only recently it had stated that "the value of institutional autonomy in Ontario outweighs the benefit, if any, that might be ascribed to a strengthening of central planning through structural change. The major role in graduate planning in Ontario must remain grounded in the universities individually and collectively."[35] Now it was urging greater centralization. On the other hand, Bette Stephenson, the new minister, wanted to hand graduate planning back to the universities. In a letter to university presidents written shortly after her appointment, she stated her intention: "In future, universities will resume their full responsibility for planning their own programs without central control. I believe that government involvement in graduate planning should end on completion of the present quinquennium."[36]

OCUA, however, continued to play from its own score. In the fall of 1979, it turned recommendations for the funding of ten new graduate programs back to COU because they had not been dealt with under the new criteria. The advisory body stated that it was no longer willing simply to accept the judgment of ACAP and COU on the criteria of uniqueness and need. Evidence must be provided. The position of OCUA hardened. It now wanted assurance from COU that the institution offering the program was the best one in the province to do so; that the program was consistent with the aims, objectives and existing strengths of the institution; and that the program should receive funding despite existing financial constraints. Angry at what they considered to be at best an unexpected explication of the earlier criteria and at worst the addition of a new "fifth" criterion, COU and the universities entered strong protests. OCUA stood its ground. The minister, retreating from her earlier statement, supported the advisory body. While reiterating the view that eventually the universities should be able to plan and control the graduate sector without direction from OCUA, Minister Stephenson declared that, for the present, more central planning and greater rationalization were necessary. Expressing the expectation that OCUA would work closely with the universities and COU on these matters, she stated that if she were not satisfied with the results she reluctantly might have to maintain OCUA and ministry involvement in graduate planning beyond the first quinquennium.

Now OCUA retreated a step. Citing "historical factors," the advisory body recommended funding for nine of the ten programs it had earlier turned back. However, it again reiterated its commitment to achieving greater rationalization in the system, and declared that in the future it would require each program to satisfy all of its funding criteria before it would make a positive recommendation. The minister agreed and, in so doing, was at pains to ally herself clearly with OCUA's firm line. In the now increasingly ambiguous and contentious situation, COU struck yet another committee, a Special Committee to Review Graduate Planning, chaired by Donald Forster, president of the University of Guelph. The views of this committee would have a decisive effect on graduate planning. As the 1970s ended, it became apparent that COU was withdrawing from use of the discipline assessment process for system planning.

●A WORSENING FINANCIAL CLIMATE

Formula funding for Ontario universities had been introduced in 1967 with the intention of providing an objective mechanism for the distribution of operating grants among the eligible institutions. At that time, the universities were experiencing a period of rapid growth. In the four-year period between 1967 and 1970, overall enrolment increased by more than 50 percent, from 80,489 to 126,367 full-time-equivalent students. All parties agreed that the formula was a notable advance, even with its shortcomings—the emerging universities required extra-formula support, and the formula weights lacked a firm costing base. In applying the formula, the value of the Basic Income Unit (BIU) was established at the outset; this value was then used to calculate the amount to be distributed to each university on the basis of its enrolment entitlement. This meant that the government was committed to fund all qualified students admitted to university. Its commitment was open-ended. Concerned about this, in 1969 the government changed the rules. In future, it would first determine the global amount of the grant and then derive the value of the BIU by dividing the number of eligible units into the global sum. This meant that the value of the BIU ceased to be an independent variable; from now on it would become a function of the number of eligible students. The operating grants formula thereby became a purely distributive mechanism. Since it was based on enrolment, however, the formula continued to serve as a stimulus to growth.

In the spring of 1971, a decision was taken to review the operating grants formula. A year earlier, as has been noted, Treasury Board had advised CUA that the value of the BIU would not exceed 6 percent, slightly less than what the advisory body had recommended. The decision to review the operating grants formula was in response to an announcement by the minister that the increase in the global grant for the coming 1971–72 year would be 2 percent (less than the amount required to meet the additional cost of the projected enrolment increase). Furthermore, in the future, decisions on annual increases would not be made until certain factors contributing to university costs (including staff-student ratios, teaching loads, the emphasis on research, and the length of the university year) had been examined. The task of providing the required additional data was given to the Joint COU/CUA Sub-Committee on Finance/Operating Grants. This committee issued an interim report in mid-1972, but no final report was ever prepared.

By this time, system enrolment growth had slowed, and some institutions were experiencing declines in enrolment. Combined with inadequate global funding, this focused attention on the need for greater funding stability, particularly for those universities experiencing enrolment declines. The Wright Report, issued in 1972, recommended that the operating grants formula be separated into two categories: one for educational purposes (an instructional funding unit), the other for "other purposes, including research" (a research funding unit). This would allow funding for research to be "de-coupled" from funding based on enrolment, and thereby provide greater stability in funding for this essential component of university activity in a period of enrolment decline. Strongly opposed by the universities on the grounds that it would substantially reduce institutional autonomy, this option was never seriously considered.[37]

To address this problem, in 1973-74 a "slip-year" provision was introduced into the formula. No longer would operating grants to institutions be based on current enrolment, but on enrolment in the previous year. This meant that universities experiencing a decline in enrolment would have a year to adjust expenditures downward before the negative financial implications of the decline took effect. It also meant, of course, that institutions experiencing an increase in enrolment would have to wait a year before benefiting from a grant increase. In the circumstances, however, this was regarded as much the lesser evil.

This modification in the formula proved a temporary palliative. Competition among the universities for new students grew. Several expanded their admissions offices and the size of their students awards programs, particularly admissions scholarships. Some introduced "open-ended" admission scholarships, awards offered to any student achieving a designated grade average on the secondary school leaving certificate. To deal with the problem, COU established a Special Committee on Undergraduate Scholarship Policy, chaired by Edward Monahan, president of Laurentian University. Reporting in December 1973, this committee recommended that COU adopt guidelines on admission scholarships to halt "open-ended" awards, which were judged to be recruiting devices, and to provide a better balance between entrance and in-course awards. A divided council adopted the guidelines on a split vote; the committee was asked to monitor results. A follow-up report in March 1974 noted that, for the second year running, the total amount allocated for admission scholarships system-wide had increased by 30 percent. The executive director of COU remarked (correctly) that this "would not go unnoticed [by the ministry] when universities are claiming financial stringencies."[38] Although some universities continued to offer open-ended awards, over the next two years the situation improved.

From its creation in 1974, funding for the system became a major concern for OCUA. One of its first moves was to develop a set of funding objectives for the system and then to employ them as the basis for its recommendations on an appropriate level of global operating funding.

This was a first step towards specifying in more practical terms the meaning of the government's standing policy that there would be a place in an Ontario university for every qualified student wishing to attend, the policy on which the original social contract with the universities had been agreed to a decade earlier.

Unremarked by the university community, in 1971 the ministry had identified a major problem affecting this policy. The government had already decided to set a limit on the total amount of operating support it would provide the universities in any given year—global operating support. But there was no limit on total university system enrolment. The global fund was limited; the number of students this amount would fund was not. An internal ministry memorandum noted that Treasury Board guidelines on global funding for the universities were based on an assumption that in the years ahead the total number of students to be supported would remain constant as a proportion of the age cohort, eighteen to twenty-four years of age. The proportion cited in the memorandum was 13.9 percent. (In the 1990s, the actual percentage would rise above 30 percent.) However, current government policy on accessibility to university was open-ended. To be sure, the meaning of "qualified" was at best loosely defined, but no serious work had ever been done to determine what percentage of the 18-to-24 age group might or should be considered a maximum. When the government's policy on accessibility was first articulated in the early '60s, the assumption had been that great economic benefits would be reaped from investment in higher education. The government no longer held this view, yet its open-ended accessibility policy continued in place. In the current environment, the memo noted, government objectives needed to be revised and clearly set out.[39] This warning call went unheeded. From that time on, the government's lack of clarity about the meaning of its accessibility policy would bedevil university–government relations.

The effort by OCUA to establish clearly the government's funding objectives represented a first serious effort to put a price on the long-espoused government objective of providing a place in an Ontario university for every Ontarian qualified and desirous of attending. The advisory body recognized the need to take into account actual enrolment. Initially, OCUA proposed a set of three funding objectives: the global operating grant should be sufficient to offset inflationary trends, to maintain and improve existing levels of service, and to accommodate enrolment increases. COU and the universities accepted these objectives. In announcing the global grant for 1975–76, the minister also accepted these objectives and stated (without offering any explanation) that the sum provided was sufficient to meet them. Since, however, the global sum was less than what OCUA had recommended, both the advisory body and COU immediately challenged this view—but to no avail. In this period, a tripartite committee composed of representatives of COU, OCUA, and the Ministry was formed to collect and publish data on expenditures on higher education in all Canadian provinces. These interprovincial comparisons showed that the level of support provided to the universities in Ontario did not compare favourably with that provided to universities in sister provinces. On the criterion of expenditure per full-time-equivalent student, Ontario's support for universities had decreased dramatically during the '70s. By 1977, Ontario stood eighth among all provinces, almost $900 (nearly 20 percent) below the average for the rest of Canada. While not the fairest comparator—Ontario had by far the largest number of students—this and other data indicated conclusively that spending on universities in Ontario had slipped significantly, and that the sector no longer enjoyed the priority it once held. These interprovincial data became a regular feature of COU publications, despite occasional threats from ministry officials to withdraw its agreement to have the data collected. Apart from causing occasional embarrassment in government circles, however, their publication had little effect.[40]

In its advice the following year, OCUA modified the objectives to meet its understanding of fiscal reality. Given current economic conditions, the objective of improving existing levels of service was abandoned as impractical, and another—the maintenance of financial viability in the system—was substituted. OCUA then developed a financial model to estimate the impact of inflation and enrolment variation on the financial requirements for the system. In so doing, it introduced two new elements: an "excess capacity" factor and a "productivity" factor. Having determined that there was excess capacity in the system, the advisory body judged that the projected modest increases in enrolment could be accommodated at marginal cost, and it recommended that a discount of 50 percent be applied to new enrolment growth. Judging that productivity could be improved, it also recommended a 1.5 percent reduction in system funding requirements to encourage the universities to improve productivity. Pleased to receive such advice, the minister accepted it.

The universities were not as pleased. They did not question the applicability of the principle of marginal costs for new enrolment, but they judged a discount of 50 percent to be too high. They rejected as inappropriate the introduction of a productivity factor to universities. COU argued that, from the universities' perspective, apparent increases in productivity might well be considered as decreases in quality. This was an argument they would not win. Meanwhile, OCUA was working to bring the operating grants formula in line with changing circumstances. Addressing the implications of maintaining the policy on accessibility, the advisory body noted the need both to fund additional growth and to provide financial stability to protect the investment already made in the event of enrolment decline.

When announcing the grant for 1975–76, Minister White requested a review of the operating grants formula. He asked that three alternatives be examined: (1) continuation of the present formula, (2) formula revision to provide a lower BIU value for new enrolment (marginal cost funding for enrolment growth), and (3) suspension of the formula in favour of distribution based on each institution's current enrolment (constant share). Among COU member universities, the formula was widely regarded as in need of amendment, but for different reasons. There was no consensus on the direction of desirable change. As a result, the collectivity endorsed the status quo. COU, with three member institutions dissenting, recommended that the existing formula be retained.

OCUA was not impressed. In the face of strong pressures to reduce public spending, using enrolment projections for the system that envisaged a slight increase in the next several years followed by a decline in the subsequent decade, the advisory council devised a complex modification in the formula. The purpose of the modification was to "contribute predictability and stability in government funding by insulating the revenues of individual institutions from reflecting all at once the full effect of enrolment perturbations, whether up or down, in any given year."[41] Expressed in the vernacular, the new formula would provide "50 percent [funding for additional enrolment] on the way up and 50 percent [funding for lost enrolment] on the way down." As the details were worked out and the implications to the individual institutions became clear, COU came on board. The minister accepted the final OCUA recommendations. The new formula embodying "averaging" and "discounts" was introduced gradually over a period of three years and was fully in place by 1978. It was made up of two components—one "fixed," the other "moving"—each comprising one half of each institution's grant. The fixed base was made up of a three-year enrolment average; the moving base was made up of a three-year enrolment base—slip-year plus the two preceding years. This second component was "rolled" annually to take into account enrolment changes. The new formula improved stability and interinstitutional equity, but it was complicated and difficult to understand. Also, it failed to halt the grumbling among those universities that continued to grow. They considered themselves hard done by.

Non-formula grants proved another matter. Because they were given only to some member universities, these grants were always somewhat contentious within the collectivity and had proved a challenge to COU. They began as Emergent Grants awarded to the four newer, small universities (Brock, Trent, Lakehead, and Laurentian), which were judged because of their small size not to be viable under the formula. Subsequently, these grants were renamed Supplementary Grants and provided to other institutions as well. By 1975, seven universities were receiving them. When OCUA reviewed the Supplementary Grants, it found no rationale for providing additional funding to Carleton, Windsor, and York. It recommended that the grant to these three be discontinued. It also recommended that Brock receive a final grant in 1976-77, and that the grants to the remaining three—Lakehead, Laurentian, and Trent—be phased out over several years. The minister accepted these recommendations. Arguing that this advice contradicted OCUA's earlier view that such grants were based on the reasonable (if not precisely verifiable) assumption that an enrolment-base formula fails to consider that universities have certain fixed costs regardless of size, COU requested a joint study to determine the appropriate level of supplementary support for the smaller universities. Its request was ignored.

Concurrent with its review of the Supplementary Grants, OCUA undertook an examination of the extra costs incurred by Lakehead and Laurentian, the two regional universities in northern Ontario, which operated in a northern environment and offered a wide range of academic programs over a vast, thinly populated area. This resulted in the establishment of a new extra-formula grant, the Northern Grant, to be provided to these two universities and to Laurentian's three affiliated colleges, Algoma, Hearst, and Nipissing. These grants provided an additional 11 percent of the Basic Operating Income (BOI) to the participating institutions. Then, in 1977, OCUA addressed the issue of the incremental costs of offering instruction in French as well as in English. Until this time, the Bilingual Grant had been provided on a largely ad hoc basis. Over the next several years, with the support of COU, a mini-formula was developed for disbursement of the Bilingual Grant to those institutions that qualified to receive it: Ottawa, Laurentian and one of its affiliates, University College of Hearst, and York's Glendon College.

In 1977, the government accepted OCUA's recommendation on the size of the global operating grant, an exceptional event never again repeated. In the following year, 1978, the grant again fell below the level recommended by OCUA, $15 million below what the advisory body had recommended and $30 million below what COU judged necessary to meet the agreed-upon objectives. In making the announcement, the minister made no attempt to relate the sum allocated to OCUA's calculation of what was needed to meet the previously accepted objectives. He simply said that he considered the sum sufficient to meet the needs of the universities, noting further that the university sector was being treated as generously as most sectors (and more generously than some) at a time when government revenues were constrained.

The universities were now hit with an unexpected actual decline in enrolment. Until 1978, although some institutions had suffered declines, system enrolment had increased annually since the early 1950s. In the first half of the '70s, annual enrolment increases, in which not all institutions shared, had averaged 5.6 percent. In addition, uncertainties not withstanding, continued small system increases were projected through the early '80s. However, in 1977–78, full-time undergraduate enrolment unexpectedly declined by 2.8 percent, producing a decline in overall system enrolment of 1 percent below that attained two years earlier. The following year saw a further decline of 2.5 percent. These declines were caused by a drop in the participation rate of secondary school graduates, for whom a university education had suddenly become less popular.[42]

In 1979, the government finally agreed to accept OCUA's recommendation on a formula for capital grants. Work had begun on a capital formula a decade earlier, but lack of agreement among the universities slowed development. With major physical expansion at an end and finances tight, in 1972 the government imposed a near moratorium on capital grants. Declaring that this state of affairs amounted to a policy vacuum, in 1975 OCUA began pressing for government funding in support of cyclic renewal—funds required for building maintenance and major renovations. In 1978, the minister accepted a recommendation from OCUA that the COU "Building Blocks" space standards be adopted as the measure of university space needs and applied to the funds made available for cyclic renewal. A minor victory, the decision represented belated recognition of the ability of the collectivity to develop and agree upon common standards for university physical plant.

The relationship between COU and OCUFA during this period deserves mention. During the late '60s, as university administrators, faculty, staff, and governing boards struggled to deal with the manifold tasks involved in the large increases in enrolment, the organizations that were established to represent the various constituencies within the university community were encouraged to co-operate with one another. In the immediate post-Duff-Berdahl era, universities all across the country undertook reforms in their internal governance structures and, as a result, the influence of faculty grew markedly. Ontario universities were in the forefront of the reforms. In this climate favouring the growth of participatory democracy, the recently organized CPUO discovered that it had a considerable amount in common with the also recently organized association representing the faculty associations in Ontario universities, the Ontario Confederation of University Faculty Associations (OCUFA). (In the same period, a similar rapprochement was occurring at the national level, between AUCC and the Canadian Association of University Teachers [CAUT].) Although the two organizations, with their different mandates, were always somewhat wary of one another, in this period they enjoyed a cordial and co-operative relationship.

In their mutual concern to strengthen the intermediate body, CUA, both CPUO and OCUFA urged the government to include academics as members. When the government agreed, the two associations undertook to provide a joint list of nominees. By the end of the decade of the '60s, CPUO was collecting and publishing data on faculty salaries and citizenship in Ontario universities. As Statistics Canada became involved on the national level, the role of CPUO/COU gradually diminished. In the early period, however, through its Committee on Academic Staff, backed by the resources of its research division, COU worked closely with Statistics Canada to develop the requisite analytical tools. Later, with the increased involvement of CAUT in faculty salary matters, COU activity in this area was much reduced. In addition to its work on faculty salaries, CPUO/COU also collected and published data on faculty benefits. Soon, data on support staff benefits were also being collected and published. Since 1978, COU has published annual reports on staff benefits in Ontario universities, a valuable ongoing contribution to the essential database.

In the early '70s, COU and OCUFA collaborated in a number of activities directly related to university faculty. In 1972, COU published *The Ten O'Clock Scholar: What a Professor Does for His Pay,* an early effort to address the myth that university faculty are underworked and overpaid. In 1973, a joint COU/OCUFA study on early faculty retirement options addressed the need to improve pensions for academic staff. A year later, the Joint COU/OCUFA Committee on Academic Career Development was struck. The report of this committee, *The Ivory Tower and the Crystal Ball,* published in 1976, analyzed in some detail the current profile of faculty in Ontario universities and outlined the kinds of actions that the universities needed to take if they were to provide adequately for the career development of their academic staff. While doubtless useful to those forward-looking institutions prepared to undertake the necessary measures, the report went largely unnoticed.[43]

By far the most ambitious joint COU/OCUFA activity involved an effort, begun in 1975, to develop a province-wide approach to the determination of faculty salaries. A joint committee comprising three university presidents and three representatives of OCUFA was struck to examine the issues and recommend an approach. After examining the issues, the joint committee proposed a system of two-tier bargaining. Several years earlier, an AUCC "preliminary study of methods of settling terms and conditions of employment in Canadian universities" recognized that any approach to collective bargaining by university faculty must include the (relevant) provincial government and suggested that such bargaining could operate sequentially at two levels. The concept of two-tier bargaining was borrowed from Great Britain. There, the University Grants Committee (UGC), which exercised considerable executive authority over the universities in that jurisdiction, undertook to bring the individual universities together to agree upon a "system" approach to the negotiation of faculty salaries. Once the universities under the "guidance"of the UGC had agreed on salaries (Tier 1), the UGC undertook to negotiate with Treasury the necessary funding to secure the previously agreed increases (Tier 2). Under prevailing conditions in Great Britain, this system "worked" for a considerable period of time. Under the two-tier system, the basic objective was to establish faculty salary schedules by first obtaining agreement within the "university system" and then to negotiate these schedules with the government paymaster. In Ontario, however, a very different regime of labour relations prevailed. Here, the universities enjoyed greater autonomy; the buffer body lacked executive authority. Since at that time no Ontario faculty association was unionized, such a proposal held a certain appeal for the local university faculty associations and for OCUFA.

The joint university presidents/OCUFA committee recommended that the proposal for two-tier bargaining be endorsed. The issue came before COU in January 1976. At that meeting, Dr. John Evans, president of the University of Toronto and chair of council, reported that "OCUFA wished to continue discussions on a (proposed) provincial salary system, and that executive heads had agreed to this." OCUFA wanted further discussions on the development of the proposal to involve COU and OCUFA staff. President Evans also reported, however, that the COU Executive Committee had decided that it would not be appropriate for the executive director (or COU staff) to participate. Such activities, the Executive Committee said, should not be undertaken under the auspices of COU, but by the executive heads as representing the universities. Council concurred. The universities were backing off. Later that spring OCUA approved the proposal, but COU was unable to achieve a consensus. With the concurrence of the ministry, the issue was referred to OCUFA. Concerned with the implications of such a proposal, the buffer body refused to endorse it. With that, the proposal died.[44] In 1978, concerned over the implications on academic staff of a negative appraisal of a graduate program, OCUFA pressed for the establishment by OCGS of a mechanism to appeal a negative program appraisal. It also requested that OCUFA be granted observer status on OCGS and that OCGS agree to hold open meetings. After due consideration, OCGS declined to provide OCUFA with observer status or to open its meetings. It also rejected the proposal to establish a formal appeals procedure, although OCGS bylaws were subsequently modified in order to meet some of OCUFA's objections.[45] COU relations with OCUFA would never again be as close as they had been.

●OTHER SYSTEM PLANNING ACTIVITIES

At the same time that COU and its member institutions were wrestling with the problems created by system enrolment swings, government grants below what they judged necessary to provide high-quality academic programs in teaching and research, and ways to improve system planning in graduate studies, other lower-profile efforts to promote interinstitutional co-operation and system planning were proceeding. Some of these involved continuation of projects begun by CPUO in the '60s; others were new initiatives. Considerable resources were devoted to these projects, with mixed results. As the '70s began, the presidents were heavily involved in university computing, library co-ordination, and a centralized university admission system. By the end of the decade, apart from the interlibrary transit system—an early success—COU was involved with only one of these projects, the Ontario Universities' Application Centre (OUAC).

UNIVERSITY COMPUTING

At the end of the '60s, university interest in the development of interinstitutional computer networks was expanding, and along with this grew CPUO's activities in support of central planning. In 1969, a Computer Co-ordination Group was established; later that same year several task forces were struck. In the fall of 1970, a Task Force on Data Communications, set up to develop proposals to meet future university computing needs, submitted a proposal for a phased development of a communications network, METANET. METANET was established to form the basis for a province-wide university computer network, the design of which was completed several months later. To oversee anticipated developments, in July 1971 an Office of Computer Co-ordination was established in the COU secretariat with a full-time director. A Board for Computer Co-ordination (successor to the Computer Co-ordination Group) was struck to supervise its activities.

The academic year 1971–72 saw an expansion of activities focused on the METANET project. A pilot program to link six locations over a three-year period was developed. Co-operative funding arrangements involving the government, the universities, and industry were proposed. The ministry put up funds for a consultant to review the plans. While agreeing that a provincial plan was technically feasible, the consultant concluded that the establishment of a central agency with authority to plan and co-ordinate the development of computer service in the universities was a prerequisite to agreement on the sharing of resources and development of specialities in each university computer centre. The primary responsibility of such a body would be to determine the appropriateness and effectiveness of METANET in rationalizing university computer services across the province.

In the fall of 1972, the COU Board for Computer Co-ordination accepted this judgment and struck a task force to address the issue. Almost two years later, in August 1974, the task force produced a white paper in which it proposed a three-stage development of a provincial plan for computer services. The responses of the universities to this plan were immediate and strongly negative. A few supported the proposal; the majority, however, rejected it as unnecessarily cumbersome and bureaucratic. Some opposed it on the grounds that it would unduly infringe upon institutional autonomy. Stung by the criticism, the task force asked to be discharged, a request that was granted.

Faced with this reality, while reaffirming its commitment to co-ordination, COU scaled down its activities in this area and restructured the Board for Computer Co-ordination. Unable to develop a meaningful program, the board recommended that it be dissolved—a recommendation that was accepted. Efforts to develop a system approach to university computing were now effectively at an end. Some concluded that the considerable resources devoted by COU over the decade in this area had been largely wasted. It was pointed out, however, that, in retrospect, recent developments in computer technology—which permitted the use of smaller, local facilities—justified the decision not to proceed with the proposed provincial network. In what some would consider to be an ex post facto rationalization of failure, it was concluded that "the successes and failures of efforts to develop co-operation amongst universities in the area of computer co-ordination provide solid evidence that easy assumptions about large-scale savings to be achieved from co-operative ventures, especially ones depending on a large centralized operation, must be carefully examined in each case prior to making major investments."46

LIBRARY CO-ORDINATION

Begun in the mid-'60s, efforts to improve co-ordination among Ontario university libraries and to develop a system approach to planning remained a high COU priority in the first half of the '70s. Although extensive duplication of library holdings was required for basic undergraduate programming, it was widely recognized within the university community that Ontario could not afford to duplicate strong research university collections in all academic disciplines. The initial task was to assess institutional library holdings and their use, an essential precondition for preparing a system plan for collection development. It was quickly determined that Ontario universities lacked adequate information about one another's library holdings and had no mechanism for accessing joint holdings. Rectifying this deficiency, then, became the first order of business.

In 1969, CPUO expanded the resources for this task by establishing the Ontario Universities' Bibliographic Centre Project (OUBCP), with a full-time research and planning officer. The centre undertook improvement of communications among the libraries, moved to strengthen interlibrary lending, conducted a study of institutional selection policies and collection development, and initiated an effort to standardize bibliographic records. The latter was to form the basis for the development of an Ontario universities' union library catalogue, judged (correctly) to be one of the major requirements for a rational system development. Despite initial concerns over the feasibility of the exercise, a decision was made to proceed. At about this time, the National Library of Canada announced plans to develop a machine-readable union catalogue. CPUO agreed to work conjointly with the federal agency on this project. The presidents, however, were cautious. "Despite the slow rate of progress to date and uncertainty about the chances of succeeding, the problem of assessing library needs cannot be ignored ... [CPUO] will have to review carefully the endeavour to assess library needs."[47] In a related area, the OCUL study of Ontario university library space requirements was also proceeding slowly.

In 1970, administrative arrangements involving library co-ordination within CPUO were again expanded. Since it was evident that a continuing staff would be required to develop and implement the planned program, the Office of Library Co-ordination (OLC) was created within the secretariat and the OUBCP dissolved. To oversee the work of the new office, a Board for Library Co-ordination, composed of three members of OCGS, three members of OCUL, and three academics, was established. The following year, 1971, was described as "one of review and reassessment in the area of library co-ordination." The results were largely negative. In the spring of 1972, COU (as it had now become) suspended all financial support for the office pending presentation of evidence of clear and satisfactory progress; the director of the office resigned. Council stated that this decision did not reflect a diminished commitment to the objectives of library co-ordination; however, it certainly showed a firm intention to see development of a sharper focus on the issues. COU's growing impatience was clearly illustrated by the response of its chair to a letter from the chair of OCUL protesting the ostensibly high-handed manner in which the executive director of COU had obtained the resignation of the OLC director. According to the letter written by Dr. Carl Williams, president of the University of Western Ontario, the resignation was a result of Council's decision to assign no budget to the office, a decision based on concern over lack of progress toward library co-ordination in the preceding five years (during which some $300,000 of council funds had been expended through the office).[48] Charged with the task of reorganizing the work of the OLC, in September the new chair of the Board for Library Co-ordination reported that his group had no specific recommendations to make. Its work, he noted, was being complicated by differences of opinion among the university librarians. Meanwhile, the opening of the new library at the University of Toronto, named after Premier John Robarts, provided much-needed additional space and the locus for the provincial bibliographic centre.[49]

In May 1973, COU approved a major report prepared by the Office of Library Co-ordination, *A Proposal for the Establishment of a Co-operative Library System for the Ontario Universities*.[50] Reiterating the basic objective of making optimal use of resources and eliminating undesirable duplication, the report acknowledged that a sound base for co-operative library collection development had yet to be achieved. However, it argued that the rationalization of research collections could occur only after discipline assessments had been completed in each academic program area and the necessary long-range policy decisions taken. Undoubtedly sound in logic, the practical implications of such an argument were not encouraging. Nonetheless, a new director was appointed to OLC and the staff expanded. (By 1978, five full-time staff were employed in the office.) With strong support from its board, efforts to improve library co-ordination were renewed.

A plan for an Ontario universities' library co-operative system listed three basic objectives: provision of superior information services to users, rationalization of collection development, and greater sharing of library resources. Since the development of a central union file of library holdings in machine-readable format was seen as essential to the attainment of these objectives, OLC undertook an ambitious program involving the development of several union catalogue projects: a central, computer-based cataloguing support system (UNICAT/TELECAT), a cataloguing system for medicine-related subjects (MEDICAT), an automated system for government documents (CODOC), a co-operative union serials system (CUSS), and a union list of maps (MAPS). A co-operative system for the purchase of major items was also instituted. The goal of system co-ordination and development, however, remained elusive. After an initial spurt of activity, activities slowed; by 1977, it was all downhill.

In 1978, a review by OCUL of the co-operative projects produced a recommendation that most be repatriated to the individual universities in order to achieve economies and to focus co-operation among groups of libraries located in geographical proximity to one another, where some success had already been achieved. Spearheaded by the University of Guelph, the universities in that region were now working together on some of the projects initiated by OLC. By this time too, it had become apparent that co-operative activities did not provide the same benefits to all participating libraries. Geographical location, the sophistication of institutional library systems, and the academic programs offered by the institutions affected the benefits accruing to the institutions. Moreover, by now it was also clear that while co-operative ventures usually provided improved service and assisted in holding down costs, there were real limits to the direct cost savings to be achieved. Furthermore, while savings might be achieved in the long run, in the short run costs often increased. In the period of constrained resources in which the universities now found themselves, approval of expenditures on library co-operation held a low priority. COU accepted OCUL's recommendation of repatriation.

Two years later, in 1980, the Management Committee for UNICAT/TELECAT, the largest of the projects administered by OLC, recommended that the consortium be dissolved. At the time, fewer than half its members were Ontario universities, and fewer than half of the Ontario universities were participating. There were continuing concerns over the cost and quality of the services being provided, and ongoing frustrations involving the administration and staffing of the program. Moreover, the structure was judged over-elaborate in light of the current and projected needs of the member institutions. After conducting its own review, Council agreed with this recommendation. On June 30, 1980, UNICAT/TELECAT was formally dissolved. Since this project was the only remaining major ongoing responsibility of OLC, the office was closed at the same time. Apart from the interlibrary transport system, this marked the end of COU involvement in library activities on behalf of the system. During the decade and a half of COU involvement, some success had been achieved in improving co-operation among Ontario university libraries, but at considerable cost. The primary objective—a provincial university library system—remained unachieved. The only continuing COU activity in the area was the interlibrary transport system. Operated out of York University, this useful, cost-effective service continues to this day.

ONTARIO UNIVERSITIES' APPLICATION CENTRE

Co-operation among Ontario universities in matters involving admission predated the establishment of CPUO. As noted in chapter 1, the universities had long been engaged together in this activity. During the '60s, the realization grew that there was a need for a centralized admissions procedure. The model was the centre in the United Kingdom that served all universities in that jurisdiction. Detailed planning began in 1969; the Ontario Universities' Application Centre opened for business in 1971. The Application Centre was designed as an autonomous, self-supporting entity. Herbert Pettipiere, former registrar of the University of Guelph and an early exponent of co-operation in admissions, headed the centre. Its operations were supervised by a Board of Management made up of representatives of the universities, the secondary schools, and the ministry. Employing state-of-the-art technology, OUAC was an immediate and resounding success. Initially serving only applicants for admission to first year, services were later extended to cover second-entry-level programs in medicine, education, and law. The ministry provided start-up funding for the first three years; thereafter, the costs of operation have been met entirely from fees paid by the student applicants. Designed to operate on a break-even basis, by charging only for the direct costs of the service these fees initially were kept low. However, in the '90s, fees were raised substantially to cover other COU services. One of the major success COU stories, the Application Centre represents an enduring example of voluntary co-operation of proven value to both the student applicants and to the universities.

INSTRUCTIONAL DEVELOPMENT

With the establishment of the Ontario Educational Broadcasting Authority (later TVO) and the opening of Channel 19 in the summer of 1970, educational television in Ontario was largely taken over by the government. However, the interest of the universities in educational technology, which went back to the early '60s, continued. Under the joint sponsorship of CUA and CPUO, Bernard Trotter, executive assistant to the principal at Queen's University, was commissioned to undertake a study to explore the relevance of a range of alternative approaches to educational technology to the Ontario university system. The resulting report, *Television and Technology in University Teaching*, was published in December 1970.[51] The report took as its starting point the application of television and other forms of technology to university-level instruction, but the emphasis was on the systematic development and evaluation of the instructional process. Visionary in nature, it suggested a fundamental review of the whole process of university instruction for the purpose of incorporating the benefits of the evolving new technology. A principle recommendation was that an Ontario Centre for Instructional Development be established. The centre would assist in improving instruction and provide support for interuniversity discipline groups that wanted to explore the production of new learning materials that incorporated the new technology and employed a course-team approach. Employing enrolment projections that indicated the likelihood of a major shortage of university places by the mid-'70s, Trotter also outlined as a possibility the creation of a new degree-granting institution offering a general degree program made up of a limited range of academic courses. These courses would employ centrally developed, integrated packages of instructional materials, including print, audio, and visual, developed by course teams and offered in regional centres across the province. Ahead of its time for Canada, it was a model of an open university.

COU and CUA now set up a joint committee to study various alternatives for the provision of additional university places, of which this was one option. When the projected increase in enrolment failed to occur, the proposal was dropped. Some proposals in the Trotter Report, however, continued to be explored. In April 1971, the presidents endorsed in principle the establishment of a centre for instructional development, and undertook to seek funding for it. Over the next academic year, the proposal was modified and became a "program" of instructional development. A central organization, with a minimal staff, would concentrate on acting as a review body to vet requests for funding for proposals from individual universities in the field of instructional development. The program would also act as a clearing house for information and provide consulting services. It would be experimental and subject to ongoing review. With funding from the ministry, in the summer of 1973 a director was named. "The Program for Instructional Development began its work in an atmosphere of mixed interest, skepticism and opposition."[52] Some good work was accomplished, but the program never flourished.

A COU review in the fall of 1974 resulted in agreement to continue the program for an additional three years at the then current level of activity, with another review planned at the end of its second year and a decision by council about its future due in the fall of 1975. When conducted, this review called for a change in strategy to promote greater institutional commitment to the program. To encourage the universities to put more of their own resources into instructional development, grants to individuals were discontinued in favour of block grants to those universities that had a clear policy on instructional development and showed a firm commitment to program objectives. Ministry funding reached $500,000 (including the costs of maintaining a central office in the COU secretariat) in 1976–77. Arguing that such funds were "seed money" and that eventually the costs should be absorbed by the institutions, funding was phased out. On recommendation from OCUA, the government ended funding in 1980. Using its own resources, COU then established a small

Office of Teaching and Learning to provide some central services: information exchange, co-ordination of interinstitutional activities, and stimulation of co-operative activities in the area. The commitment was for two years. When a review indicated that, in a period of serious budget constraints, instructional development did not enjoy high priority among member universities, council discontinued activity in this area. In June 1982, the office was closed and its assets were transferred to the University of Waterloo.

HEALTH SCIENCES

At the same time COU was winding down some of its co-operative activities, new ones were being developed to meet the changing circumstances of Ontario universities. One of these was the Office of Health Sciences. CPUO was involved with the health sciences early on. In 1966, the committee published a brief paper, *The Health Sciences in Ontario Universities: Recent Experience and Prospects for the Next Decade.* The Council of Ontario Faculties of Medicine (COFM), comprising the deans of the five faculties of medicine in Ontario universities, was an early affiliate of COU. In 1973, the Application Centre inaugurated the Medical Applicants Service, for students applying for admission to Ontario faculties of medicine. That same year, an informal group composed of the executive heads of those universities with health science centres, plus the University of Guelph (which had a college of veterinary medicine), established an informal group that met from time to time to discuss matters of mutual interest. In 1978, at the initiative of COFM, a small Office of Health Sciences was set up in the COU secretariat to provide administrative and secretarial services to these groups. Two years later, in 1980, the Ontario Council of University Health Sciences (OCUHS) was formally established and became an affiliate of COU. That same year, a Liaison Committee for Health Sciences was established and became a COU affiliate. With growing pressures to contain health care costs and the perceived relation between these costs and the size of the university medical training establishment, the need for improved communication and co-operation among the universities with faculties of medicine and health sciences centres grew. In the coming decade, the activities of these groups, particularly COFM, would increase greatly.

● BURGEONING CANADIAN NATIONALISM

As noted in the previous chapter, Canadian universities came under fire in the late '60s for their failure to pay sufficient attention to matters

Canadian. The criticism focused principally on large numbers of non-Canadians being appointed to faculty and the (implied consequent) failure to give adequate attention in academic programming to Canadian issues and culture. Ontario, as the largest province and with the most universities and highest enrolment, was a particular target. As the '70s began, new factors were added. The recent maturing of Canadian graduate schools resulted in a growing cadre of young Canadian scholars and researchers seeking professional appointments. At the same time, the slowdown in enrolment growth, combined with growing financial constraints, was producing a sharp reduction in the number of new faculty appointments being made. In addition, although enrolment in graduate schools was continuing to increase, fewer Canadians were enrolling. As a result, both the number and the proportion of non-Canadians in Ontario graduate schools was increasing. The emerging picture showed qualified Canadians unable to obtain appointments in Canadian universities at the same time that large sums of public funds were being spent in graduate schools to educate non-Canadians. Strong pressure from the media and politicians developed to reserve Canadian universities for Canadians, both faculty and students.

Concerned about the issues, in 1970 the Committee on University Affairs requested from the universities data on the citizenship of faculty and graduate students, broken down by department. Outraged at this intrusion into university autonomy, the universities reacted with hostility, arguing (among other points) that such a request violated the Ontario Code of Human Rights. It did. The following year, CUA repeated its request. This time, after a meeting between COU and CUA, at which a compromise agreement was reached, the universities began to provide data. However, feelings remained bruised. Within the university community, where scholarship was considered to be international in character and citizenship not a meaningful criterion for determining an academic appointment, the firm position taken by COU was seen as proper and justified. Many in the broader community, however, did not share this view. The universities were seen as truculent and unresponsive in dealing with a policy issue of some consequence.

The issue did not go away. In 1975, an all-party Select Committee on Economic and Cultural Nationalism of the Ontario legislature tabled a report that was strongly critical of what it considered to be the Ontario universities' continuing failure to appoint more Canadians to faculty. It recommended the introduction of hiring quotas for non-Canadians.[53] Under pressure from the opposition, the minister informed COU that he was not satisfied with the continuing high number of non-Canadians being appointed and asked them to do something. In response, the executive heads agreed to assume direct responsibility for the appointment of faculty in their institutions. They undertook to see that all qualified Canadian applicants would receive careful consideration and that a non-Canadian would be recommended for appointment only if no qualified Canadian was available. At the same time, however, they refused to discriminate between Canadian citizens and landed immigrants. Since the human rights code considered persons in both categories to be Canadian, both categories of applicant would be treated in the same way—as Canadians.

This did not end the criticism of Ontario university hiring practices; however, it did avoid the imposition of harsher measures. By the end of the decade, the percentage of Canadian citizens on the faculty of Ontario universities rose to near three-quarters (74.1 percent), while the number of new faculty appointments going to non-Canadians declined both in absolute numbers and as a proportion of the total. For 1978–79, data on new faculty appointments (excluding visiting professors) showed that 90 percent were Canadians or landed immigrants, and only 10 percent non-Canadians.[54]

During this period, the federal government also became involved. Concerned over the growing number of foreign nationals entering Canada on student visas to enrol as graduate students and then applying for work permits to allow them to take up teaching and research assistantships at a time when many recent Canadian university graduates were unemployed, Employment and Immigration Canada proposed requiring universities to advertise all such assistantships. The Association of Universities and Colleges of Canada (AUCC), strongly backed by COU, successfully resisted this initiative. The controversy intensified in the mid-1980s with the publication by AUCC of volume 3 of a study commissioned by that organization on Canadian studies in the country's universities.[55] Adopting a simplistic approach to data on the citizenship of faculty in Canadian universities that failed to distinguish between Canadian citizens and landed immigrants, the report urged the federal government to take direct action to improve the number and proportion of Canadians employed in the universities. Once again striking a responsive chord with politicians, this provoked questions in Parliament by opposition members that led to further involvement by government in university appointments procedures. Employment and Immigration Canada subsequently imposed strict requirements on the advertising of faculty positions in Canadian universities and used its power to grant or withhold immigrant visas to restrict the hiring of non-Canadians, even visiting professors. Consultations with the university community represented through AUCC, and arguments between the federal ministry and the universities over which academic fields should be exempt from these regulations, continue to this day.

●ADVOCACY

Concerned over the public's widely perceived lack of understanding about the nature and role of universities in society, at the June 1975 meeting of council the COU executive committee proposed that the traditional low profile approach of the universities be abandoned and increased effort be placed on external public relations. (An earlier Sub-Committee on Public Relations, established in the mid-'60s and never very active, had been defunct for some years.) It was agreed that the universities should take steps to improve their public image, and the executive was asked to pursue the issue. However, six months later, when the executive proposed an expenditure of up to $22,500 on a public opinion survey, the ensuing discussion "reflected considerable skepticism about the value of such a project, and also reflected concern that the public would look askance at the universities' spending money on a public relations survey during a period of austerity."[56] On a divided vote, the proposal was rejected. It would be three years before council took up the matter again.

In December 1977, COU struck a Special Committee on the Public Image of the Universities, headed by B.C. (Burt) Matthews, president of the University of Waterloo. Reporting a year later, the committee recommended that council establish public relations as a priority and allocate the necessary resources to initiate a program to provide more information about Ontario universities to the general public. An allocation of $40,000 for the coming year, 1979–80, was proposed. When council adopted the report in January 1979, at the suggestion of the executive the budget was increased to $75,000 per year for an initial period of two years. The Office of Communications, staffed by a full-time professional, was opened in July 1979.[57] Quickly justifying its existence, it has been a permanent part of the COU secretariat ever since.

In 1977, Edward Monahan, retiring president of Laurentian University, was appointed executive director of COU, succeeding Dr. Macdonald. He would serve three terms, retiring in 1991 after fourteen years.

●SYSTEM UNDER STRESS

Following the disappointing announcement of the global grant for the coming year, 1978–79, and in the midst of the troubling discussions with OCUA over the future of graduate planning, COU held an extended discussion about the state of the system. The discussion was based on two papers prepared in the secretariat for the executive committee. The first, *The Present State of the Ontario University System*,[58] stated bluntly that there were clear signs that the system was becoming unstable. The announced level of funding for the upcoming year (1978–79) was seriously short of what the universities required. Early data indicated a further decline in the participation rate, and there was growing concern both within and without the university community over the ways in which the universities were responding. Under strong pressures to maintain revenues, many universities had begun to take action to protect or improve their share of the enrolment market. Advertising and secondary school liaison activities were expanding, as was the staffing of admissions offices. There was a further increase in the number and value of admissions scholarships. Besides producing criticism that such allocation of scarce financial resources was inappropriate, concern was expressed about the potential lowering of academic standards at a time when the universities were criticizing poor academic standards in the schools.

This concern is illustrated by a proposal from its executive committee regarding first-year admission requirements and council's reaction. At its September 1978 meeting, council received a recommendation from the executive committee that first-year students who had not obtained an average of 60 percent on six grade thirteen subjects—the agreed-upon minimum academic standard for university admission—be declared ineligible for counting towards formula funding in their first year. This provoked vigorous debate, after which the recommendation was approved: sixteen in favour; seven against, with two abstentions. Given this result, the executive committee was asked to "review implementation and presentation in the light of the vote." When the executive reported back at the following meeting, it proposed that that the earlier motion be circulated to member universities for information and that no penalty be imposed "for now." This recommendation was approved, with two abstentions.

The issue came before council again some fifteen months later, in March 1980. At this meeting, a motion to reaffirm the earlier decision to have funding withdrawn was defeated—eleven in favour, thirteen against. The absence of good data, it was argued, precluded an accurate assessment of the size of the problem. More research was needed. The executive director was instructed to write the minister requesting a joint review. There was no response from the ministry. The matter came before COU again in January 1982 when a research report was presented. The data showed that the numbers of first-year students admitted without having met the minimum admission requirements was small, probably less than 2 percent of the system total. However, five institutions had admitted more than 5 percent of the first-year class without confirming that they had met the minimum academic requirements. This time, council reaffirmed its position on minimum admission standards, instructed that the report be circulated to the minister and to OCUA, and recommended that OCUA recommend withdrawal of funding for students who lacked the minimum. At the same time, it noted, "while universities should not, in times of financial constraint, be seen to be admitting large numbers of students unable to meet minimum entry requirements, they should nevertheless exercise individual judgment when these restrictions were inappropriate on compassionate or other extraordinary grounds."[59] By this time, however, the attention of council and the other major system players was largely focused on other matters—the Fisher Report had been issued and all were anxiously awaiting the government's response.

As the 1970s ended, other more important matters concerned council. The operating grant formula continued to be criticized; various (conflicting) proposals were being made to amend it. There was a growing feeling that system issues were not being effectively addressed either by COU or by OCUA. Some universities were taking their case directly to the government. While clearly entitled to do so, such special pleading was increasing the prospect of greater government control. At the same time, universities were being criticized for poor management (some were running deficits), another factor that could lead to government control.

Judging it time for COU to exercise some leadership, the executive committee proposed that council invite OCUA to join in the establishment of a commission to develop plans for the system in the 1980s. The commission would be asked to study institutional role differentiation, relations between the universities and the CAATs, financing (including tuition fees), the distribution mechanism, and the nature of the collectivity. It was also proposed that the commission report not later than July 1979 and that its report be a public document.

A second COU paper, *Stabilization of the Ontario University System*,[60] dealt with the need to stabilize the system, in particular to modify those factors contributing to greater competition among the universities. To deal with problems during the period in which the proposed commission would be at work, several grant distribution options were outlined for discussion purposes. They included a freeze on each institution's share. Other proposals were also made: that the COU Guidelines for Communication with Undergraduates be reaffirmed and published; that a set of guidelines on undergraduate scholarships based on the principles stated by the Monahan Committee be developed and approved; that students admitted to university lacking a 60 percent average in six Year 5 subjects be ineligible for funding in their first year; that the Supplementary Grants be continued at current levels but that no university receive any special grant beyond those currently in place; and that consideration be given to a further discount on funding for new students.

This set of proposals proved too much for council to swallow. There was no consensus. After considerable debate, it was proposed that the chair should meet informally with the chair of OCUA to report on this discussion, ascertain OCUA's views and its plans in relation to them, and report back at a special meeting. At this meeting, the executive committee reported that OCUA had no interest in joining the proposed commission. The advisory body was planning to publish its own white paper and proposed that COU go it alone. This suggestion was rejected. In September 1978, council agreed to establish a Committee on Long-Range Planning. Its mandate was to study matters affecting long-range planning, both individually and collectively; to recommend strategies; and to maintain an ongoing review. Chaired by Percy Smith, professor of English and former Vice-President Academic of the University of Guelph, who would serve part-time for a period of two years, the committee was provided with a budget of $45,000.[61] Its first task would be to prepare a COU response to the OCUA white paper on system issues.

The other recommendations from the executive suffered a mixed fate. The proposal that COU recommend that Supplementary Grants be held at current levels was tabled after a vote showed fourteen in favour and seven against. The proposals to reaffirm guidelines on undergraduate admissions practices, on undergraduate scholarship policy, and on communications with undergraduate applicants were passed, but only after long debate and on split votes. Since they were only guidelines and it was evident that some member institutions would choose not to abide by them, in practical terms the vote was meaningless. The proposal that COU affirm a minimum requirement for admission to first-year university of 60 percent on six Year 5 subjects, and that those admitted with a lower average be ineligible for formula funding, was passed, but only after the number of subjects required was reduced to five and the stipulation that students not meeting the minimum should be ineligible for funding was removed. These results amply demonstrated that COU was becoming unstable. Institutional self-interest was replacing concern for the collectivity. Concern for the maintenance of high academic standards was declining in the face of a need to expand enrolment to increase revenues. Consensus was less and less likely to be obtained on any issue seen by members as adversely affecting their institutional well-being, a clear sign of trouble.

Essaying a look ahead, COU characterized the future in one word: uncertainty—uncertainty over finances, over enrolment, over staffing, over the structure of the system, and, above all, uncertainty over the role and place of universities in society. That year, in its annual brief to OCUA, entitled *The Price of Restraint,* council calculated that the minimum financial requirements for the system called for an increase in the global grant of 6.9 percent in each of the next three years. If tuition fees were to remain frozen, the annual increase in the operating grant would need to be 9.6 percent. To illustrate the seriousness of the universities' plight, OCUA modelled two extreme alternatives. Were there to be no increases in operating grants and the revenue shortfall covered by tuition fee increases, tuition fees would rise 20 percent per annum and double in three years. Were the revenue shortfall to be covered by reductions in academic staff, a reduction in faculty complement of 15 percent (some 2,000 positions) would be required. Both options, of course, were rejected by COU as unacceptable.[62]

The OCUA white paper *The Ontario System: A Statement of Issues,*[63] published in September 1979, addressed the major problems facing the system and outlined some options. One option was increased government support; other options included rationalization of satellite university campuses, merging undergraduate programs offered by neighbouring universities, and the development of different roles by different universities. The paper urged both the universities and COU to devote more attention to planning. Under the heading "Autonomy and Control," the advisory body reopened the issue of structure. Noting that in its spring hearings it had been impressed as never before by the opposing views held by the universities and various provincial organizations about the appropriate roles and effectiveness of the two major provincial bodies, COU and OCUA , the advisory body set out several alternatives: maintain the current structure, abolish OCUA, provide OCUA with limited executive authority, or transform OCUA into a university grants committee. This reopened a debate that had lain largely dormant since the publication of the Wright Report almost a decade earlier.

In setting out these options, OCUA reiterated its own view that COU should be assuming greater responsibility for system planning, and stated that it would continue to press council to accept such responsibilities. Given the reduced financial circumstances of the universities, OCUA was convinced of the need for greater co-operation and co-ordination among the universities, a reduction in program duplication, and further rationalization and differentiation in the system. It was looking to the institutions to develop plans that would emphasize role differentiation and to COU to play a larger role in system planning and co-ordination. At the same time, OCUA itself began to exert more authority in system planning in the graduate area.

In its draft response to the OCUA white paper, the COU Committee on Long-Range Planning came out in favour of granting OCUA limited executive authority. It acknowledged that such authority would need to be appropriately circumscribed and methods defined for giving it effect. Nonetheless, it judged that in the current circumstances, greater central authority was called for. This proposal provoked long and vigorous debate; in the end, there was no agreement. Council "received" the report and transmitted it to OCUA "for information," with an accompanying note that the matter continued to be under discussion within COU.[64]

When 1970s began, the mood of the presidents had been one of quiet optimism. As the decade ended, this optimism had been replaced by a growing sense of unease and uncertainty. Their organization was now described as "a marvel of compromise and inconsistency to many both within and outside it … [it was experiencing] anxiety, even schizophrenia."[65] External pressures to expand and extend interinstitutional co-operation and co-ordination in the interests of the common good of the system were growing. Council seemed increasingly unable to respond effectively. As the financial climate grew chillier, the universities were looking more and more to their own interests, not to the good of the collectivity. Some members of council would have liked to see the roles of both OCUA and COU reduced. In such an environment, the leadership that council had exercised in system planning was fast disappearing; the future of both bodies was becoming uncertain.

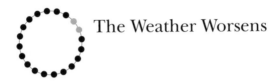

CHAPTER 3

The Weather Worsens

AS THE 1980s BEGAN, the mood in the universities was sombre. This was in marked contrast with the air of quiet confidence and optimism that had pervaded the community a decade earlier. Before the decade was half over, two serious efforts would be made by the government to address system issues. Both would prove unsuccessful. During the same period, COU involvement in system planning would become much diminished, principally as a result of its own decisions. OCUA involvement would expand. The leadership role of COU and its overall effectiveness was negatively affected.

The COU assessment of the basic problem facing the universities was aptly described in the title given its triennial report covering the three-year period 1978-79 to 1981-82: *Squeezing the Triangle.*[1] The universities had always considered the quality of their academic programs to be the highest priority. For two decades, they had been endeavouring to implement public policy that promised a place in an Ontario university for every qualified student who wished to attend, a policy that they accepted. Continuing inadequate funding—the term "underfunding" had yet to enter the lexicon—was, however, beginning to threaten access to quality undergraduate education. Three factors—accessibility, quality, and funding—imagined as three sides of an equilateral triangle, were exerting strong pressure on one another. If this pressure were not relieved soon, COU argued, there would be an implosion.

At COU, the prevailing mood of uncertainty was overlaid with a growing fractiousness among the member institutions. Because the annual increases in the level of global funding were failing to keep pace with continuing high inflation, and because tuition fees were controlled, the only way for universities to increase operating revenues was to expand enrolment, even though the grant for new students was at a discount. Competition among the universities for students was increasing. Some members were complaining of predatory actions by their sister institutions, and calling for action by council. The buffer body,

Notes to chapter 3 are on pp. 220–222

OCUA, was now promoting institutional differentiation as the preferred means of rationalization. It was urging COU to become more involved in system issues. Given the circumstances, apart from a substantial increase in the level of public funding, any change in the system would affect member institutions differently. In a zero-sum game, inevitably there would be some winners and some losers. In such conditions, a voluntary association like COU had very limited room to manoeuvre. At the same time, the number of government regulations affecting the universities was increasing. COU, as the recognized representative of Ontario universities, was being drawn more frequently into acting on behalf of its member institutions. The first half of the '80s would be the busiest ever experienced by the COU secretariat. The number, range, and complexity of the issues council was now being called upon to address would impose a severe test on senior members of staff. Measured by effort, the results were outstanding; measured by clear benefits to the collectivity, they were much less so.

On the face of it, relations among COU, OCUA, and the Ministry of Colleges and Universities (MCU) were good, even cordial. The new chair of OCUA, William Winegard, former president of the University of Guelph, had served a term as chair of COU. Burt Matthews, a former president of the University of Waterloo who would succeed him, was also well known to COU. Premier Davis, in his previous role as minister of Colleges and Universities, had presided over the expansion period. A strong minister, Dr Bette Stephenson, was now in place. Both were regarded as friendly toward the universities. Benson A. (Ben) Wilson, the assistant deputy minister of Colleges and Universities responsible for the university sector, was a well-respected senior civil servant who understood the university community and enjoyed its confidence. The decision a decade earlier to establish a strong research arm within the COU secretariat had paid off. Well-staffed and led, the COU research division provided the database and analytical capacity for much of the research that supported system planning. Because its work was widely accepted as sound and objective, both OCUA and MCU maintained only modest in-house research capacity. Nevertheless, the centripetal pressures placed on the universities by OCUA and the government, in combination with the centrifugal pressures generated within council itself, provided a potentially volatile mix.

●ACADEMIC PLANNING IN A COLD CLIMATE

In the academic year 1979–80, government funding again fell below that judged necessary by both COU and OCUA. The next year, with inflation running in double digits, both councils requested an increase of more than 12 percent; the government provided little more than half of that. Overall, the increase amounted to 7.1 percent. However, this included an increase of 7.5 percent in tuition fees, plus institutional discretion to increase tuition a further 10 percent. Although the students were angry and others in the university community expressed objections, with few exceptions the financially hard-pressed universities increased tuition fees to the maximum allowable. Three major COU committees were at work: one on university research, one on long-range planning, and a third on graduate planning. In the same period, OCUA published two papers: *System on the Brink: A Financial Analysis of the Ontario University System 1979*, which described the universities' financial problems, and *System Rationalization: A Responsibility and an Opportunity*, in which the advisory body argued for greater differentiation among the institutions in their programming, and for more centralized planning.[2]

The COU Special Committee on Provincial Support for University Research was established in November 1979 under the chairmanship of James Ham, president of the University of Toronto, in response to the expressed interest of Premier Davis in the subject. Working rapidly, the committee's report was presented to COU in March 1980; it was promptly endorsed by council and forwarded to the premier.[3] The Ham Report proposed an approach to provincial research policy that would emphasize Ontario as a research-based province committed to "living by its wits," a jurisdiction where the universities would be strongly supported in both pure and applied research. Its principal recommendation was for the creation of an Ontario Council for Research and Productivity. The proposed council would assist in the formulation of policies to promote a more active collaboration in research among government, business, industry, and the universities; identify specific needs and opportunities for research and development; and recommend funding in areas judged important for the improvement of productivity. The report also called for a new federal-provincial policy on research in Canada. The premier was supportive, the cabinet less so. It would be a year and a half before the government responded with an announcement of the establishment of a Board for Industrial Leadership and Development (BILD).

At the same meeting at which it approved the Ham Report, COU received a report on undergraduate program planning from its Committee on Long-Range Planning, known as the (Percy) Smith Committee. The committee's earlier report on graduate planning had recommended that some executive authority for planning be granted OCUA. This had provoked controversy within council and failed to be endorsed. Its second report, *Challenge of Substance: A Report on Undergraduate Programmes in Ontario Universities*, would suffer a similar fate.

The committee found much duplication and little imagination in undergraduate program offerings. Its report stated that the provincial picture "reflect[s] the disposition of each university to view its sister universities as competitors, to put it bluntly, in a struggle for survival, rather than in a common enterprise for the public good." The committee's review of undergraduate programming disclosed a good deal of duplication in popular program areas such as Spanish and African studies, with a corresponding lack of interest in some of the newer areas such as Middle East and East Asia studies. This finding led it to note wryly that a common argument in favour of university autonomy is that it encourages diversity; however, "it seems not to prevent the operation of an opposing principle: that necessity is the mother of imitation."[4]

To improve effectiveness, quality, and economy in undergraduate education, the committee argued that "a far greater amount of discussion and planning should go on between and among universities with the needs of the system and the Province in mind." But the insistent pressures of competition for students, fostered by the formula, inhibited this. COU had been aware of the need for improved planning but lacked a mechanism for ensuring that improvements be made. Recommendations to strengthen system planning by an earlier COU committee on planning, the Special Committee to Assess University Policies and Plans (Guidon Committee), were formally approved in 1976; however, no effort was made to implement them.[5]

The (Percy) Smith Committee made two main recommendations: (1) that each university undertake to advise the others immediately of all proposals for new undergraduate programs, and (2) that COU establish a standing committee on undergraduate programming. Such a committee would examine the changing needs of the Ontario university system and the best means of responding to them; identify new areas and encourage orderly program development; and encourage discussion among the universities on undergraduate programs and policies from a system perspective. The Council of Deans of Arts and Science gave the committee's report a mixed reception. After a sharp debate, COU adopted the first recommendation and referred it to the Ontario Council of Academic Vice-Presidents (OCAV). The rest of the report was simply "received." At the same time, in full knowledge that the committee needed to be re-staffed, including the naming of a new chair, council chose not to do so pending a response from the academic vice-presidents' group.

Later that same year, three more reports from the (Percy) Smith Committee were tabled at council. *University Laboratory Equipment: A Vanishing Resource,* which contained no recommendations, was approved and forwarded to OCUA. A report on undergraduate enrolment, *Numbers in the Air*, which described the problems inherent in undergraduate enrolment planning based on projections of manpower needs, the imbalance in accessibility across the various regions of the province, and the evident lack of concern in individual institutions for taking system enrolment needs into account, was "received." The third, a report on faculty, *The First Essential*, produced vigorous discussion. Commenting briefly on the recommendations of a 1976 report on academic career planning prepared by a joint COU/OCUFA committee, the (Percy) Smith Committee noted that while this earlier report had been approved by COU, no further action had been taken. Concerned with longer-term implications of funding constraints and a stable enrolment for the future pattern of faculty salaries and faculty age profile, and with the implications for the nature of the university of the growing movement towards faculty unionization (seen by many in the universities "with great misgiving"), the committee recommended that COU invite OCUFA "to join in a careful study of the causes, processes, and effects of faculty unionization in Ontario, with a view to reaching common understanding and to ensuring the well-being of the universities"—a proposal that OCUFA was known to oppose. In the end, this report also "was received."[6] With the increasing militancy of many local faculty associations and the growth in the number of these associations moving towards collective bargaining, relations between COU and OCUFA cooled.

At the December 1980 meeting of council, the executive director reported that the academic vice-presidents' group had agreed to meet three times a year to report to one another on new undergraduate program proposals at their institutions, "for information." Given this information, COU decided to take no further action. The Committee on Long-Range Planning was allowed quietly to expire. The Ontario Council of Academic Vice-Presidents only fitfully met its commitment to exchange information on institutional undergraduate program planning; it had little effect. With money in short supply, fewer proposals for new undergraduate programs were coming forward; at the same time, when planning new programs the institutions were little inclined to consider what others were planning or to take into account system needs. Nor (owing to a lack of financial incentives, among other factors) was any university inclined to undertake the arduous task of closing an academic program.

The tussle between OCUA and COU over responsibility for system planning continued, each urging the other to become more heavily involved. With the publication by OCUA of *System Rationalization: A Responsibility and an Opportunity* in the fall of 1980, the argument was extended to the undergraduate level. Back in 1977, the advisory body had raised the issue of how greater savings might be affected. In a letter to university heads outlining issues to be discussed at the hearings that year, the question was raised: "Are savings possible by the merger of one institution with another or through the merging of certain specific services such as libraries, computing, campus planning, other support services and even teaching in geographically proximate institutions [or indeed system wide]?"[7] OCUA was trying to encourage institutional differentiation. In its 1978 annual report, the advisory body noted that "graduate (program) rationalization and disciplinary evolution have been considered in isolation. Council believes that future rationalization and planned evolution must take into account the interaction between the graduate and the undergraduate sectors and the institutional profiles which thus emerge."[8] The view of OCUA was clearly stated in its 1980 paper *System Rationalization*. Ontario has a university system and each university is a part of that system. Yet, the universities have failed to recognize this; they seem unconcerned. To OCUA, this stemmed from their apparent assumption that "somehow or other, an acceptable total provincial array of programs would follow automatically from the sum of the plans of each institution." Such a view, it stated, was no longer adequate. Future planning would have to be based on a clear recognition that Ontario has a university system, one in which each university has a particular role to play. If this were to be accepted, each institution could plan on the basis of its particular role and new academic programs would be developed in light of system needs and institutional strengths.[9]

Echoing the opinion of the COU Committee on Long-Range Planning, the OCUA paper bluntly asserted the need for greater system-wide consolidation and rationalization to prevent and eliminate undesirable duplication, to protect existing strong programs, to preserve opportunities for innovation, and to ensure resources be effectively used and be available in areas of need. A review of undergraduate programming over the previous twenty years showed little attempt to co-ordinate program planning and a minimum of interinstitutional co-operation. While accepting the general principle that it is desirable to leave as much planning as possible in the hands of individual universities, OCUA stated that more central control was now necessary. OCUA agreed with the basic approach proposed by the (Percy) Smith Committee; however, it considered the committee's recommendations inadequate. Given that the chair of OCUA, William Winegard, and the chair of the COU Long-Range Planning Committee, Percy Smith, earlier had served together respectively as president and Vice-President Academic at the University of Guelph, it is somewhat ironic that at the same time COU was rejecting these recommendations of the Smith Committee for having gone too far, OCUA was criticizing the committee for not having gone far enough.

Ocua divided undergraduate programs into three categories: core programs in arts and science, professional programs, and quasi-professional programs. For programs in the first category, an exchange of information among the universities was considered sufficient. For those in the second category, ministerial approval should be required for funding. For programs in the third (middle) category—quasi-professional programs—the advisory body thought that COU should monitor developments and undertake the necessary program co-ordination.

The divergent views of COU and OCUA on undergraduate planning were soon put to the test. In the spring of 1980, the University of Waterloo put forward a new undergraduate program in geological engineering, a quasi-professional program, and asked the advisory body to review it. (Ministry policy dating back to 1974 stated that approval of funding for professional programs would be granted only upon recommendation from OCUA. The policy, however, was not widely known and had not been uniformly implemented.) The advisory body promptly referred the matter to COU. Council requested comments from its member institutions, the Committee of Ontario Deans of Engineering (CODE) and the Association of Professional Engineers of Ontario (APEO). Both associations favoured the new program, but opinion among university faculties of engineering was mixed. At the debate in council, some members took the view that COU "could not and should not take on the role of an undergraduate ACAP." On a straw vote, council was divided: thirteen in favour, eleven opposed and two abstentions.[10] COU then advised OCUA that, while there was consensus that it should play a major role in reaching decisions on funding of new undergraduate programs, it was not in a position to specify what this role should be without further discussion within council and further dialogue with the advisory body. COU had failed. OCUA decided to move on. It set up its own academic committee to review the program. (The committee's recommendation was positive.)

In the fall of 1981, without warning the minister announced a temporary funding freeze on all new undergraduate programs and invited OCUA to develop procedures to handle requests for exemption from the freeze. The advisory body responded immediately. OCUA noted that it "has seen no clear evidence that COU is willing to accept the responsibility... [and] there is need for control. Therefore, OCUA is prepared to accept the responsibility of recommending on funding for undergraduate programmes."[11] Its newly formed Academic Advisory Committee (AAC) would undertake the work and apply the three-fold division of undergraduate programs previously outlined. Unable to find consensus among its member institutions on what role it should play in undergraduate program planning, COU ceded the ground to OCUA. OCUA's role, however, was limited to recommendations on funding for new programs under the established rubrics. The advisory body made no serious effort to develop a mechanism for the system planning of undergraduate programs. Rationalization of existing programs and the development of new ones remained in the hands of the universities. It would be more than a decade before COU again became involved in this area, when it instituted a program under the direction of the academic vice-presidents' group (ACAV) to undertake regular "audits" of the quality of undergraduate academic programs.

Concurrently, a parallel devolution of COU leadership took place at the graduate program planning level. In the fall of 1980, in accordance with then existing procedures affecting discipline assessment, COU submitted six new graduate programs to OCUA, with a recommendation that they be funded. In each case, documentation was provided to meet four of the current criteria for funding: successful appraisal, need, uniqueness, and enrolment. Council, however, declined to address the fifth criterion—that the programs be consistent with the aims and objectives of the institution offering them, and be deserving of funding despite the current financial constraints. Its justification for this omission was this: it was inappropriate for COU to become involved in the application of non-academic (that is, financial) considerations to decisions affecting the academic programs of any member university. COU would continue to undertake program appraisals; it would expect to be consulted on other matters and would remain free to give advice. But it would not make decisions involving non-academic considerations. Such decisions would be left to OCUA.

This decision reflected the views of the COU Special Committee to Review Graduate Planning (Forster Committee), now completing its work. Its final report was presented to council in March 1981. The committee argued that the circumstances affecting graduate planning and programming had changed greatly since the discipline assessment process had been introduced a decade earlier. Graduate enrolment peaked in 1975. Since then, the average annual increase in the number of new graduate programs was 1 percent. In this context, the committee concluded, complex planning controls were both unnecessary and undesirable. Because the players (COU, OCUA, and MCU) had been preoccupied with micro-planning and program-by-program regulation over the past few years, little effective system planning had taken place. Such micro-planning needed to cease. Survival now would depend on flexibility, not control. What was needed in the current circumstances was a focus on sectoral planning in which universities with recognized academic strengths in given sectors would be allowed to mount new programs subject only to rigorous academic appraisal. Discipline assessment should be abandoned in favour of continuing rigorous appraisal, including periodic appraisal of all graduate programs on a regular cycle. COU's role should be limited to broad system planning and careful monitoring of quality by means of program appraisal. If decisions on funding were to be made, let OCUA make them and employ its own academic advisory committee to do so.[12] Discipline assessments already underway in philosophy and social work continued; that in philosophy was completed only in 1984. Nevertheless, the decade-long effort by COU to promote system planning at the graduate level by means of the discipline assessment process was at an end. The Advisory Committee on Academic Planning (ACAP) was dissolved in June 1981.

The consequences of this decision were substantial. From now on, COU would be involved only in graduate program appraisals. When combined with Council's parallel decision to opt out of undergraduate program planning, taken for essentially the same reasons, COU effectively removed itself from any leadership role in system program planning, creating a vacuum that thereafter was never adequately filled.

The mandate of OCUA's new Academic Advisory Committee (AAC) was to provide expert advice on graduate program planning based on the advisory body's funding criteria (including societal need and institutional appropriateness), to monitor the COU appraisals process (now involving periodic appraisals as well as appraisals of new programs), and to review the annual compilation by COU of doctoral macro-indicator data. In 1983, alarmed over the large number of successful appraisals, AAC requested that it be provided with the CVs of all consultants employed in the appraisal process. The resulting fuss was resolved by an agreement with OCGS that these would be provided only in "very critical cases." Still unhappy about the apparent lack of rigour in some appraisals, a year later (1984), AAC proposed that in selected cases it be provided with the total documentation used in an appraisal. Fearing that this would result in AAC "second guessing" an appraisal, COU strongly resisted this proposal. After discussion between the two bodies, in April 1985 agreement was reached on an external audit of the appraisal process. Entrusted to a small committee chaired by Stefan Dupré, a former chair of OCUA, the results settled the issue. In a report issued in April 1986, the committee stated: "The overall finding of this Committee is that, in our unanimous and unqualified opinion, the Appraisals Process which is currently in place produces reliable and credible judgements of the academic quality of existing and proposed graduate programmes in Ontario."[13]

Judgments on the success of the Ontario graduate program planning process differ depending on the assessor. One perceptive external observer concluded that "[Ontario] universities, holding to hallowed notions of institutional autonomy and academic freedom, had not really accepted the legitimacy of provincial co-ordination except as superficial rhetoric ..., yet their own efforts at voluntary co-ordination, under the banner of 'collective autonomy' had, with few notable exceptions, simply not been up to the task."[14] An insider has a different view. "Overall it is fair to say that the general quality of graduate study in the province was higher as a consequence of these efforts, although the cost effectiveness is hard to estimate. There can be little doubt that had the universities not been vigorously working at establishing a reliable planning process, OCUA or the Ministry would have found it convenient to impose some less acceptable control."[15]

With the benefit of hindsight, both judgments seem partly correct. Had the universities acting collectively through OCGS and COU not defended institutional prerogatives, a more centralized and therefore less flexible approach likely would have been adopted. At the same time, the universities' unwillingness to broaden their planning horizons to include system considerations reflected a failure to recognize legitimate system requirements. Concern for academic quality—the driving force behind COU's continuing involvement in the appraisal process—was surely an essential condition of good system planning. It was, however, not a sufficient condition. COU and the universities' determination to protect institutional autonomy, combined with the voluntary mechanism they developed to promote system planning, in the end proved unequal to the task. Their continuous opposition to the establishment of a system-planning agency with requisite executive authority left a vacuum that remains unfilled to this day. Had academic program planning developed with system considerations more firmly in mind, the broader community, including students and taxpayers, would have been better served.

While system program planning remained the major preoccupation of COU in this period, council dealt with several other matters with system implications. In the spring of 1980, a private members' bill was introduced into the legislature to provide degree-granting status to the Canadian School of Management. COU intervened at the committee stage to oppose the legislation, arguing that the institution did not meet minimal academic standards for the offering of degree programs. Confronted with such negative views on an issue involving quality, the committee decided not to proceed. The bill died on the order paper. At about the same time, a new degree-granting institution was established in the province by means of a private member's bill. Redeemer Reformed Christian College, a liberal arts college sponsored by the Dutch Reformed Church, received a charter to grant baccalaureate degrees in arts with a religious designation. Because of its denominational ties, Redeemer was ineligible for provincial grants. COU did not become involved. The college opened in Ancaster in the fall of 1981.

In the fall of 1980, concerned about reports that Ontario would soon have a shortage of highly qualified manpower in computer science and some areas of engineering, the Ministry of Colleges and Universities issued a white paper on polytechnic education in Ontario. The paper raised a number of questions about the ability of the post-secondary institutions in the province to meet future labour market needs in this area. Given Ontario's two-track post-secondary system, the paper asked: Was there any need to develop a "middle level" composed of polytechnic institutes? Were the present two sectors sufficiently involved in polytechnic education? Should there be greater co-ordination between the university and CAAT sectors? OCUA and COU were both invited to comment.

Given their current financial problems, most universities were not keen to see any funds diverted to new projects. The COU response was lukewarm. Its brief stated that data did not suggest an impending manpower shortage, that universities and colleges of applied arts and technology (CAATs) had the matter under review, and that co-operation across the university–CAAT interface existed and could be expanded. The institutions were open to further co-operation; the big problem was lack of funding. Appendices attached to the COU brief provided data on the current state of play across the university–CAAT interface. Far from making the case for close co-operation, these data illustrated how little co-operation actually existed. In the entire system, there were only six joint university–college programs: three at McMaster University and one each at Toronto (at Erindale College), Windsor and York universities. Only two universities— Brock and Laurentian—had formal provisions providing advanced standing to graduates from CAATs. Transfers of students between the two sectors were minimal. Over the five-year period, 1974–79, less that 2.5 percent of those admitted to university came from a CAAT, while about 5 percent of those admitted to CAATs came from a university. Over the period, CAAT enrolment had increased and now constituted more than half of the total enrolment in the post-secondary sector. University enrolment had declined, from 52.3 percent of the total in 1974 to 45 percent in 1979. In the midst of everything else that was going on, this issue was quietly dropped. Another decade would pass before serious efforts were undertaken to bridge the university–CAAT divide.

Growing financial pressure on the smallest university in the province, Trent, which offered mainly undergraduate programs in arts and science in a more faculty-intensive Oxbridge approach to teaching, produced a small relaxation in formula funding regulations. Early in 1981, on recommendation from OCUA, the minister approved a new non-formula grant, the Differentiation Grant, to assist Trent University. The executive director of COU wrote the chair of OCUA enquiring about the rationale for the new grant. In his reply, Chair Winegard stated that the grant was to make up for the lack of flexibility in the funding formula. It was being provided to Trent because that university was willing to accept a particular role for itself as a mainly undergraduate arts and science institution offering no professional programs. He noted that other universities were free to apply for a Differentiation Grant. Indeed, he said, OCUA would have liked more institutions to differentiate themselves and accept restrictions on their programs. However, none would be compelled to do so.[16] This information was conveyed to the universities, but there were no other takers. By now, the earlier decision of government to establish all Ontario universities as equal in terms of their degree-granting rights had become a major deterrent in the efforts of OCUA to introduce a more differentiated system.

● TWO MAJOR REVIEWS: THE FISHER COMMITTEE AND THE BOVEY COMMISSION

At the beginning of the decade, strong pressure from the universities led to the decision by the government to strike a committee to conduct a comprehensive review of the Ontario university system. By this time, meetings of university executive heads and board chairs with the premier had become an annual event. At the August 1980 meeting, the universities made an impassioned plea for increased government support. Without making any commitment, the premier asked for details. In a brief prepared within the COU secretariat, *The Situation of the Ontario Universities,* the universities gave their reply. The universities were no longer able to reconcile publicly endorsed objectives with the level of funding being provided. Year-to-year accommodations could no longer be made to continuing shortfalls in funding. Quality, in some cases even viability, was now threatened. The brief sketched three possible ways in which the growing gap might be closed: (1) ad hoc adjustments in academic programming, (2) additional funding, or (3) a scaling down of the level of university operations. The first option was rejected as not in the long-term interest of either the universities or the province; the second option was the one the universities preferred. The brief emphasized, however, that the primary issue was where the government stood.[17]

According to the brief, part of the problem lay with the operating grant formula. "It offers no incentive for contraction in order to sustain quality, either within a university or in the system as a whole.... [Moreover,] because it remains, despite the dampening factors, to a significant extent enrolment driven, it continues to provide stronger incentives for competition than for co-operation among institutions."[18] What was required was a modification in the formula to encourage the universities to make voluntary adjustments in programming and to improve interinstitutional co-operation. As well, the university–government structure needed to be re-examined. A clearer definition of the respective roles of the individual institutions, COU, OCUA, and the ministry was required.

The brief offered some proposals on structure. "What COU should *not* [italics in the original] do is assume the authoritative role with respect to plans and policies of specific member institutions. To do so would be to make it, at least for these purposes, the de facto governing body of a University of Ontario."[19] COU should reduce its involvement in system planning; OCUA should assume greater responsibility. The intermediate body should have its membership strengthened by the addition of more academic members and be restructured to the point where it would enjoy the confidence of both the universities and the government sufficiently to assume such responsibilities, a confidence it now clearly lacked.

The COU brief also proposed increased funding by means of an amended formula, one that offered incentives to universities to reduce programming and to expand interinstitutional co-operation. The brief argued that, if this were to be done, COU might then be able to perform an expanded role in fostering voluntary co-operation and planning among its members, and a strengthened OCUA might be given some executive authority. This was a new approach—reform of the operating grants formula to provide financial incentives to the universities to rationalize programs and to differentiate themselves from their sister institutions. No details were provided; these, the brief stated, had yet to be worked out. The brief insisted, however, that the first requirement was for the government to articulate clearly public objectives and then redesign funding arrangements in light of them.

Presented in mid-November, the COU brief received immediate attention. Four days later, the minister stood in her place in the legislature to announce the establishment of a Committee on the Future Role of Universities in Ontario. Chaired by the deputy minister of Colleges and Universities, Harry Fisher (and known thereafter as the Fisher Committee), it was a blue-ribbon group made up of persons with broad knowledge and experience at both the institutional and system levels. Its mandate was to develop a public statement of objectives for the universities in the 1980s in operational terms; to consider appropriate modification in the funding mechanism; to define more clearly the joint roles of the individual universities, COU, OCUA, and the government; and to recommend such policy changes as it judged necessary to improve the ability of the universities to meet the agreed-upon objectives. It was asked to produce a preliminary report by the end of February and a final report by the end of June 1981.[20] Working with vigour and despatch, the special committee produced a preliminary report on time; its final report was published in August 1981.

The activities of COU did not cease during the period in which the Fisher Committee was at work. Nor did those of OCUA or the ministry. Debate continued within council on system planning issues, as did negotiations between COU and OCUA on these and other matters. The government made decisions on funding. The operating grants for 1981–82 provided an overall increase of just over 10 percent, including a further increase of 10 percent in tuition fees plus an additional discretionary 10 percent. Although somewhat higher than expected, the increase fell short of what both COU and OCUA had judged that the universities needed. With inflation running above 12 percent and further increases in enrolment, the universities continued to struggle. COU now calculated the accumulated shortfall in operating grants to be almost $260 million, nearly 20 percent of the projected system revenue for 1981–82.

The interim report of the Fisher Committee, issued at the end of February 1981, invited comment on a variety of options covering finance, planning, and structure. The COU response reiterated its view that the principle problem was lack of funding and that there was a pressing need for the government to take a position regarding its public policy objectives. The COU position was also firm on the issue of system structure. In its interim report, the Fisher Committee dismissed the possibility that COU could successfully manage system planning, and it proposed a strengthened OCUA. COU agreed about its own inability to manage system planning and on the need for a strengthened OCUA. However, it was not prepared to go as far as the committee in granting executive authority to any central agency. The COU response stated that structure is concerned with means, not ends. The problem, council stated, lay in the inadequate specification by the government of goals for the system. The government had stated very broad objectives and expected a high level of social responsiveness to these objectives through wide-ranging accessibility. How was the system to be managed if insufficient funds were provided? The committee identified a major structural issue: the degree to which the system requires planning authority. The thrust of its observations, however, was that the worse the financial future, the more outside intervention into university decision making would be required. COU did not find this argument compelling, except possibly in extremis. Undoubtedly, the tougher the financial outlook, the harder the decisions that would need to be taken. "But it does not necessarily follow that these decisions should be taken centrally. Over the past few years, the universities have adapted, albeit with difficulty, to significant underfunding without central direction. We are not convinced that the outcome is a system of lower quality than might have been achieved through system planning with centralized authority."21

The final report of the Fisher Committee, published in 1981, added a strong voice to the chorus of those urging increased government support for the universities.[22] In keeping with its mandate, the committee made recommendations across a broad spectrum. To maintain accessibility, it urged that tuition fees be kept low and student assistance improved. A number of proposals were made for modifying the structure of the system. The major focus, however, was on the public policy objectives for the universities and the amount of public funding needed for their implementation. Here the committee came out strongly in support of the position long held by the university community. It recommended that the government reaffirm the objectives stated by OCUA as still valid and that it provide a level of support sufficient to enable the universities to meet these objectives. This level of funding, it said, should be sufficient to meet the costs of inflation and to provide for the career development of faculty and support staff. It should also include an additional $25 million per annum for replacement of furniture and equipment.

To emphasize the implications of this option, in the final chapter of its report the Fisher Committee provided a sketch of a scaled-down Ontario university system. It predicted that "Ontario would have one comprehensive university..., not more than four full-service universities offering a more restricted range of... programs at all degree levels ... [and] four or five special-purpose institutions ... Of the remaining institutions, some may have to be closed, and others ... restructured. These institutins would offer high-quality undergraduate instruction in arts and science and perhaps the early years of programs in high demand." Adopting this option, the Committee said, would require significant direct intervention by the government ("No amount of tinkering with current structures will be satisfactory"). Once restructured, however, it believed that the resulting more limited system composed of "basically autonomous institutions within clearly defined limits" could function well.[23]

The advice of the Fisher Committee to the government was blunt. Either increase funding—the committee's preferred option—or scale back the system. A third option—maintaining the status quo, which the committee termed "muddling through"—was decisively rejected. The preferred path forward was to increase funding sufficient to enable the universities to maintain quality at their current level of operations. The less preferred, more drastic path was a major reduction in the scale of provincial university operations sufficient to enable the institutions to maintain quality at the level of financial support provided. Adopting this option, the committee said, would involve a reduction in accessibility in both geographic and program terms, and would adversely affect the breadth of university research. Its adoption also would require amending the legislative acts of the universities.

If adequate funding were to be provided, the Fisher Committee judged that the existing, essentially decentralized system of academically autonomous universities could (and should) be maintained. University governing bodies and senior administrative officers, however, needed to assume greater responsibility for re-orienting their institutions to changing societal needs and sharpening their respective institutional roles. They also need to take steps to ensure that systematic reviews of their institution's mission and effectiveness took place. The committee accepted a reduced role for COU, agreeing that the voluntary association could not easily adopt policies contrary to the interest of any of its members and that, if it did, it could not enforce them. It recommended that OCUA be strengthened and given responsibility for overall system planning and co-ordination. With clearly defined institutional roles, adequate funding with a revised formula and modified roles for COU and OCUA, the Fisher Committee concluded that the Ontario university system could continue and prosper.

The university community was much encouraged by the Fisher Report. The big question was how the government would respond. Throughout the fall and winter of 1981–82, COU and the universities pressed for a response. The government hesitated, pleading economic uncertainties compounded by the ongoing debate betwee the provinces and the federal government over support for health care and post-secondary education under the Established Programmes Funding legislation. Although it would not become clear for some months, the government had immediately rejected the Fisher Report. No direct response was ever given. The government's response came, however, in February 1982, with its announcement of the operating grants to the universities for the coming year. It contained both good news and bad news. The good news was that there would be an increase in operating grants to the universities of more that 12 percent (12.2 percent), which was above inflation. Formula tuition fees would be allowed to increase by the same amount, and the further institutional descretionary increase of 10 percent would continue to be allowed. The bad news was that the government had effectively chosen the option firmly rejected by the committee. Public policy objectives would be maintained; government funding would not be substantially increased. It was to be "muddling through."

In announcing the increase in funding for 1983–84, Minister Stephenson stated that this relatively generous allocation was intended to provide the universities with breathing space, a period in which to adjust their expenditures and programs (presumably downward) in light of continuing fiscal restraint. In informal conversations with university representatives, the minister made it clear that the publicly stated objectives for the system continued to hold, and that the third option—scaling down the system—had been rejected. Further than that, however, she would not specify. If the universities had any lingering doubts that they were now firmly located low in the government's priority spending list, these were removed several months later when the provincial treasurer (who had opposed giving the universities so large an increase in operating grants) removed their exemption from the provincial sales tax. The effect of this "new" 7 percent tax was to reduce their grant revenues below inflation and leave them struggling as hard as ever.

In interviews given much later, some of the principal government players told the story. The judgment of the Fisher Committee that funding levels needed to be increased to maintain academic quality had found no support within either Treasury Board or the ministry. (COU's proposal that the deputy minister, Dr. Fisher, chair the committee, had proven to have been without avail.) The Policy and Priorities Board of cabinet was of the view that the BIU value of the operating grant could continue to be reduced if done at a slow and consistent rate, and was convinced that no university should or would be closed. Neither cabinet nor the premier was prepared to close down any institutions.[24]

The spring 1982 COU brief to OCUA on system funding requirements, forlornly titled *Once More, with Feeling*, expressed the universities' frustrations. According to council, the cumulative system shortfall since 1977–78 now amounted to over $350 million, more than 27 percent of projected global university revenue for 1982–83. Admittedly, about half of this total represented foregone increases in salaries for staff. The remainder, however, reflected real reductions in expenditure: reductions in staff complements and across a range of non-salary expenditures—mainly library acquisitions, laboratory equipment, and physical plant maintenance. The interprovincial comparisons showed that Ontario, which had stood fifth among the provinces in 1974–75, was now in tenth and last place, $1,500 below the national average on expenditure per full-time-equivalent student.[25] Except for one year, 1987–88, Ontario would continue to occupy last place for the remainder of the century. It was the same sad story for capital funding. Selecting 1 percent of the value of total university space inventory as calculated by COU "Building Blocks" as the minimum amount required annually for cyclic renewal (building renovation and replacement), OCUA calculated that by 1980–81 the accumulated shortfall in capital funding in Ontario universities exceeded $47.1 million.

Occupied with other pressing priorities, the government was not listening. Nor did the media or the public appear to be concerned. In these circumstances, while continuing to press the Ontario government for more funding, COU increased its lobbying efforts with the federal government and expanded its activities to inform politicians and the public about the plight of Ontario universities. As the '80s continued, COU involvement in advocacy accelerated. By the end of the decade, advocacy activities would be consuming a major portion of Council's staff and financial resources.

The financial difficulties of Ontario universities, like those of their sister universities in the other provinces, were exacerbated by political arguments between the federal government and the governments of the provinces. When the Government of Canada ceded responsibility for post-secondary education to the provinces in 1967, it discontinued direct grants to Canadian universities. It then entered into an agreement with the governments of the provinces whereby it agreed to cover 50 percent of each province's expenditures on post-secondary education. This commitment was later capped, and 10 years later, in 1977, the earlier agreement was succeeded by the Established Programmes Funding (EPF) legislation. Under this legislation, the federal government undertook to transfer income tax points plus specific cash transfers to the provinces to assist them in covering the costs of health care and post-secondary education. Although an unconditional block transfer from the federal government to the governments of the provinces, the funds were intended to cover both health care and post-secondary education. In what was later to become a major bone of contention between the parties, at the time, for administrative purposes, the cash grants under EPF were arbitrarily assigned by the federal government in the same proportion as had applied under the previous arrangements in 1975–76, i.e., roughly two-thirds for health and one-third for post-secondary education. Later, in the '80s, when spending on health care began to climb across the country, the portion of EPF dollars spent by most provinces on health climbed above the two-thirds proportion and that spent on post-secondary education correspondingly declined.

The EPF legislation was never popular with the federal government. It quickly realized that, since the funds constituted an unconditional grant, very little political mileage could be gained from the large sums being transferred to the provinces. When in the early '80s, governments at both levels began to face the negative effects of high inflation, decreasing revenues, and increasing pressures for spending, particularly on health care and social services, pressures developed to have the EPF agreement renegotiated. The federal government wanted to reduce its commitment; most provincial governments wanted to expand it. Concurrently, faced with escalating costs, most provinces, including Ontario, began allocating more than two-thirds of the transfer funds to their health care and social services budgets, thereby reducing the dollars available for post-secondary education.

As the '80s began, the Association of Universities and Colleges of Canada (AUCC) expanded its lobby activities with the federal government. The two principal targets were EPF and increased federal expenditure on research through the federal research granting councils. Because of its strong research arm, not to mention Ontario universities' interest in these matters, COU became heavily involved. Employing data provided by the federal government on total dollar transfers under EPF, COU calculated that a larger and increasing proportion of Ontario universities' operating grants was now coming from the federal government, not from provincial resources. Displeased, the Ontario government promptly challenged the validity of the data, thereby producing a dispute that to this day remains unresolved.

In 1982, COU submitted a brief to the Parliamentary Task Force on Federal–Provincial Fiscal Arrangements. The brief urged the federal government to remain involved in financing Canada's universities and to undertake once again to provide a clearly designated sum for their support.[26] Informed in advance, the minister quietly encouraged this action, while voicing her opinion that it would not likely accomplish anything. She was right. Protracted federal-provincial negotiations over EPF were one of the reasons the Government of Ontario gave for not responding to the Fisher Report. Unable to obtain agreement with its provincial partners, the federal government then unilaterally discontinued the revenue guarantee, one of the three main components of the EPF arrangement. This action resulted in a reduction of transfer payments to Ontario, thereby further potentially adversely affecting Ontario universities. Despite this, COU continued as a strong ally of its federal counterpart, the AUCC, in lobbying the Government of Canada to increase financial support to universities. The COU Research Division became the main source of Canada-wide data collection and analysis, and senior secretariat staff were heavily involved in the drafting of briefing papers focused on federal issues. Arguments between the federal government and its provincial partners over funding for post-secondary education continued through the 1980s, each level blaming the other for deficiencies in the level of financial support being provided these important institutions.[27] Over the period, the Government of Canada gradually reduced the amount of funding provided by its cash transfers under EPF. The universities and their representative associations (ACCC and COU) protested, but to no avail.

Back in Ontario, two government decisions had an impact on the system. One was the imposition of a substantial increase in undergraduate fees for visa students; the other was action taken to address the fact that some Ontario universities were beginning to run deficits. In the early '80s, undergraduate enrolment of foreign (visa) students in

Ontario universities rose sharply. The first two years of the decade saw an increase of more than 30 percent. Unexpected, this increase was the result of a combination of two factors, both of which lay outside the control of the universities. Improved economic conditions in Southeast Asia encouraged many of the middle class there to seek higher education for their children. The number of local university places were few, and competition for them was fierce. A degree from a British, U.S., or Canadian university carried a certain academic cachet. East Asian students, mainly middle-class ethnic Chinese from Hong Kong and Malaysia, discovered Ontario as a place where a university education of high quality was available at low cost. Catering to this clientele, the number of private secondary schools, which promised entry to an Ontario university to their graduates, mushroomed in Toronto. In 1980, the British government instituted a policy of full-cost tuition fees for visa students; as a result, for British Commonwealth students accustomed to going to Great Britain for higher education, Ontario universities became a real bargain.

Struggling to balance their books, Ontario universities regarded this new source of potential enrolment with mixed feelings. Some eagerly embraced this new source of enrolment. The arrival of these readily identifiable foreign students, however, did not pass unnoticed, particularly when some universities were now placing enrolment limits on their popular professional programs. Some Canadian students denied a place in limited enrolment programs complained (as did their parents) that they were being discriminated against in favour of non-Canadians. The situation was aggravated when a major Canadian television network (CTV) aired a prime-time "exposé" on the subject with barely disguised racist overtones. The program produced a spate of public protest. At the same time, several of the private "visa schools"—which were not carefully monitored by the Ministry of Education—went bankrupt and left their students stranded in a foreign country. The government was being pressed to take action. Two options were available: establish a quota on visa students or hike their fees (or do both).

Long on record as being in favour of low tuition fees, but not keen to have enrolment quotas imposed by government, the universities faced a dilemma. A small group within COU met informally to work out a compromise. System enrolment projections predicted a steady rise in undergraduate enrolment over the first half of the '80s, to be followed by a slight decline in the second half of the decade. Prospects for increased funding were poor. In an effort to pre-empt an anticipated government decision to increase visa-student tuition fees substantially (the Government of Quebec had already implemented a large increase in tuition fees, although tuition remained lower there than in the other provinces, and exempted students from la Francophonie *outre mer* from this increase), the group proposed that COU negotiate with the minister a new arrangement covering visa students. The proposal: maintain formula tuition fees for both graduate and undergraduate visa students at the current levels, and establish a quota on undergraduate visa students eligible for inclusion in the enrolment count for funding purposes. To control undergraduate numbers (where the problem lay), a quota of 5 percent of total undergraduate enrolment would be imposed for visa students both system wide and at each institution. Universities would be free to enrol undergraduate visa students above the quota and to set tuition fees for them; however, the university would not be able to include these "supernumerary students" in the enrolment count for BIU funding.

When the proposal came before COU in December 1981, those universities that stood to lose funding vigorously opposed its adoption. The motion was defeated, eleven in favour, fifteen opposed.[28] With the universities unable to agree, the minister made a decision. Tuition fees for all visa students were sharply increased. For those institutions that had opposed a quota, it proved to be a pyrrhic victory. To make a point, the ministry placed the additional revenue generated by the higher fees (some $33 million in the first full year) in a special fund, and at year's end distributed the sum among all of the universities on the basis of each institution's share of system Basic Operating Income (BOI), not on the basis of the number of visa students each institution had registered. By this means, those universities that enrolled more than their system share of foreign students were deprived of any increased revenue from the higher tuition fees.

The introduction of higher tuition fees for undergraduate visa students had an immediate effect. In the first year of its application, first-year registration of visa students declined by 27 percent. It also had an effect on COU, though not an immediate one. This episode would later play a role in reducing further the confidence that some executive heads had in COU's ever being able to agree on those decisions that, while clearly good for the system, would adversely affect some member universities. It was another in the growing number of instances in which the voluntary association was proving to be ineffective.

As a consequence of the lengthening period of underfunding, some universities had begun to run deficits. This drew the attention of the minister. Early in 1982, she issued a statement that the government was not prepared to provide funding to cover deficits. She requested OCUA (now led by Burt Matthews) to provide advice on what action should be taken to prevent and eliminate "unmanageable deficits." In response, OCUA recommended legislation (already in place in some provincial jurisdictions) that would limit the power of governing boards to approve operating deficits and would cap the level of deficit at 2 percent of the annual operating budget. This advice was quickly accepted. Shortly thereafter, Bill 42, an Act to Amend the Colleges and Universities Act, was introduced. It would provide the minister with authority to place into trusteeship any university that ran a deficit of more than 2 percent of annual operating revenues, which a ministry review judged to be unmanageable.

The universities, led by COU, vigorously opposed the legislation. They argued that it would reduce institutional flexibility in dealing with changing financial circumstances, a flexibility that to date had proven successful when the institutions were forced to operate in a climate of severe financial constraint. Negotiations with the ministry succeeded in having all but one of the objectionable clauses removed from the draft bill. The minister, however, refused to budge on the section describing the powers of the supervisor, who under the legislation would have authority to overrule decisions of university boards. On second reading of the bill in committee, COU argued the universities' case. The two opposition parties, in a minority government, supported the stand of the universities and blocked the bill in committee stage. The bill died on the order paper. The primary objective of the minister was achieved, however, when the boards of governors of those institutions with escalating deficits took a firmer hand in controlling expenditures. Over the next several years, the incidence and size of universities' year-end operating deficits were sharply reduced.[29]

Government underfunding of the universities, however, continued. By 1982, after so many years during which grants had failed to match cou's judgment of what was required, COU abandoned the annual exercise of recording the accumulated shortfall, seeing it as lacking both relevance and credibility. What COU insiders termed "the tragedy of the commons" was now underway. Undergraduate enrolment began to rise again. To meet their commitment to accessibility and to gain the additional income that tuition fees provided, the universities took in more students. Each year more sheep were being put out to graze on a field of inadequate size to permit their being well nourished. Adopting a more pragmatic approach to university funding requirements, COU now focused on the level of funding required to prevent further deterioration in quality, without mention of "catch-up." Its briefs to OCUA now stipulated only the level of funding judged necessary to enable the universities to maintain the level of operations of the previous year. Data were also presented to illustrate how grants to universities on a per-student basis compared with grants to secondary schools, to hospitals and to prisons on a per-student/patient/prisoner basis. These comparisons were unfavourable to the universities.

Advice from OCUA to the government largely supported the universities' case. But the government was not listening. This led COU to conclude that "the continuing failure of government to accept it [OCUA's recommendations on funding] meant that council [OCUA] served increasingly as a buffer protecting government from the demands of the universities."[30] While not entirely fair, such a comment reflected the view of an increasing number of members of the university community about OCUA, a view that arose as a result of the withdrawal of COU from system planning and the increasing involvement of OCUA in the management of the system, including its de facto exercise of some executive authority, which had produced a shift in the balance of power within the structure of the system.

Although the government did not accept the recommendations of the Fisher Committee for increased funding to the universities, it did move on the earlier COU proposal to expand support for research. In the speech from the throne opening the 1981 spring session of the legislature, the government announced the establishment of a Board for Industrial Leadership and Development (BILD) to administer a proposed massive new program of industrial expansion. The new board, BILD, would provide funds to support university research in the form of equipment grants, and assist in the development of high tech centres where the resources of government, the private sector, and the universities could be pooled to stimulate research and development. The plan also called for the creation of an Innovative Development for Employment Advancement (IDEA) Corporation to act as an agency to promote the new policy. Although a grand plan, its implementation was very slow. Almost a year passed before a board of directors was named for the Idea Corporation, a further six months before a chief executive officer (Ian Macdonald, president of York University) was put in place. Funding for research projects proved equally slow and meagre in amounts. In the first year, 1982–83, a total of $8.3 million was provided in grants to universities for the purchase of research equipment, welcome indeed but relatively insignificant in light of the objectives. With inflation continuing in double digits, the government was having great difficulty in controlling spending, so much difficulty in fact that it decided to impose wage and price restraints.

By 1983, dominated by the intractable questions about funding, university–government relations were at an impasse. An effort to revise the operating grants formula had failed. Informal meetings continued between the minister and the COU executive committee, but without any tangible results. Enrolment was rising, and revised projections indicated that the increase (due primarily to an increased participation rate among females) would continue. The "tragedy of the commons" continued to be played out. Although the grants formula was now heavily discounted against new students, some universities continued to take in large numbers. This produced a sharp split within COU. Some universities, mainly the larger and more established institutions, set enrolment caps and kept firm control over expansion by raising admission requirements. Others, mostly the smaller, newer ones, plus York University, were prepared to increase enrolment substantially. The views on formula revision of these two groups differed markedly; indeed, the positions of the two groups were incompatible. Institutions that did not favour increasing enrolment while funding remained so low were anxious to maintain the value of the Basic Income Unit (BIU); their representatives argued for larger discounts on new enrolment. They held that, as long as increases in funding remained below inflation, the formula should be set aside in favour of fixed institutional shares. Those institutions that had increased enrolment wanted full funding for these increases. Their representatives argued that their institutional share of the operating grant was unfairly low since, due to the discount on new enrolment, it had not increased proportionate to their share of total enrolment. While meeting the same educational responsibilities as their more affluent sister universities, these universities argued, they were forced to operate on "discounted" dollars.

Repeated efforts by COU to develop policies to address this issue proved unsuccessful. Universities became less willing to divulge their enrolment plans. An effort to obtain agreement among the universities that none would increase first-year intake unless additional funding was provided failed. In the spring of 1983, institutional plans and projections for first-year admissions that fall were surveyed and reported to council. When preliminary fall registrations were posted, however, they showed little correlation with the earlier institutional projections. The spring survey projected a system decline of 0.2 percent in full-time undergraduate enrolment; fall registration data showed a system increase of 3.5 percent overall, with some universities showing large increases.

Provincial wage restraints, introduced that fall, compounded the universities' financial difficulties. The government announced a cap of 5 percent on increases in compensation for the coming year, and signals were given that the increase in university operating grants would reflect this limit. COU calculations indicated that a global increase of this amount distributed by the existing formula would produce a range of institutional increases above and below 5 percent. With inflation running in double digits, across the province university faculty and staff bargaining units were already balking at the prospect of salary increases being held to 5 percent. Any university that received less than a 5 percent increase in its operating grant could be in serious financial trouble.

In December 1981, COU debated the contents of a draft brief to the provincial treasurer on the matter. The draft, prepared in the secretariat, proposed that the formula be suspended and each university receive the same increase. Two university heads, Ronald Watts of Queen's University and Douglas Wright of the University of Waterloo (both heavy hitters), wrote the minister directly to plead their university's case. Both institutions had decided to cap enrolments in order to maintain quality. As a result, whatever the size of the global increase in operating support, their institutional share would be less. Should the global increase be limited to 5 percent, they argued that their universities would be in serious financial difficulties, an outcome they judged to be unfair. President Ian Macdonald of York protested in the strongest terms the COU proposal to suspend the formula. York, he said, had increased enrolment over the past several years. On a BIU per-student basis it was now, (apart from Brock University) the worst-funded university in the system and could not sustain a formula freeze. He urged council to press for a continuation of formula funding and an increase in the operating grant for 1984–85, sufficient to allow each university to receive an increase of at least 5 percent. Were COU unwilling to do this, he argued, it should recommend a global increase of 8 percent and include a provision that no university receive less than 5 percent, with those falling below this minimum being subsidized on a proportional basis by those falling above it. Unable to agree, council took no decision.[31]

Concerned about the continuing chorus of criticism from the university community over the lack of funding to the system, the government decided to conduct another review. On the final day of sitting before the 1983 Christmas recess, Minister Stephenson stood in her place to announce the establishment of another commission—the Commission on the Future Development of the Universities of Ontario. It was asked to present the government with an action plan to better enable the universities to adjust to changing social and economic conditions; The Commission was to proceed on the basis that annual increases in the public resources provided to the universities would reflect a desire to protect their integrity and strengthen their ability to contribute to the intellectual, economic, social, and cultural foundations of society, as well as reflect the commitment of the government to fiscal restraint and prudent management of public funds.[32] This was certainly a tall, if not inherently contradictory, order. Edmund Bovey, a retired business executive, was named chair. He was joined by two other commissioners—Fraser Mustard, a former vice-president, Health Sciences, at McMaster University, and Ronald Watts, a former principal of Queen's University and chair of COU—both well known and respected members of the Ontario university community, with prior service respectively on OCUA and COU.

The commission set to work immediately. A preliminary report in the form of a discussion paper, *Ontario Universities 1984: Issues and Alternatives*, was issued six months later. It focused on four major concerns: quality, accessibility, adaptability, and differentiation. After an extensive series of public hearings during the fall, the final report, *Ontario Universities: Options and Futures*, was presented to the government in December 1984 and released to the public. Respecting the premise implicit in its terms of reference that no substantial increase in funding could be expected, the commission broke new ground. Its wide-ranging recommendations constituted a complex set of interdependent proposals that were far from traditional in the Ontario context. The commission recommended an increase in capital grants, additional support for faculty renewal, a separate "adjustment fund" to assist universities to close or amalgamate academic programs, and increased tuition fees. It acknowledged an urgent need for improved interinstitutional planning and co-ordination and greater institutional differentiation. But it favoured an enlargement of "institutional differentiation within a competitive context rather than by formal designation and central control." It proposed a "competitive system within which institutions are rewarded for the distinctive functions they perform and the quality of their activities and in addition are provided with the capacity to be flexible and innovative ...."[33] The commission also recommended a new approach to the distribution of operating grants—a "corridor" system to allow variations in an institution's enrolment within a narrow band (the corridor) derived from the institution's current funding base without affecting the size of its operating grant. Proposals on system structure were also made.

Attention focused immediately (and almost exclusively) on two recommendations: one for a temporary reduction in system enrolment, the other for an increase in tuition fees. The first was necessary, the commission had stated, to permit the universities time to improve the quality of undergraduate programs, judged to have fallen below minimum acceptable standards; the second was necessary to provide them with the additional revenues necessary to maintain quality. Student and faculty associations, the media, and the minister quickly rejected both recommendations. The government was not prepared to sacrifice its long-standing policy on accessibility in the interests of restoring academic quality, mainly because it did not accept the universities' argument that quality had suffered. Many senior university administrators, who reluctantly judged both recommendations necessary in the current financial circumstances of the institutions, supported them. Their support, however, was muted. Apart from a flat rejection of these two recommendations, the government ignored the Bovey Report. It was quickly consigned to the high shelf already occupied by the earlier Fisher Report. Nothing changed.

●LIAISON WITH THE MINISTRY OF EDUCATION

This period recorded one of the few examples of collective autonomy involving institutional self-denial. It involved a decision of those Ontario universities with faculties of education to reduce the intake into their bachelor of education degree programs. In the wake of the MacLeod Report and encouraged by the Ministry of Education, faculties of education in Ontario (including those newly established when the teachers' colleges were closed) expanded enrolment. By the mid-1970s, however, with the school-age population in the province levelling off, the teacher shortage ended and an oversupply was developing. As a result, the government began to put pressure on the universities to reduce intake into this professional program area. So serious was the issue taken by the ministry that it struck a commission headed by a former director of OISE, Dr. Robert Jackson, to conduct an enquiry. Addressing the issue, the Association of Deans of Education in Ontario Universities, an affiliate of COU, came up with a proposal the reduce intake by more than one third (from some 7,200 in 1975-76 to some 4,500 in 1978-79). Recognizing the cyclical nature of the job market for teachers, however, the deans were not anxious to reduce their faculty complements. They proposed that a reduction in "pre-service" enrolment be compensated in part by an increase in "in-service" courses, courses offered to assist practising teachers to upgrade their qualifications. Because York University had recently inaugurated a four-year combined baccalaureate program (the only one in the province), which had yet to achieve a "critical mass," it was exempted from the enrolment cut. After approval by COU, negotiations with the ministry followed. After a considerable time, the package proposed by the deans and COU was agreed to and implemented.[34]

Cou also became involved with the ministry of education across the interface between secondary schooling and Ontario universities. In 1978, when the minister of education inaugurated the Secondary Education Review Project (SERP), COU agreed to participate, although it limited involvement to those issues in which the universities had a direct interest, principally university admission requirements and the preparedness of secondary school graduates to undertake university-level studies. SERP was followed in 1981 by a ministry policy paper, *Ontario Schools: Intermediate and Senior* (OSIS), which proposed a substantial change in Ontario secondary schooling. The proposed new policy directly affected the universities. Grade 13 was to be replaced by Year 5; the curriculum offered in this university preparatory final year of secondary schooling—now to be called Ontario Advanced Courses (OACS)—was to be revised. Both the number of required courses and the total number of courses required for the completion of the Secondary School Honours Diploma (SSHD) were to be reduced. The purpose of this latter change would be to make it possible for a student to "fast track" and complete secondary schooling in four years rather than five. To the surprise of some experts, not many secondary school students elected to take the fast track.

After the abolition of provincial secondary school leaving examinations in the early '70s, a wide variation in the performance of secondary school graduates in first-year university programs was noted. This led university admissions officers as well as faculty to conclude that grading standards differed widely in secondary schools across the province. As a consequence, in its presentations on SERP, COU had recommended the introduction of standardized achievement tests in English and Français, and in mathematics at the end of secondary schooling. Such tests, it was argued, would assist the universities in handling applications for admission more equitably, especially when offering places in programs with limited enrolment, and in awarding scholarships. These recommendations were now repeated. At the same time, the universities indicated willingness to provide discipline experts from among the faculty to assist in determining course content for the new OACS. COU also pointed out that success with the new secondary school curricula would require changes in teacher education. On another matter, which seemed not to have occurred to the ministry, it was pointed out that when a reduction of secondary schooling from five years to four came into effect—a reduction the universities in principle did not oppose—there would be a "double cohort" of students entering university. Steps would need to be taken to ensure that this did not adversely affect the students involved. Some preliminary planning was begun. However, for a variety of reasons, including the fact that most students elected not to fast-track, no double cohort occurred. It would be more than twenty years before the "double cohort" entered Ontario universities. Year 5 was formally removed from the secondary school curriculum in 2002 and the first "double cohort" entered in September 2003.

As the review of secondary education continued and it became evident that COU would remain involved, in 1985 council appointed a Secondary School Liaison Officer, a part-time position, and gave him an office in the secretariat. John Ricker, former dean of education at the University of Toronto, was the first appointee. Richard van Fossen, former chair of the English department at the same university, succeeded him. The decision to establish this office clearly signalled the interest of the universities in this area and their willingness to dedicate resources to the important task of secondary school curricular reform. Welcomed by secondary school teachers and principals, as well as by ministry staff, this decision proved to have been a wise one. Over the next decade, the universities were able to influence in a positive way the curricular and other changes that constituted this reform of secondary school education in Ontario. While much good was accomplished, not all COU proposals were accepted. Proposals on achievement testing, opposed by the teachers' federations, which feared that such tests might be used to evaluate a teacher's performance, were ignored. A proposal that official secondary school transcripts provide full disclosure of all courses taken and grades awarded, opposed by the ministry on the spurious grounds that such disclosure would violate a student's right to privacy, was also ignored.

● SOME CO-OPERATIVE SERVICE ACTIVITIES

While the financial difficulties facing the universities were worsening and relations with the government deteriorating, other council activities were proving more productive. In 1981, at the initiative of the executive heads, several of whom were growing concerned over the expansion in number and value of athletics scholarships being offered by some Ontario universities, COU struck a Task Force on University Athletics, chaired by Neale Taylor, president of Wilfrid Laurier University. Its report, presented in December 1982, resulted in a council decision to strike a Special Committee on Intercollegiate Athletics, with an expanded membership and mandate. The new committee included representatives from the two Ontario intercollegiate leagues: the Ontario Universities' Athletic Association (OUAA) and the Ontario Women's Intercollegiate Athletic Association (OWIAA). Its mandate was to examine the organizational structure and programs of intercollegiate athletics in Ontario, including institutional philosophies, programming, and scheduling; the financial support, including corporate support, being provided them; and the relations between OUAA, OWIAA, the Canadian Interuniversity Athletic Union (CIAU), Sports Canada, and COU. Donald Rickert, executive director of the Donner Foundation, was named chair. Following the report of this committee, at a special meeting in May 1985, council approved (with the University of Toronto abstaining) the establishment of the Ontario Commission on Intercollegiate Athletics, with a part-time executive secretary and an office in the COU secretariat.[34]

The commission, a semi-autonomous body external to the two leagues, was to oversee their operations, and to serve as a link between them, the universities, and COU. Over the next few years, operating without fanfare and with minimal resources, it obtained agreement among COU member institutions to continue the ban on athletic scholarships; inaugurated an audit system covering the recruiting and supervising of student athletes; improved scheduling in both leagues; successfully promoted the equalization of opportunities for women athletes at both league and intramural levels; and developed new guidelines covering the corporate sponsorship of university athletic events, in particular sponsorship by breweries and distilleries. It continues to exist.

Not all of the activities initiated by COU in this period were successful. Because of the large number of elementary and secondary students now enrolled in French immersion and other core French programs in Ontario, in 1982 the French Studies Committee of council recommended the establishment of a centre to assist members of university French departments in offering effective second-language training and other university departments in offering a selection of their courses in the French language. Carleton University and the University of Ottawa developed a joint proposal for the centre, and COU undertook a search for funding. This initiative was complicated by a competing proposal subsequently developed by the Ontario Institute for Studies in Education (OISE), necessitating an evaluative process that caused some delay. Despite strong support from its Commissioner of Official Languages, the federal government declined to provide funds. So, too, did the Government of Ontario. Although supportive in principle, given their financial circumstances the universities were unwilling to see the necessary funds come off the top of their global operating grant. In the end, the project was abandoned. A similar fate befell the recommendations of the COU Committee on the Disabled. The committee was struck in response to a growing awareness of the need to improve opportunities for the disabled to gain access to higher education, and it was encouraged by the ministry. It developed proposals for an action plan that would begin with a comprehensive survey of students' needs. However, funding was required. After numerous unsuccessful efforts to obtain government funding to undertake the survey, the committee was discharged. Nonetheless, the efforts of this committee provided some stimulus for the universities to take this issue more seriously than otherwise they might have.

One of the by-products of the focus on accessibility to university that marked the early 1980s was a growing awareness of a larger body of potential university students—mature persons of various ages and backgrounds unable to attend university full-time. Advances in technology now made it less difficult to meet the needs of this group. After undertaking a study, in 1983 COU formed its Distance Education Committee.

With limited resources, the committee compiled a directory of available distance education courses and programs and began the task of working toward the development of an agreement to cover the transfer among universities of credits gained via this mode. A proposal for the development of a province-wide computer-conferencing network to assist students involved in distance education was abandoned due to lack of funding.

In 1985, COU decided to become more proactive in the area of gender equity, an area in which it had already been involved for more than a decade. Its first report on the status of women had been published in 1975. Now council struck a Status of Women Committee. From this time onwards, COU involvement in this important area would be sustained. From the outset, the committee worked closely with the provincial government agency involved in the issues of pay equity—equal pay for work of equal value—advising on the best ways of allocating monies from the provincial Employment Equity Incentive Fund to the university sector. It also wrote an employment equity manual for universities. With strong leadership from succeeding chairs and ongoing support from the research division, this committee came to play a substantial role in improving the status of women (students, faculty, and support staff) in the universities and beyond. Data on student applicants/registrants, student enrolment and participation rates, degrees awarded, full-time faculty (new hires, rank, salaries, and full-time support staff by gender), with relevant comparisons between males and females, were collected and published. In 1994, COU struck a companion group, the Committee on Employment and Educational Equity. Working in close co-operation with the Status of Women Committee, its task was to develop equitable and accessible educational opportunities for all groups in Ontario universities. In 1996, the COU Status of Women Committee took over from the ministry responsibility for the publication of a series of statistical reports on the status of women in Ontario universities.[35] Published biennially, this publication provides a series of statistical reports on the progress of women in Ontario universities that in some cases goes back to the late 1970s. As such, it constitutes the single most important resource for monitoring changes in the participation of women in Ontario universities.

● A NEW GOVERNMENT

During the fall of 1984, while the members of the Bovey Commission were busy writing their report, members of the government were preoccupied with the race to succeed Premier Davis. Pending the election of a new party leader and a predicted general election soon to follow, the government was in a holding pattern. The treasurer, Frank Miller, known not to be a strong supporter of the universities, was elected party leader and became premier. Shortly after, a small group of COU representatives met with the new treasurer, Larry Grossman, and the new minister, Ken Norton, to press for a response to the Bovey Report. The minister (described afterward by a member of the COU delegation as not very well informed) notified the group that the government would not be conducting a review of the report until after the upcoming election and that no major decisions with respect to its recommendations could be expected before the fall of 1986, some fifteen months hence.[36]

The election was called for May 2. In the run-up, the government announced a new program to assist university research—the University Research Incentive Fund (URIF), but few funds ($10 million) were committed to the program. Working with ministry officials, COU developed a plan for their distribution and some money was disbursed. (The next government cancelled the program.) In the election, the Conservatives, who had held power in the province for more than forty years, were defeated. University matters were not an election issue. However, in opposition, the Liberals had been critical of the government for its failure to fund universities adequately and had made a commitment to change this. Hope within the university community for some improvement, therefore, was high. This hope was increased when the new premier, David Peterson, announced his cabinet. The Ministry of Colleges and Universities was again given its own minister, something it had not had since the abortive effort by the preceding government in the late '70s to amalgamate it with the Ministry of Education. The new minister, Greg Sorbara, was a rookie MPP. However, Allan Adlington, Vice-President Administration of the University of Western Ontario, became the new deputy minister. The new government moved quickly to inject additional funds into the universities. In mid-October, a $50 million University Excellence fund was announced. Its three-fold objective—improvement in the quality of undergraduate instruction, support for excellence in research, and renewal of the professoriate—was derived from recommendations in the Bovey Report.

In order to discuss their mutual problems, the executive heads of Ontario universities were now meeting informally outside COU meetings. As well, the presidents of the self-styled "research intensive" universities—McMaster, Queen's, Toronto, Waterloo, and Western—had begun to meet among themselves. Meetings of the executive heads were reported on at COU. Meetings of the smaller group, dubbed by fellow members of COU as the "MacTwit Group" and regarded by them with some suspicion, were not. Meeting in the summer of 1985 shortly after the election, the executive heads seized the initiative and invited the new minister to meet with them. Buoyed by his agreement to do so and in the positive climate thereby created, they formed three task forces. Although they were working outside the formal council structure, the executive heads decided to consider the three task forces as informal committees of COU. Each was charged with the development of proposals to be brought to council for ratification and action. George Connell, president of the University of Toronto, chaired Task Force A (on planning). Its task was to develop a comprehensive planning proposal that would include system enrolment demand and capacity, academic programming and research, relations with the CAATs, and internal affairs. Harry Arthurs, president of York University, chaired Task Force B (on funding). It was asked to develop proposals for amending the formula on operating grants. Alan Earp, president of Brock University, chaired Task Force C (on communications). It was charged with developing a long-term advocacy strategy for COU.

All three reported to COU in the fall of 1985, with decidedly mixed results. Task Force A proposed a study of the existing enrolment capacity of all COU member institutions, to begin with a survey. Council accepted this proposal. Two months later, however, President Connell reported that institutional responses had been disappointing. Few universities had responded fully, some not at all. Given the lack of institutional support, the task force decided to stand down for six months, after which it would reassess the situation. It would never take up its work again. Task Force B fared little better. President Arthurs reported that two alternative funding models were being developed, along with criteria to test them. Two months later, when the results were presented, council could not agree on how to proceed. Some suggested a tripartite committee (COU, OCUA, and MCU); others suggested that COU go it alone. A motion that council take no action was lost on a straw vote. Given the lack of agreement, the chair of COU was asked to discuss the issues with the deputy minister.[37]

With COU unable to agree on the road ahead on funding, the matter was left in the hands of OCUA. In an effort to mobilize support behind a proposal to move to the "corridor" system recommended by the Bovey Commission, the advisory body held a series of meetings with the universities. Senior members of the COU secretariat staff attended these meetings and provided technical support. Council, however, was not otherwise involved. Once again, COU was unable to provide any leadership in dealing with system issues affecting planning and funding.

Proposals from Task Force C, on communications, received a more positive response. Its recommendation that COU expand advocacy activities and retain the services of an external consultant was adopted and immediately implemented.[38] This represented a major step forward in council's advocacy activities, and marked the beginning of its use of consultants to support these activities. COU retained the services of Public Affairs Management (PAM), a small firm with strong ties to the new Liberal government. The firm's first assignment was to conduct an "audit" among senior government officials to determine their attitudes to the universities. PAM's confidential report, tabled at the December 1985 meeting of COU, made sober reading.

The report stated that the government felt that it had made a serious commitment to the support of post-secondary education in the province, a significant departure from its predecessor. Yet the response of the universities had been muted, with comments ranging from surprise to hostility. Senior politicians and bureaucrats recognized the importance of the universities to the government's economic and social goals. However, the perception of many was clouded by their view that university faculty were overpaid and underworked. Some members of this group exhibited genuine skepticism about the universities' claims of high productivity and low pay. Consequently, there was great resistance to providing the universities with increased operating grants, which could be applied to salary increases, rather than providing them with targeted funds to promote specific government objectives. Many of these officials, not strong proponents of university autonomy, considered that more direction by government was required. Within government, however, divergent views were held about how best to achieve conflicting government objectives. Some favoured broader accessibility; others argued for a university system more geared to the promotion of employment-related programs. How to rationalize the university system was a live issue within the government, although it remained unfocused. The universities enjoyed little public support and had little political clout; there was little public pressure to increase funding. Efforts by the group of five research-intensive universities (the MacTwit Group) to plead their special case had annoyed both the premier and the treasurer. More targeted funding was on the way. "It is clear that if the universities fail to come to grips with this question [their inability to develop consensus on key issues], the government will unhesitatingly and without regret impose policies which may not be suitable for all institutions."[39]

This frank assessment prompted some immediate decisions. A PAM recommendation that COU sponsor a study of faculty compensation by an external, independent expert to counter the negative views within government was immediately accepted. After lively debate, a recommendation that COU undertake a tour of the province to take the universities' case to the broader public was also approved. Realists argued that, if the universities were to be seen as credible within the wider community when they complained about inadequate funding and argued a decline in the quality of their operations, they would have to show instances in which program quality had declined. Others remained unprepared to admit actual declines in quality lest it adversely affect their prospects to attract students. These misgivings notwithstanding, the tour was undertaken in the early months of 1986. Although institutional participation was somewhat spotty, the exercise succeeded in raising the profile of the universities and was judged a success.

The practical problems facing COU and its member institutions in making the case that Ontario universities were being underfunded can be illustrated by reference to the publication in 1984 of a monograph by a pair of academic researchers at the Ontario Institute for Studies in Education. Given a title borrowed from Charles Dickens, *Please, sir, I want some more*, the work provided an overview of Canadian university finance and expenditures by province in the period 1974–82, with particular reference to Ontario, and analyzed the situation of the universities in a period of financial restraint. The authors had undertaken a survey of the views of Canadian university presidents and deans on the decline in public funding for universities, and its consequences. Although the sample was small (a questionnaire had been sent to 625 persons, which produced 182 usable responses, of which one-third [61] were from Ontario), nearly three-quarters of the Ontario respondents judged that the overall quality of academic programs in their institutions had improved over the preceding decade. And on the criterion of peer assessment employed by OCGS in its appraisal of Ontario graduate programs in the period, 1977–82, none of the Ontario respondents reported any deterioration in programs with which they were involved. These responses led the authors to conclude this: "Possibly the greatest failing of the universities in the public debate on funding has been to make quality the pre-eminent policy variable and then be unable to provide any evidence at all as to how quality has been affected by declines in funding." While acknowledging that such measures are not necessarily any better measure of quality, they urged the universities to develop "output" measures to support their case. Two years later, the principal researcher followed up with an article equally provocatively titled, "If the cuts are so deep, where is the blood"?[40]

Meanwhile, the Peterson government was planning for a greater investment in the universities, particularly on the research side. The speech from the throne opening the spring 1986 session of the legislature announced a major initiative in research, a result of recommendations from a special task force on research chaired by Deputy Minister Adlington. A high-powered Premier's Council was to be formed, with membership from government, business, and the universities. Its basic objective was, "to steer Ontario into the forefront of economic leadership and technological development."[41] Over a ten-year period, $1 billion was to be made available to this council to fund research and development. This large sum included funds for the establishment of university chairs in designated disciplines and for the establishment of university centres of excellence. Funding for the faculty renewal component of the University Excellence Fund, initially provided for one year, was extended for a period of five years to fund 500 faculty positions.

The establishment of university centres of excellence would have a significant effect on the future course of university research in the province. Moving quickly under the chairmanship of Dr. Fraser Mustard, a member of the Premier's council and former member of the Bovey Commission, within a year seven centres of excellence were selected from among twenty-eight applications, of which the majority (five) involved interuniversity consortia. When new money was put on the table for research, the willingness of the universities to co-operate with one another for a share was amply demonstrated. While council was not formally involved in these developments, members (particularly those in the MacTwit Group) and senior COU staff became heavily engaged.

In tabling the provincial budget in spring 1986, the treasurer announced an increase of 4 percent in the university operating grants for each of the coming two years, 1986–87 and 1987–88. An additional $100 million in capital funding was announced, $66 million for the universities and $34 million for the CAATs. This was certainly good news. Yet (as if to confirm the earlier PAM assessment) the reaction of the universities was mixed. Some complained that the government seemed to be giving with one hand while taking away with the other. Universities were being provided with a significant increase in funds targeted for specific purposes, but increases in the level of basic operating support were less than the amount required to maintain current levels of operation. Those holding such an opinion failed to accept that Ontario universities had now entered a new era, one in which a higher (though still small) proportion of their income from grants would come with strings attached. The era of "targeted funding" had arrived in Ontario.

In this same period, the federal government began to show a renewed interest in university research. The federal granting councils— the Medical Research Council of Canada (MRC), the Natural Sciences and Engineering Research Council of Canada (NSERC), and the Social Sciences and Humanities Research Council of Canada (SSHRC)—adopted the "matching fund" concept in dealing with grant applications from the universities. A National Advisory Board on Science and Technology (NABST), similar to the Ontario Premier's Council, was established in 1987 and began to develop its own program for centres of excellence. The object was the same: to draw the universities, the private sector, and government together in a technologically driven industrial strategy to improve economic prospects, this time at the national level. Through ACCC, COU and its member universities were more than bit players in these developments. When the new federal Department of Industry, Science and Technology was established in 1990, Dr. William Winegard, president emeritus of the University of Guelph, former chair of COU, and now a member of Parliament, was named as minister.

Overall, the atmosphere improved within both the universities and COU. The May 1986 PAM report to COU was positive. The report stated that the universities had succeeded in raising their profile and had made impressive gains. COU had "initiated a mobilization and cohesiveness in the university system not seen in many years."[42] But there was still a long way to go. Executive heads should maintain their efforts and focus on educating their internal communities. COU should become even more proactive and develop a long-term advocacy strategy. Accepting this advice, the COU Committee on Communications continued to be active. A "consumer warning" pamphlet was prepared and distributed to Ontario secondary schools. Employing comparative data on funding levels in other Canadian provinces and selected U.S. jurisdictions provided by the research division, the pamphlet warned of possible declines in quality unless more resources were allocated to the universities. "Days of Action" in various cities were planned for October. The one outside the legislature involving Toronto, York, and Ryerson universities, serendipitously held immediately following the announcement that that a U of T professor, John Polanyi, had won a Nobel Prize, was well attended. The event received widespread publicity and was considered a great success. Assisted by COU secretariat staff, OCUA consultations with the universities on formula revision continued; progress, though, was slow.

Despite the increased resources being devoted to advocacy, COU and its member universities experienced continuing difficulties in making the case for additional funding with the government and the public. "Underfunding" was proving to be a tough sell. The universities' case rested on a basic hypothesis: quality and funding are causally related. Decreases in funding produce decreases in quality. "It is clear that funding has decreased, therefore,..." However, to tough-minded bureaucrats, wary politicians and a somewhat cynical public, the evidence was not very compelling. Interprovincial data published by COU clearly showed that in Ontario, public expenditures on universities had declined significantly relative to public funding in the other provinces of Canada. But, it was countered, given its very large university student population, Ontario should be expected to achieve economies of scale. Therefore, the point was moot whether the data showed that Ontario universities were underfunded; perhaps universities in the other provinces were being overfunded. Moreover, data showing declining expenditure per student, increased faculty-student ratios, increased teaching loads, increased class size, reduced capital, library and equipment budgets, etc., though accurate, were "input" measures. They showed what was going into the system. Few, if any, "output" measures, which some argued were better measures of quality, were included in the universities' argument. Ontario university leaders (admittedly for good practical reasons) continued to be very reluctant to state clearly where academic program quality was declining. It would be another half decade before COU and Ontario universities took seriously the need to develop output measures, and then only after having been pressured to do so by a government task force on accountability.

Meanwhile, university enrolment in Ontario continued to grow. In recognition of these continuing increases, in the fall of 1986 the government injected a further $50 million into the operating grant base. For a time, university complaints ceased. A cabinet decision that funds for new enrolment would be provided at 95 percent of the value of the BIU settled the argument as to whether new enrolment growth should be funded at average or marginal cost. Inevitably, the decision pleased some universities but displeased others. Because of its public commitment to accessibility and its sensitivity toward criticism from parents and students, the government continued stubbornly to resist the universities' request that they be allowed to increase tuition.

● A REVIEW OF COU STRUCTURE

When striking the three task forces to press the universities' case with the new Liberal government, the executive heads recognized that their decision could have implications for the future of COU. At the time, however, they did not see this as a matter of high priority. When the task force reports came before council, some academic colleague members expressed mild concern over the secondary role consigned them. Most, however, were greatly heartened by what they regarded as an excellent initiative. At the January 1986 meeting of COU, reporting on behalf of the Colleague Caucus (as it was now starting to be called), Gerald Booth, the academic colleague from the University of Windsor, stated that considerable division had arisen among the colleagues about how they might best serve council. Recent policy debates, in particular those over formula revision, had shown COU to be badly divided. Should colleagues participate in council as "instructed delegates" from their institutions, committed to vote with the executive head? Or should they be free to take their own positions? In the ensuing discussion, all agreed that if academic colleagues were to participate more effectively, they should come to council meetings better prepared. However, the issue of whether or not they should come to council as instructed delegates from their member institutions was not addressed. Everyone also agreed that, in future, the Nominating Committee should make more use of the academic colleagues when making nominations for committee membership, and that the COU chair, who served as chair of the Nominating Committee, should consult with the academic colleagues when exercising this responsibility. It was also suggested that colleagues should serve longer terms. There was consensus that member institutions should recognize the desirability of providing greater continuity when selecting colleagues. How this might best be done, however, should be left to institutional discretion.[43]

As part of the ongoing effort to strengthen COU and raise its profile, during the winter of 1987 the executive director undertook a tour of member institutions. The issue of council structure was raised in many of his meetings. The need for more rapid response to emerging issues was of particular concern. Academic colleagues wanted to be more involved in council decision making. They felt responsible to their senates, but these academic bodies were not geared to rapid decision making. By the time university senates became seized of the issues, often the opportunity for decisive action had passed. This created a practical dilemma. When the executive director reported to the executive committee on his visits, that group decided (once more) that COU structure and functions should be examined. In September 1987, a memorandum from the executive committee to council outlined two options. The first, supported by the majority of the executive, was intended to make COU a more effective policy-making body. The second, proposed by U of T president Connell, would have COU vacate the policy field entirely and leave OCUA, in consultation with COU, to deal with policy issues.

President Connell, who as chair of council had participated in the earlier inconclusive efforts to find consensus on revising the operating grants formula, on system program planning, and on visa student fees, argued that it was unrealistic to expect a body such as COU to develop and maintain consensus on important policy issues. Members' institutional interests were too diverse; a voluntary association such as COU could not be expected to achieve consensus or, lacking consensus, to coerce member institutions. OCUA should be the body to play this role. COU should continue to undertake research and policy analysis, co-operative service activities, and general supervision of the system. However, it should reduce its system planning and advocacy role. In the ensuing debate, the

Connell option was rejected. For the majority of council members, the suggestion that OCUA should assume a larger policy-making role risked the creation of a policy vacuum in which the voice of the universities would go unheard.

Once again, around the COU table expediency carried the day. The fundamental differences were papered over and recourse made to a familiar remedy. COU should continue to be involved in system-policy issues; it should strive constantly for consensus on broad basic principles. Issues on which the collectivity failed to achieve consensus should be acknowledged. When a majority position was reached, it should be presented as such, along with the minority view(s). Every effort should be made to have an open and frank discussion of all relevant issues around the council table, with a free exchange of data and information. Greater effort should be made to involve all member institutions in council activities and to improve discussion of policy questions. More COU meetings should be held outside of Toronto; more guests—for example, the minister, other ministers and deputy ministers—should be invited to attend council meetings.[44] These essentially palliative measures were readily agreed to; the secretariat was charged with overseeing their implementation. Some changes were made. An increasingly stretched secretariat staff did what it could to expand the information flow and to improve the conduct of council business. However, the secretariat could process only the information it received, and the "important" was sometimes sacrificed to the "urgent." Not directly addressed, the underlying malaise affecting the collectivity remained unresolved.

A short time later, the COU Committee on Communications asked PAM to undertake a second audit, this time of member institutions and their relations with COU. The PAM report, tabled in May 1988, provoked a storm. Based on interviews with COU members and senior administrative officers in the universities, its message and recommendations—which included one that the academic colleagues be removed and COU again become a presidents' club—proved too hard to swallow. Council's response was to shoot the messenger. A year later, COU decided to examine this "subject of recurring concern" once more. This time, however, a university executive head from outside Ontario would lead the review.[45]

Dr. Arnold Naimark, president of the University of Manitoba and at the time president of ACCC, was chosen as chair. This Committee to Review the Structure and Role of COU reported in May 1990.[46] The report divided COU activities into two broad categories: service and policy. It found all but unanimous agreement that the COU's service functions were being conducted efficiently, effectively, and beneficially. The high quality and value of COU service activities was widely acknowledged both within and outside the university community in Ontario and beyond.

In the area of policy and advocacy, however, the Naimark Committee discovered sharply divergent views, dependent upon the perspective of the commentator. Given the zeal with which Ontario universities guarded their autonomy and the prolonged period of financial constraint to which the system had been subjected, the report stated that it was very difficult to gain agreement on any issue that ultimately produced divergent financial and/or political implications for COU member institutions. Therefore, "for the collectivity to speak with one voice and then act ... is a rare event."[47]

Notwithstanding such difficulties, the Naimark Report recommended that COU continue to operate in both the service and the policy areas, although it was recognized that the balance between the two would continually shift. On the issue of structure, the committee recommended that the academic colleagues be retained. Its survey of current COU members had shown that only a small minority—five executive heads and one colleague—supported the option of a two-tier council, in which executive heads and colleagues would have clearly separate roles. A second option—that colleagues be granted the same rights as executive heads, endorsed by four colleagues and one executive head—was rejected as not viable. Three-quarters of the colleagues favoured the option of retaining colleagues and clarifying their role. Fewer than half of the executive heads favoured this option, but there was no agreement among them on an alternative. Only one executive head supported the abolition of colleague membership. The committee, therefore, recommended that the role of an academic colleague be clarified as involving participation in COU activities, but not institutional representation. Colleagues should be full-time academics, not administrators, elected by the senior academic body of their institution for two-year renewable terms. They should report regularly on COU activities to their institutions through this body. Executive heads should meet frequently with their academic colleagues to discuss council business, but colleagues should not come to meetings as instructed delegates. One colleague, the colleague member of the executive committee, should serve as the senior colleague and chair the Colleague Caucus.

Like the earlier PAM audit report, the Naimark Report was very critical of the activities of the Group of Five (the MacTwit Group), judging that it served only to weaken COU. However, unlike PAM, which had recommended its disbanding, the Naimark Committee took a more pragmatic approach. It accepted that such groups would likely continue to exist. While urging that all COU member institutions should be encouraged to work together, it recommended that council develop internal mechanisms to allow special-interest groups to work within the collectivity and to report on their activities to council. To deal with ongoing tensions among the member institutions, it recommended the establishment of a COU Committee on Policy and Planning separate from the executive committee. Among its other responsibilities, this committee would monitor the activities of any subgroups (such as MacTwit) within council. The report also recommended a number of ways in which COU activities might be streamlined, and made less formal and more accessible to colleague members. All of the recommendations of the Naimark Report were adopted; most were promptly implemented. A committee on policy and planning was struck, but it proved ineffective. The hoped-for improvement in the ability of council to deal effectively with controverted policy and advocacy issues remained unfulfilled.

COU was not the only major system to undergo a review during this period. In 1988, the government named John Stubbs, president of Trent University, to undertake a comprehensive review of OCUA. His charge was to make recommendations on its mandate, role, membership, structure, and staffing. For its submission, COU dusted off the section of its earlier brief to the Bovey Commission dealing with the buffer body. In it, COU recommended that OCUA be given a sharpened and strengthened mandate, provided with a strengthened membership and staff, and given more resources. It also proposed that the advisory body become more proactive in the policy area and reduce its regulatory activities, and that its advice be made public when rendered, and, if not accepted, the reasons given.[48]

The Stubbs Report described the gradual evolution of OCUA. During the 1970s, it had acted primarily as a buffer between the universities and the government. It had been both "reactive" (dealing with specific requests from government) and "proactive" (publishing policy papers on systems issues). More recently, a combination of changing circumstances had pushed it toward becoming a regulatory body. Given the growing complexity of the provincial university system and its limited resources, OCUA had become less and less able to exercise effectively its primary function of providing advice to government on broad policy matters affecting the system. To remedy this, President Stubbs recommended changes very similar to those contained in the COU brief. OCUA should play a larger and more formal, though still advisory role, in system planning and co-ordination, employing the approach advocated by the Bovey Commission: a strengthening of system planning and interinstitutional co-ordination through a mix of funding incentives and disincentives. He recommended that a new order-in- council spell out more clearly the broad policy and operating responsibilities of the advisory body, that it be given a mandate to comment on policy initiatives emanating from other ministries (such as the Ministry of Health, which had an impact on the university system), that it be provided with additional resources to augment its research capacity, and that it abandon some of its regulatory activities.[49] Apart from approving a modest increase in the staff complement of OCUA, the government ignored these recommendations.

● ACCOUNTABILITY COMES TO THE FORE

It had always been understood that Ontario universities were to be accountable for the expenditure of the public funds they received—accountable to their governing boards, faculty and students; and to the government, and through it to the taxpayers. When government grants became their principal source of revenue, the universities accepted and clearly acknowledged this accountability. In the early years, however, there were few rules about how this accountability should be rendered, a situation that prevailed into the 1980s. In that decade, the growing complexity of public finance and the concurrent pressures to justify public expenditures produced a new set of auditing principles and practices covering the public sector. Auditors embraced new accountability principles and developed new rules for this sector.

Because Ontario universities are private, autonomous institutions, each with its own governing board responsible for financial matters, for a time they remained relatively immune from the pressures to have their accounts reviewed in accordance with the new rules. Since the '60s, they had been required to have their books audited annually by independent external auditors and to file these reports with the ministry. With the advent of formula funding, the ministry and the universities agreed upon a set of regulations covering eligibility for receipt of operating grants. As well, clear rules on institutional eligibility for capital funding were established. Taken together, these fulfilled the accountability requirements as set down by the ministry.

In the early '80s, the provincial auditor began to question the adequacy of these relatively simple requirements. Armed with a new Audit Act granting his office wider powers, he decided that the university sector ought to be included within his jurisdiction. First hints of the auditor's interest came in 1983, but it took another three years before this interest took formal shape. In late 1986, the deputy minister informed the executive heads of the provincial auditor's announced intention to conduct an "inspection" audit of Ontario universities, and he invited comments.[50] They came immediately. Given the legal status of universities as private institutions and the long tradition of respect for university autonomy, the universities questioned whether the Audit Act gave the provincial auditor authority to conduct audits in the universities. They also queried what was involved in an inspection audit. Consequently, the executive director of COU wrote the auditor indicating that the universities would like to discuss the matter.

Seeking support for his proposal, the provincial auditor then wrote to the chair of the Public Accounts Committee, the all-party legislative body to whom his annual report was presented. He informed the committee of his intention to undertake inspection audits of the universities and invited its members to consult their respective caucuses to obtain their parties' views on the proposal. Informal enquiries by the executive director of COU disclosed that, though both the Liberal and NDP caucuses were inclined to support the universities' view that the provincial auditor lacked authority under the Act to proceed, neither party was prepared publicly to say so. An informal meeting between the provincial auditor and representatives of the universities was held at which the suggestion was made that he meet with the universities' external auditors. He declined to do so and affirmed his intention to proceed with an inspection audit of one small university. He invited COU to select the university, from among Brock, Trent, and Wilfrid Laurier. Council declined to do so. COU then decided to seek a legal opinion as to the precise meaning under the Act of an "inspection audit"; in particular, what limits, if any, could be applied to the scope of such an audit. All of the universities agreed that, pending receipt of the legal opinion, none would respond to the provincial auditor. Consulted informally, the provincial treasurer indicated that, although there was a general lack of support within the government for the auditor's initiative, no official statement to this effect could be expected. The universities were on their own.

In May 1988, the auditor announced that he had chosen Trent University as the site for the first inspection audit of an Ontario university. Shortly after, COU received the legal opinion it had requested. This opinion held that the auditor was entitled to audit the financial records of universities, but not records dealing with purely academic matters: for example, faculty appointments, promotions, tenure, sabbatical leave, and teaching loads. While of some use, the legal opinion left unresolved the question of how any difference of opinion between the university and the auditor on what constituted an "academic matter" would be settled. Given this legal opinion, some members of council argued that the limits of the auditor's powers under the Act should be tested in court. Others counselled full co-operation. In the end, aware that the auditor was not amused at this resistance to his plans, a COU working party assisted Trent in the development of a list of financial accounts that the university would make available.

The report of the Trent University audit, included in the auditor's 1988 annual report, contained a number of critical remarks concerning

Trent's practices; in particular, a financial settlement with the former president approved by the executive committee of the university's board of governors without authorization from the full board. The ministry was also criticized for an "overpayment" of operating grants to Trent on behalf of students "dubiously" registered as honours rather than as pass students. Subsequently, the ministry was able to show that it had granted Trent permission to count these students as honours students but had failed properly to record the decision. The action of the Trent board executive committee, while technically within its authority, left a bad taste. From the perspective of the universities, this was not an auspicious beginning to the audit process.

In the two following years, two more inspection audits were carried out, one at the University of Guelph, the other at the University of Toronto. In both cases, some minor errors were uncovered. In the fall of 1990, the provincial auditor sought to broaden his powers, requesting that the Audit Act be amended to permit him to conduct "value-for-money" audits of the universities. In a submission before the Public Accounts Committee, which was reviewing the request, the deputy minister took a position in support of the universities. His brief argued that such an amendment was contrary to the tradition of university autonomy, that it was not necessary to ensure proper accountability, and that the legislation under which his ministry operated did not permit it to require the universities to submit the kinds of data necessary to conduct this type of audit.[51] Although clearly sympathetic to the auditor's proposal, the committee decided to take no further action. Several more years would pass before the continuing rearguard action of the universities to hold the auditor at bay was lost. In the meantime, with a new government, the universities would come under direct pressure from the ministry for increased accountability.

As the 1980s drew to a close, the frustration level of the universities began again to rise. Significant amounts of new funding had been provided. But continually rising enrolments, inflation, and the imposition of new financial obligations imposed by new government regulations continued to erode the universities' ability to move ahead. The government continued to preach accessibility, but, in the eyes of COU and the universities, over a lengthening period of time it had stubbornly refused to provide the requisite base funding. COU held regular informal meetings with the new minister, Lynn MacLeod, but with little positive effect. In September 1988, first-year enrolment increased by 6 percent. Funding for 1989–90 was increased by approximately the same amount. However, the spring 1989 provincial budget introduced a new payroll tax that would cost the universities an estimated $24.5 million per year. A government reorganization saw the Ministry of Colleges and Universities abolished in favour of a new single Ministry of Education and Training (combining three formerly separate ministries: Education, Colleges and Universities, and Training). Sean Conway, a senior member of cabinet, was named to head the new ministry.

Ministry attention now focused on the CAATs, where a major review, called *Vision 2000,* was underway, and on the ongoing reform of secondary schooling. Operating grants for the coming year, 1990–91, were increased by slightly more than 8 percent, which included 3.15 percent for new enrolment. However, when the cost of meeting new legal requirements—increases in unemployment insurance (UI) program and Canada Pension Plan (CPP) premium payments, the new employer health tax and pay equity—was factored in, the global increase amounted to less than 3 percent. Less than that predicted by ministry officials, this produced new cries of anguish from the universities.

The government provided an additional $18 million in the spring 1990 budget, to be distributed pro rata among the institutions. The results of negotiations with OCUA over revisions to the institutions' corridors produced further ructions. On average, the increase amounted to 8.89 percent; however, increases to individual institutions ranged from 1.15 percent to 18.22 percent. The smaller universities, plus York University (with an increase of 14 percent), were among the favoured few. Those universities whose increase amounted to less than 5 percent, mainly the larger ones, were outraged. With the economy becoming unstable and a recession predicted by some experts, the government decided to go to the people in the third year of its mandate and called a summer election. When the ballots were counted, to the surprise of many (including Bob Rae, the leader of the New Democratic Party (NDP), who would become premier), the Liberals were defeated and a majority NDP government elected.

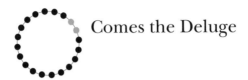

CHAPTER 4

Comes the Deluge

THE DECADE OF THE 1990S would be unlike any of the preceding ones for the voluntary association that represents Ontario universities. Described by COU Chair Ron Ianni, president of the University of Windsor, as "tumultuous," it would see more changes to the provincial university system than had taken place over the whole of the preceding two decades. Most of these changes produced adverse—some would say perverse—effects on the quality of higher education, the institutions providing it, and the association dedicated to its service. The decade would see a continuation of the expansion in enrolment, though at a somewhat slower pace, that has given Ontario one of the highest university participation rates in the world. At the same time, it would see a massive contraction of public funding, which would change for the foreseeable future the way universities in Ontario are financed.

In 1995, Ontario universities found themselves in a new environment with the advent of a new Conservative government elected on promises to reduce government spending and taxes, and to promote private enterprise and competition. No longer able to count on the public purse to provide subsidies in the amounts received over the preceding two decades, the universities would be driven to increase fees substantially and to seek major support from the private sector. In addition to being forced to learn to operate with sharply reduced government grants, the universities would also be forced to compete with one another both for funds and for students.

After 1995, Ontario universities competed with one another for a share of "targeted" public funds, both capital and operating grants—grants now available only for academic and research programs identified by government as being of high priority in light of its economic objectives. They also competed with one another in raising the private funds now required to enable them to secure the "matching" government grants—grants available only to institutions able to raise the required matching amount. In addition, in the new, more competitive environ-

Notes to chapter 4 are on pp. 222-225

ment, universities competed with one another for "high-flyer" students, offering financial incentives such as scholarships and bursaries to entice them to enrol in their institution. Some universities, principally the older and larger ones, with their larger endowments, more influential alumni, and greater access to private funds, found themselves in a better position to compete than did others. The university playing field was no longer as level as it had been. Although all were equally universities, clearly some were now more equal than others. These changes affected both the individual institutions and the provincial university system. They also affected COU.

The '90s would see four presidents (as the chief executive officer was now called) of council. Edward Monahan retired in 1991 after almost fifteen years in office. Peter George, dean of Social Sciences at McMaster University, succeeded him. He served only three years before returning to that university to become president. In 1994, Bonnie Patterson, dean of Business at Ryerson Polytechnical Institute (later becoming Ryerson Polytechnic University), was named president. She, too, served three years before accepting the presidency of Trent University. The incumbent at the time of writing, Ian Clark, with a distinguished career in both government and business, was named president in 1998.

As the 1990s began, COU altered its priorities and expanded advocacy activities. Later, when forced by budgetary pressures to re-examine these priorities, a decision was taken to accord research a lower priority and to reduce this activity. The universities felt increasingly threatened when the new NDP government, elected in 1990, failed to respond to their urgent requests for more funding and for permission to increase tuition fees, and at the same time imposed new regulations on them. Relations between COU and the ministry, always delicate, became strained. So, too, did relations with OCUA, now increasingly seen by the universities as an arm of government. The protection of university autonomy again became a major issue. Many of the new regulations imposed by the government on the universities were part of its general efforts to improve equity and fairness in the public sector. They were being applied broadly across the entire public sector. To COU and its member institutions, however, they were signs of overregulation that threatened university autonomy. COU rhetoric grew more strident; tempers sometimes flared; (arguably) council's effectiveness diminished. No longer engaged in leading the development of a provincial university system, COU was now frequently engaged in defensive action to protect university autonomy.

When the new Tory government did away with OCUA, another significant change occurred. For some time, COU had been advocating in favour of higher tuition fees and greater support from the private sector. It was pleased at the new government's enthusiasm for more private-sector support, but was staggered by the size of the reduction in government grants. The universities now had to come to terms with substantially smaller public subsidies in a new, more competitive environment. So, too, did COU. The policy parameters had changed drastically; so, too, had the balance among the players. With the disappearance of OCUA in 1996, a new element was added. The system triad became a duo: the ministry and COU. In this new structure, the balance of power lay overwhelmingly with the ministry. COU now found itself asked by the ministry for advice on matters of the government's choosing—and not always in the interests of the universities. It was also asked to manage government policy, something it had long criticized OCUA for doing. At the same time, council's ability to provide carefully researched and fully documented advice was somewhat less than it might have been, owing to its reduced research capacity.

● ADVOCACY

Like the new premier himself, the universities were surprised at the results of the summer-1990 election. The new premier, Bob Rae, young, brilliant, and charismatic—a student radical some twenty years earlier as an undergraduate at the University of Toronto—was someone who understood the importance of universities to ensure a strong Ontario. But he was the head of an untried populist government that was preoccupied with other, higher priorities and was facing an economic downturn. Universities were not at the top of his government's policy priority list. Aware of this, the universities did not have much expectation that in the immediate future Rae would be leading the charge for increased funding. Still, they were optimistic that he would listen. The appointment of Richard Allen as minister of Colleges and Universities was taken as an early hopeful sign. A history professor on leave from McMaster University and a former opposition critic, Allen was a member of the academic community with good knowledge of the provincial university system. At his first meeting with COU, the minister made a favourable impression when he promised to put forward a strong case in cabinet on behalf of the universities and to press for increased funding. (Deputy Minister Thomas Brzustowski, a former academic colleague from the University of Waterloo and later vice-president Academic of that university, was probably the most troubled person to leave that meeting, for he knew that the minister would not be able to deliver on many his promises.)

University matters had not been featured in the summer election campaign, and COU had not become involved. Nevertheless, council moved quickly to implement an advocacy strategy directed to the new government. A *Recovery Plan for Ontario Universities* was drafted. Efforts were initiated to develop a coalition in support of the plan that included faculty, students, and support staff. A new public relations firm, Hill and Knowlton, with close ties to the NDP government, was retained. Because the window of opportunity was not likely to remain open long, time was of the essence. A meeting with the premier and the treasurer was requested. A special meeting of council was convened to approve the proposed plan. The *Recovery Plan*, based on an earlier proposal emanating from Queen's University, *Ontario Universities: A Plan for Action*, called for an integrated effort involving government, the universities (including their alumni), and the private sector to work together to provide more resources for higher education.

The principal objective was to restore the level of funding provided to Ontario universities in 1978, the last year in which the funding level recommended by OCUA had been implemented. To close the gap, a large sum—$410 million—would be required. The plan proposed that this amount be "returned" to the universities over a period of four years through a combination of increased government grants and increased tuition fees. Under the plan, two-thirds of the required amount would come from government, and one-third from the students, through a $550 increase in tuition fees. The revenue produced by the fee increase would be paid into a trust fund to be administered by OCUA. Adjustments would be made to Ontario Student Assistance Program (OSAP) regulations to protect students of limited means. As well as these proposed increases in university revenues, university alumni and the private sector would be encouraged to increase their support of universities.

The debate on the plan within council was lively. No member opposed having a plan, but some members expressed grave reservations about this plan's proposal for a sharp increase in tuition fees. Concern was also expressed that the proposed coalition involving faculty associations and student groups (described as fragile) would not hold. A proposal that the fee increase be voted on separately was put to a straw vote; it failed to pass. A proposal that a large-scale rally in support of the universities be held in Toronto was also challenged; one colleague member stated that he would not be willing to cancel classes to allow students to attend. In the end, it was agreed (with four negative votes) that, despite the risks, COU should proceed.[1]

Events moved quickly. At a meeting with a small COU planning committee in early December, the minister indicated that he was attracted to several aspects of the *Recovery Plan*. He was particularly pleased that a coalition with broad support within the university community was being formed. Shortly thereafter, however, the premier stated publicly that his government would not permit any increases in tuition fees. At a press conference some days later, COU unveiled its *Recovery Plan*. Two of the coalition partners, the Ontario Confederation of University Faculty Associations (OCUFA) and the Ontario Federation of Students (OFS), boycotted the event. They held their own press conference, one at which they severely criticized the plan's proposal to increase tuition fees. The proposed rally was never held. The COU position differed markedly from that held by the faculty and student associations. Both faculty and students continued to hold firmly to the view that the government should contribute the funds necessary to meet its public policy objectives. Tuition fees should not be increased. COU and its member institutions, with a better appreciation (perhaps) of fiscal realities, no longer expected the government to make up the full revenue shortfall from the public purse. Although the case was not put in precisely these words, they were arguing that the private sector—i.e., the students and their parents—should be expected to contribute a share. The universities' emphasis was on the paramount need for substantially increased revenues, some of which, they argued, might reasonably be expected to come from the private sector: from students, alumni, and the corporate sector. This argument did not play well with many faculty and students, though not all members of these estates opposed the plan. More significantly, it did not play well with the government.

As 1991 opened, the economic situation of the province continued to deteriorate. The government imposed spending restraints. The minister now declared himself unable to support any of the *Recovery Plan*'s proposals for increased spending. At the May 1991 COU meeting, the plan was declared dead.[2] Resigned to the prospect of little if any financial relief through increased government grants in the near term, COU settled down to an advocacy campaign to persuade the politicians and the public about the pressing need to improve university revenues. Obtaining increased revenue from higher tuition fees became a central element in the program. The battle, bruising at times, would prove long and difficult and, ultimately, was lost.

After the failure of the Bovey Commission, COU had moved to develop and maintain a long-term advocacy plan on behalf of Ontario universities. In the growing fractiousness among its member institutions, achieving consensus (never easy) continued to remain elusive. In the mid-1980s, the National Universities' Week campaign, a campaign sponsored by AUCC and in which COU played a leading role, achieved some modest success. This led to a National Forum on Post-secondary Education, jointly sponsored by the federal government (through the Secretariat of State) and the provincial governments (through the Council of Ministers of Education). The forum was held in Regina in the fall of 1987. Brian Segal, president of Ryerson Polytechnic Institute and at the time chair of the COU Committee on Communications, served as co-chair. Although the forum did not lead to any commitments from either the federal or the provincial levels of government, the organizers judged it a success for raising public consciousness of the importance to Canada of its institutions of higher education.

Following the National Forum, the COU Committee on Communications proposed an Ontario counterpart to serve as the anchor of a new, long-term advocacy strategy for council. The plan, *Ontario Universities into the 21st Century*, would call upon COU to sponsor a public enquiry into the major policy issues confronting Ontario universities as they moved toward the new millennium. To be led by a high-level committee composed of both university and non-university representatives, the exercise would take the form of a series of public town hall meetings to be held at various locations across the province. A broad cross-section of the public would be invited to discuss a series of basic policy questions in a workshop format. The questions would be prepared in advance and supported by position papers provided by COU. These regional meetings would culminate in a large plenary session to debate the workshop findings; votes would then be held on a series of policy proposals. The results would provide a basic policy platform on higher education in Ontario. A report would be published describing these results and used for ongoing advocacy purposes.

Debated over several meetings of COU, this ambitious proposal initially received cautious support. Its potential was recognized; however, concerns were raised about the costs, both financial and in terms of personnel. Fear was also expressed that the proposed format might produce results that the universities could not control. It would be a big gamble, one requiring a major investment without adequate assurance that the desired results would be obtained. Several draft position papers were prepared and examined; none was found acceptable. The project was quietly abandoned.[3] Once again, the inherent conservatism of COU member institutions yielded a decision not to act.

While agreement on a long-term strategy remained elusive, COU advocacy activities increased. Led by its Committee on Communications, sustained efforts were made to clarify and focus more sharply the messages the universities wanted to convey to government and the larger public. COU *Briefing Notes* was now published more frequently and in larger numbers. The *Queen's Park Newsletter*, directed at MPPs, was begun. Two occasional brochure series were inaugurated: *Dividends*, which focused on what universities provided by way of added value to society; and *Neighbours*, which detailed how universities were involved in their local communities. Meetings were organized with party caucuses, with individual ministers, and with senior government bureaucrats. Tours of secondary schools were undertaken—eight in the 1988–89 school year. COU continued to be heavily involved in the annual National Universities' Weeks. The COU lobby on behalf of Ontario universities was now a major activity. It was hard work, and the payoff was not obvious. Moreover, it was proving to be a substantial drain on the time and energy of senior secretariat staff, already heavily burdened with other duties.

As part of its evolving long-term advocacy strategy, in 1990 council approved the establishment of a new advocacy agency, the Alliance for Ontario Universities. Its task was to build a broad coalition across institutional and sectoral boundaries in support of Ontario universities. COU provided an initial funding for a period of three years; the Alliance office was located in the COU secretariat. It was, however, a separate organization with its own staff, and the plan was to make it a self-supporting agency with its own quarters as soon as was practicable. Always closely involved in the development of COU advocacy activities, the Alliance never achieved its anticipated effectiveness. Part of the reason for its failure to meet expectations was the creation, at about the same time, of another organization with a similar purpose—the Friends of Ontario Universities (FOU). Headed by the president of the Alumni Association of the University of Waterloo and strongly supported by that university, FOU aimed to mobilize Ontario university alumni in local communities across the province in support of the universities, in particular to serve as local, community-based political action groups at election time and on other occasions when advocacy on behalf of the universities could be useful. In theory, the two advocacy organizations would be partners. Their basic objectives were the same; their respective plans were potentially complementary. It did not work out that way. The Alliance and FOU were often competitors, seeking support from mostly the same sources. Efforts to co-ordinate their activities were continuous; the results were disappointingly meagre. Much time and energy was expended on attempts to gain agreement about what should be done, and not enough on getting it done.

Now a major COU activity, advocacy was proving to be a costly one. COU annual budgets clearly show the shift in emphasis. When the Office of Communications was opened in 1979, its budget amounted to some $80,000 and represented less than 10 percent of council's total annual operating expenditures. By 1993, council was spending more than $785,000 on advocacy. This included $412,170 for the Office of Communications, $226,000 for the Alliance, and a contribution of $150,000 to FOU. Together, these outlays represented one-third of total COU expenditures that year, exclusive of the portions of budget for administration and research covering the salaries of senior staff, who now were devoting much of their time to advocacy. Much of this funding was coming from the Ontario Universities' Application Centre (OUAC), which that year contributed $681,000 to COU. At this time, OUAC was covering some 22 percent of Council's operating budget. As the 1990s progressed and COU revenues (like those of its member institutions) were compressed, these numbers declined slightly, although not as a proportion of total council expenditures. Following a review of Alliance operations in 1994, its COU support was reduced to $20,000; this support was phased out entirely the following year. The Alliance struggled on for several more years at a much-reduced scale of operations; it finally ceased to exist in 1997.

COU support for FOU continued at a substantial level for several years. Eventually, however, pressure to reduce the COU budget, combined with dissatisfaction over the results obtained, led to the decision to terminate funding. In establishing the parameters for the COU budget for 1996–97, the Committee on Policy and Planning reviewed the activities of FOU. Noting that COU had contributed more than $500,000 to FOU between January 1992 and January 1995, the committee concluded that, its efforts notwithstanding, the Friends organization "was not able to deliver the kind of lobbying effort that COU had hoped for." It recommended that funding for the Alliance cease in April 1996, that discussions be undertaken with FOU to incorporate ways of including the Friends network into COU advocacy activities, and that a business plan be prepared to incorporate this activity within the COU budget. These recommendations were adopted.[4] FOU continued to operate for another two years before finally ceasing to operate in the fall of 1998.

The ability of COU to sustain these large expenditures on advocacy was substantially assisted by a policy change introduced in 1989 affecting the operations of the Ontario Universities' Application Centre (OUAC), whose financial operations are overseen by council. When the centre opened in 1971, it had been agreed that, after the initial start-up grant from the ministry, the centre should be self-supporting through the fees charged the student applicants. It was also agreed that fee levels should be based on the not-for-profit principle and kept as low as possible. A comprehensive review of the centre conducted in 1988, on the retirement of the founding director, recommended continuation of the mandate and operations of OUAC. This included continuation of the self-supporting and not-for-profit financial principles. Endorsed by the OUAC Board of Management, these recommendations were accepted by COU. In 1989, to meet the cost of planned new services, the basic application fee was increased by $1 to $18 per applicant. That same year— against the express opposition of the OUAC Board of Management—COU instituted a surcharge of 10 percent on OUAC gross revenues to support council's advocacy program. The rationale, not readily accepted by all, was that the students would also benefit from COU activities on behalf of Ontario universities. This surcharge added some $90,000 to the COU coffers. A year later, in 1990, the surcharge on OUAC revenues was increased to 30 percent. That year, Council's need for increased revenues was prompted not so much by a larger expenditure on advocacy (although spending had gone up) but by the sharply increased costs of accommodation for the secretariat. This was caused by the decision of the University of Toronto to cease providing the secretariat space in the Robarts Library. As a result, COU was forced to acquire space for its secretariat off campus at current commercial rates. This added $300,000 to council's annual operating budget, with absolutely no compensating value added.

Once the decision had been made to use OUAC revenues to augment the COU budget, the temptation to continue the practice proved irresistible. Few outside COU were aware of the new source of income and there were few critics. During the efforts in 1990 to promote the short-lived plan for recovery, however, the president of the Ontario Federation of Students, who had learned of the new surcharge, wrote COU a strong letter denouncing the use of students' money in support of advocacy to increase tuition fees. In the spring of 1992, $500,000 was transferred from the OUAC operating surplus to COU. This sum was used in part to cover an overrun in the budget for administration and research "due to unanticipated severance costs and increased costs for accommodation."[5] In 1992, OUAC undergraduate application fees were increased from $18 to $23, and a $27 special cost-recovery fee added to cover other expenses incurred by the centre. This raised the fee for individual applicants to $50. Transfers from OUAC were now covering some 22 percent of COU operating expenditures. By the end of the decade (1998–99), OUAC was contributing almost a million dollars ($956,000) annually to COU, a sum that amounted to more than 30 percent of COU revenues.[6]

In the more competitive environment of the late '90s, OUAC modified some of its procedures. Student applicants were now permitted to choose more than three universities by paying an additional charge, and they were allowed to make two amendments to their initial choices without charge. At the same time, some changes were made in the way OUAC surplus revenues were distributed. These revenues, which had been transferred directly into the COU operating budget, were now directed to member institutions on a pro-rated basis; institutional membership dues to council were increased by a similar amount. The rationale for this change was that, since some applicants do not attend university, it was inappropriate that they should be supporting COU. However, the earlier principle abandoned a decade earlier—that application fee revenue should cover only the direct cost of applications for admission and not be used for other purposes—was not reintroduced. OUAC exercised a monopoly on application for admission to Ontario universities. Prospective students were willing to pay the fees charged; COU and the universities needed the revenue.

The greatly increased emphasis on advocacy, dictated by the changed circumstances of the universities, produced a realignment of council priorities. Just as the universities came under severe budget restraints that required them to assess priorities and reduce expenditures on those that were accorded a lower priority, so, too, did COU. In the first half of the 1990s COU endured a series of difficult budgets. In two of these years, an operating deficit was recorded. To help meet the costs of advocacy, the budget of the research division was reduced and, with it, the staff complement—not once but several times. After a review of the operations of the division in 1993, eight of the division's regular annual reports were dropped and another ten reduced in scope. Only seven were kept unchanged. During the budget discussions in the spring of 1994, the president of COU asked that the organization be judged first as an advocacy organization and then as a service provider. Several council members expressed dismay that the balance of resources had been transferred to strategic advocacy; one urged that rigorous research output be maintained as a requirement. While acknowledging the problematic nature of such considerations, the president argued that in a period of severe restraint, some trade-offs were necessary.[7] Ironically, after the election of the new Tory government in 1995, which produced a substantial reduction in ministry staff and operations, and the demise of OCUA, neither the ministry nor COU possessed the requisite system research capacity. The "knowledge is power" principle adopted by COU in 1969 when it made a commitment to having a strong research arm had been sacrificed on the altar of advocacy. (This loss has been compensated in part by a considerable increase in the number of COU-sponsored conferences and publications devoted to the importance of universities in contemporary society.)

● UNIVERSITY-GOVERNMENT RELATIONS: THE RAE YEARS

The position of the New Democratic Party on some major university issues was well known before it came to power. A populist party, it favoured expanding accessibility and strongly opposed increasing tuition fees. In the beginning of its mandate, however, it was unclear how the new government would choose to deal with the universities. Given the large number of inexperienced members, including most of the cabinet, it was several months before a clear pattern of behaviour began to emerge. When it did, it became apparent that this government intended to put its own stamp on how university affairs were to be handled and that it would be more interventionist. Accessibility, equity, and accountability became the focus. Funding remained constrained.

In Ontario, participation rates were now among the highest in the world and enrolment continued to increase. Government, therefore, directed its attention to improving accessibility to a university education for identified disadvantaged groups: Aboriginal peoples, francophones, women, and single parents. Small amounts of targeted funds were provided for these purposes, but these amounts were taken "off the top" of the basic operating grants. The universities were expected to improve services for these groups without any new money. At the same time, stronger anti-discrimination and pay equity regulations were enacted across all sectors in receipt of public funds, including the post-secondary sector, and greater emphasis was placed on accountability for the expenditure of public funds. As the government's agenda developed, the minister's early commitment to be a strong advocate for the universities and to be readily accessible to COU went unfulfilled.

Nor did the government feel bound by previously established rules or practice. The Programme Adjustment Fund established by the previous government was maintained, but the rules were changed without consultation. In the spring of 1991, the minister announced continuation of the fund and asked OCUA to administer it. But the $17.2 million committed by the Peterson government was reduced by $3 million. Further, only 90 percent of the funds would be disbursed to the universities on the previously announced pro rata basis; the other 10 percent would be awarded on a competitive basis—a small but significant change to the universities. When OCUA examined the proposals submitted by the universities competing for these funds, it recommended funding for seventy-five of them. Shortly after, the minister announced funding for only twenty-six. In many cases, the recommendations from OCUA were ignored and the ministry imposed its own decisions. Universities that found themselves left out were angry. At COU, a proposal was made that council object in the strongest terms and urge reconsideration, and that all institutions defer accepting the grants pending reconsideration. Objections were registered; the minister was asked to reconsider, but no changes were made.[8] None of the "winner" universities chose to defer its acceptance of the funds.

At the same time, the government applied its populist philosophy to those agencies, boards, and committees to which it named members. Bodies dealing with university affairs, including OCUA, became more broadly representative and composed of stakeholder groups. Members now were drawn from a much broader constituency within the university and college sectors: faculty, students, and support staff. Moreover, appointments were frequently based on the political persuasion of the appointee. Some appointees had little experience with post-secondary education matters; they brought new, and not always relevant or congenial, interests to the table. The easy familiarity that had formerly marked relations within and among these university groups (criticized by many in the new government as illustrative of a too-cosy relationship among the parties) was lost. Discussions now were often strained and agreement became more difficult to reach.

In the fall of 1991, a new university policy unit was established in the ministry. With the release of the *Vision 2000* report on the CAATs, increased attention was being given to the college sector. The ministry began to consider how to deal with the universities and the colleges of applied arts and technology as two components of a single post-secondary sector, something that had not been contemplated seriously since the time of the Wright Commission some two decades earlier. The ministry indicated that OCUA would continue to play a central role in university affairs; the ministry also stated that it was not obliged to consult with this advisory body on all matters affecting universities. Word filtered out that the ministry was planning to set up a common data unit to cover both the universities and the CAATs.

Following his inspection audits of three Ontario universities, the provincial auditor requested more authority to undertake audits of universities. The Report of the Standing Committee on Public Accounts to the legislature in July 1991 supported this request and recommended amendments to the Audit Act to give the auditor greater authority to undertake audits of universities. Ths included the discretion of conducting "value-for-money" audits. That fall, the minister appointed the Task Force on University Accountability, with a mandate "to develop recommendations for a framework to provide for the clear accountability of Ontario's universities to the public." Its focus would be on institutional accountability. Composed of twelve members, the task force was chaired by William Broadhurst, a senior partner in a major accountancy firm (Price Waterhouse) with wide experience in university affairs and a member of OCUA. He was the only member of that body named to the group.[9] Having previously indicated his intention to ensure that university governing bodies become more representative of the internal and external communities they were committed to serve, the minister asked the Broadhurst Task Force to examine university governance structures and their role in accountability. The Task Force was located in the COU secretariat; the research division provided research support. Concurrently, the minister asked OCUA to provide advice "on whether and how to establish a system of program reviews as a means of ensuring public accountability for academic quality." Both groups would report in 1993.

At the December 1991 meeting of COU, the minister indicated that plans were being developed for a comprehensive review of the entire post-secondary sector. Its purpose would be to bring greater coherence across the university-college binary divide. The major emphasis would be on equity of access and quality of instruction, especially at the undergraduate level. The minister stated that while university funding remained a high priority, because the government was facing a serious financial crisis, it was impossible to predict funding levels over the next few years. Although some funds would be made available for repairs and maintenance, there would be no capital grants to universities in the coming year. He urged council to recognize that doing battle with the government on these issues was counterproductive, and he expressed the hope that he could count on COU support. This was the meeting at which the chair of the COU Government Relations Committee (formerly the Committee on Communications), President Arthurs of York, trenchantly observed, "Predictions were dire, expectations minimal and concern monumental."[10]

In January 1992, the provincial treasurer announced levels of operating support for a three-year period. There was to be a 1 percent increase for 1992–93 and a 2 percent increase in each of the following years, 1993–94 and 1994–95. (These latter increases would not be realized.) As the minister had previously signalled, apart from small sums for repair and maintenance, capital grants dried up. Early in 1992, Minister Allen advised the executive heads of the universities and the CAATs of his plans to reshape the post-secondary system to ensure that programs and services could be delivered more efficiently to the maximum number of students without loss of quality. That summer, he established the University Long-Term Restructuring Committee. Its task would be to determine how to make the universities "responsive to the continuous or lifelong education, training, and knowledge needs of a modern economic society and democratic society ... [while] ensuring the fullest possible response to the government's equity/access agenda within an environment of constrained public resources."[11] The committee was asked specifically to provide advice on institutional specialization and differentiation; program rationalization with potential for cost savings; options for strengthening the quality of undergraduate teaching; alternative program delivery mechanisms leading to cost savings; criteria for eligibility for public funding, including use of full-cost recovery and private sector delivery; restructuring of the academic year; and exploration of stronger linkages with employers and labour to introduce more work experience. Composed of nineteen members and constructed along the now-familiar stakeholder lines, the committee was co-chaired by the deputy minister and the chair of OCUA.

The establishment of this committee was greeted with dismay by the universities. While prepared to accept that such a group of stakeholders might appropriately discuss system goals and objectives, COU was firmly of the view that detailed planning for the system ought to be left to OCUA (weak as it was). After rejecting a suggestion that COU launch its own review of the system structure, with obvious reluctance council named members to its assigned seats on the committee. As its first task, the committee was instructed to identify and establish priorities among the issues it intended to address. Ignoring the minister's caveat that no additional public funding should be expected, and exercising a considerable degree of creative obfuscation, in December 1992 the committee submitted an interim report in which it identified several areas of study that it planned to examine over the next eighteen months. The following month, a major cabinet shuffle saw the establishment of a new, "super" Ministry of Education and Training, combining elementary, secondary, post-secondary education, and training. David Cooke, a senior member of cabinet, was named to head the new ministry. A new deputy minister, Charles Pascal, was appointed. A former member of the COU secretariat, former president of Sir Sandford Fleming College and, more recently, a leader of the *Vision 2000* review of the CAATs, Pascal had broad experience in both the university and college sectors.

The new minister did not respond to the *Interim Report of the University Long-Term Restructuring Committee*, nor did he make the report public. The committee ceased work. By spring 1993, the government recognized that it had seriously underestimated the cost and the effectiveness of its efforts to combat the recession. These efforts were failing; the budget deficit was rapidly rising. Government spending would have to be reduced. Discussions were initiated in all of the public sectors, including the university sector, to negotiate a "social contract" in which each sector would be asked to agree to reductions in public spending. It was proposed that the reductions be achieved mainly through reductions in salaries and wages. In the face of these developments, the work of the University Long-Term Restructuring Committee was formally suspended. It would never reconvene.

The results of the two accountability reviews arrived in 1993. In May, the Broadhurst Task Force issued its final report, *University Accountability: A Strengthened Framework*. Instructed by the minister to focus on the accountability of individual institutions, the task force developed an institution-based accountability framework grounded in university governing bodies. The framework focused on two essential accountability functions: board approval of policies and procedures governing institutional performance, and board monitoring of these. Although satisfied that most Ontario universities already had appropriate accountability policies in place, the task force judged that, too often, governing bodies were insufficiently involved in monitoring institutional performance. It made a number of recommendations to remedy this defect. To support the proposed strengthened institutional accountability framework, the task force recommended creation of an external, arm's-length monitoring agency: "an Accountability Review Committee, located within the Ontario Council on University Affairs, but independent from it, to monitor and report on the effectiveness of the accountability frameworks of Ontario universities."[12]

Two months later, OCUA submitted its advice on accountability for academic programming. It stated that, while the OCGS appraisals process had been providing accountability for the quality of graduate programs since 1968, there was "no province-wide systematic quality review process at the undergraduate level." Following the lead of the Broadhurst Task Force, the advisory body recommended "monitored (institutional) self-regulation": each institution should have policies and processes in place to review academic program quality—and these should be subject to audit by an "Academic Quality Audit Committee," whose members would be publicly appointed.[13]

COU was already involved in the accountability issue. In 1988, the Council of Senior Administrative Officers (CSAO) had undertaken a review of accountability. Never intended to be formally adopted or published, the report, which contained a set of guidelines on university accountability directed to governing bodies and senior administrators, was commended to the attention of COU members and their governing bodies. At the time, this CSAO report, University Accountability, received almost no publicity within the university community or outside it.[14] Like a number of policies approved by the voluntary association that were not congenial with the prevailing views in member institutions, these guidelines were largely ignored. The principles espoused in this 1988 report and many of its specific suggestions, however, had attracted the attention of the Broadhurst Task Force. They were now embedded in its report, where they had to be taken more seriously.

The institutionally based accountability framework developed by the Broadhurst Task Force, drawn largely from the earlier CSAO report, placed the locus of accountability with the governing board—properly constituted, organized, supported, and empowered—which had responsibility for the development and approval of appropriate policies and procedures governing institutional performance, and for monitoring them. In the changed environment, apart from some cavils over what should constitute appropriate performance indicators, COU and its member institutions had no difficulty accepting the accountability framework recommended in the Broadhurst Report. Most institutions now began to improve internal procedures covering accountability. COU, however, voiced opposition to the proposed independent Accountability Review Committee to support strengthened institutional accountability frameworks. It would be one more external body with which the universities would have to deal. Moreover, it would be part of OCUA, now regarded by COU as a body that had been co-opted by government.[15] Preoccupied with other matters, the minister made no decisions on the recommendations in either report. Neither of the external monitoring agencies recommended by Broadhurst and OCUA was ever put in place. A year later, an even more ambitious effort by the ministry to establish an Education Quality and Accountability Office (EQAO), with "responsibility for addressing issues of educational quality and accountability in the elementary/secondary sector and the post-secondary sector," failed to survive the defeat of the NDP government.[16]

The issuance of these two reports on different aspects of university accountability served as a stimulus to COU. In the course of its work, the Broadhurst Task Force had asked the COU Council of University Planning and Analysis (CUPA) to provide it with advice on the development of an appropriate array of objective performance measures and outcomes indicators. The early results of this work, which included both "input" and "output" measures, were included as an appendix in the report. A COU/CUPA committee continued work on these indicators. Over the next several years, COU approved a comprehensive set of indicators, which individual COU member universities then began to implement. This provided an effective response to those in government who had been expressing dissatisfaction with the universities' (ostensible) lack of accountability.

On the other accountability matter—academic quality review of undergraduate programs, for years COU had stubbornly defended the exclusive right of each university to manage its own affairs in this matter. Despite the lip service paid to the need to develop system procedures for measuring academic quality, nothing effective had been done. Now, under pressure from OCUA, COU finally moved. The Ontario Council of Academic Vice-Presidents (OCAV) developed an undergraduate program review process similar to that proposed by OCUA. Each university would undertake regular academic quality reviews of its undergraduate programs; OCAV would monitor the results and publish them. Approved by COU, the process began in 1997. Under this process, each institution undertakes an undergraduate review audit of its undergraduate programs using guidelines mandated by COU. It had taken more than fifteen years to institute a system in which the academic quality of undergraduate programming would be formally judged on a regular basis and the results made public. Similar to the graduate program appraisal process, the audit lacks any direct system-planning component, something the COU Committee on Long-Range Planning (the [Percy] Smith Committee) and OCUA had recommended almost two decades earlier.

The spring and early summer of 1993 saw COU and its member universities heavily involved in the "social contract" exercise. Facing a rapidly rising provincial deficit resulting from its unsuccessful efforts to stem the negative effects of a serious recession, the Rae government decided to take firm steps to reduce spending in all sectors. The result was Bill 48, the Social Contract Act, passed into law in July. Under the terms of this Act, each public sector, including the universities, was required to negotiate with the government over the amount of public funds it would receive. The objective was to reduce government transfer payments overall by $2 billion, principally by lowering salary bills. The universities' share in this reduction amounted to some $110 million. COU spearheaded the negotiations in the university sector. One COU member institution, Wilfrid Laurier University, opposed the decision of council to act on behalf of the collectivity, arguing that Ontario did not have a university system and that each autonomous university should be free to negotiate its own contract with the government. This view did not prevail. The negotiations at the central university panel proved difficult, acrimonious, and destabilizing. In the end, agreement was reached, but only after OCUFA and other union groups had left the table. With a central agreement in place, all COU member institutions (some with gritted teeth) then succeeded in finalizing local arrangements in time to qualify for a proffered discount. In the universities, as everywhere else in the public sector, salaries were frozen and all employees were forced to take unpaid holidays that became known as "Rae days."

One by-product of the Rae government's determination to reduce expenditures was the decision of the ministry, in 1994, to withdraw OHIP (health insurance) coverage for foreign students attending Ontario universities and colleges. Stepping into the breach, COU immediately struck a special committee to search for alternative sources of coverage. The committee was able quickly to reach an agreement with Ontario Blue Cross to provide essentially the same coverage as had formerly been provided by OHIP, and at a significantly lower cost to the student than that available from individual private health insurance carriers.[17] Here is an instance in which council, faced with an immediate problem, was able to provide a remedy that served both the collectivity of institutions and an important segment of the academic community.

Growing desperate to find new sources of revenue, COU and the universities intensified their advocacy activities, focusing principally on proposals to increase tuition fees. That year, the global operating grant to universities for 1993–94 was reduced by 6.3 percent, the first-ever absolute decline. Fear grew that government funding would decline further; it did. A COU discussion paper, *Tuition Fee Reform*, released in August 1993, became the basis of a renewed lobby campaign in the fall that included all MPPs. Council's position was clear and straightforward. Tuition fees should be increased to provide a greater proportion of the revenues required by the universities. These increases should be accompanied by reforms in student assistance programs to provide needy students with an ability to access higher education, including the introduction of an income contingency loan repayment plan (ICLRP). In November, COU sponsored a large conference on provincial renewal to which representatives of business, labour, government, and academe were invited. It focused on the important role of universities in economic renewal. Lobbying of MPPs was now almost continuous.

These efforts met with partial success when, in March 1994, the government announced that it was allowing tuition fees to be increased by 10 percent in each of the coming two years, 1994–95 and 1995–96—a decision calculated to add some $200 million to university revenues. However, no mention was made of an income contingency repayment plan.

In November 1993, the now fragile relations between COU and the government, the result of the acrimony generated in the social contract negotiations, were further shaken by the minister's announcement that he was asking OCUA to provide him with advice on the university funding mechanism, with a view to modifying it to achieve some specific policy objectives. Described as a review of the allocative mechanism, the minister's intentions went well beyond this. Stating bluntly that "the universities cannot continue to do business in the same way," he asked for an examination of the issues in order to achieve an appropriate balance between teaching, administration, research, and community service; to develop mechanisms for accountability in the use of resources in these areas; and to propose a funding system that would contain mechanisms and incentives for achieving the necessary combination of efficiency, economy, and reallocation to achieve identified priorities. These priorities were identified as: increasing accessibility for non-traditional students; greater emphasis on teaching; a more integrated educational system that permits easy movement from one sector to another; a funding mechanism that encourages sharing and co-operation among universities, colleges, and others; and incentives for program co-operation, restructuring, and greater differentiation.[18] Minister Cooke was asking OCUA to take up where the University Long-Term Restructuring Committee had left off, and he was serious. In taking up the task, OCUA would be equally serious.

The universities were angry that, in the midst of all of the problems created by reductions in funding, the increased number of regulations, and the social contract being imposed on them, they were to be called on once again to justify their activities—to undergo yet another exercise at the end of which they expected to be called upon to do more with less. OCUA's response to the Resource Allocation Review (RAR), as it came to be known, was immediate and strong. A number of research projects were commissioned; several research bulletins were issued. A discussion paper, *Sustaining Quality in Changing Times: Funding Ontario Universities*, was published. Noting the pressure on government to ensure that public investment in the universities was strategically focused and that there was sufficient flexibility within the system to target that investment as circumstances dictated, the paper forthrightly addressed the matter of institutional autonomy. In examining the desirability of having the universities become more responsive to public priorities, the paper suggested that the high degree of autonomy currently enjoyed by the universities might need to be reduced.[19]

Since (in the view of OCUA) the current funding mechanism did not spell out plainly what the public was obtaining from its investment in universities, the advisory council stated that the government ought to be clearer about what it is purchasing on behalf of the public and the universities ought to be clearer about what they are delivering. The discussion paper then went on to examine alternative approaches to funding. Three funding models were outlined. Model A, a modified version of the then current corridor system, would produce incremental change by removing some of the deterrents to the achievement of policy objectives. Model B, a reversion to the former enrolment-based funding, would be more enrolment sensitive and therefore in a period of enrolment growth more compatible with the government's current accessibility policy. Model C would substitute an entirely new funding mechanism—a "Purchase of Service System"—that would fundamentally change the university-government funding relationship. Under this model, the government would become an active partner with the universities in determining each institution's mission and the balance of its activities among teaching, research and community service.

Although OCUA expressed no preference among the three models, the university community immediately concluded that it favoured Model C, since this option had greatest potential to provide the government with the increased policy flexibility it clearly was desirous of obtaining. Under this model, the funding of teaching would be separated from the funding of research, something OCUA appeared to favour because it would permit shifting the balance of resources to instruction in a period when enrolment was increasing and funds limited. As well, this model could be employed by government to direct universities in accordance with whatever other policy objectives it might have. The chorus of criticism from the university community that greeted the publication of the discussion paper made the already strained relations between COU and OCUA much worse. OCUA was harshly criticized for failing to provide a thorough assessment of future enrolment demand and of the precise nature of the accessibility problem (the alleged crisis on which the need for the review was predicated), for not giving proper consideration to the quality of education, for ignoring graduate education, for prejudging the need to change the balance between teaching and research, and so on and on.[20] The advisory body was also roundly criticized for having abdicated its role as an independent buffer body by aligning itself too closely with the government's interventionist agenda. Considerable hostility and more than a few angry exchanges marked OCUA's subsequent consultations with the university community. Relations between the president of COU and the chair of OCUA became very strained. Relations between the deputy minister, a strong supporter of OCUA in this task, and the president of COU also deteriorated. In this period, COU was not highly regarded by the ministry; nor (partly as a result) was it proving very effective in its advocacy efforts.

Despite severe criticism from the university community, OCUA held its course. In its final report, submitted to the minister in September 1995, the advisory body stated, " council believes that the system of publicly funded legally autonomous universities should be maintained, but that provision for more effective system co-ordination and planning and for government to express the public interest should also be made. It is recommended that this be accomplished primarily through modifications to the funding allocation system and associated policy mechanisms."[21] The new allocation system recommended by OCUA would be cost-based and include negotiated activity levels and outcomes. Instruction would be funded separately from research. There would be system level assessments of societal need to assist in determining the requirement for both new and existing programs in the professional and quasi-professional areas. Program quality reviews would be implemented for all undergraduate academic programs. Transfer of credits for first- and second-year courses among Ontario universities would be mandated as a condition of institutional eligibility for formula funding.[22]

Clearly, adoption of such a set of recommendations would move the yardsticks of autonomy significantly in favour of government. Funding would be altered directly in favour of government objectives. In a period of financial constraint, the funding of additional enrolment in a period of overall restraint would be achieved by reducing provincial support for research. The way would be opened for a multi-tier university system.

Closer relations between the universities and the colleges would be mandated. The university community was outraged. Both COU and OCUFA, and their institutional members joined in a chorus of criticism. By this time, however, the minister and the government that had requested the advice were no longer there. An election had intervened in which the NDP government had been replaced by a Conservative one. OCUA's advice was submitted to a new government with a much different agenda, one focused on reduced public spending and deregulation.

COU characterized the OCUA advice on resource allocation as a relic of the previous government, designed to address an accessibility problem that did not exist. Accepting OCUA's advice, COU said, "would impose new administrative and bureaucratic burdens on both government and the universities at a time when flexibility was what was needed." The operating grants mechanism, council argued, represented "a singularly inappropriate tool" on which to build a new university–government relationship. The new minister was urged to delay indefinitely any major changes to the funding formula on the grounds that replacement of the existing arrangements would be needlessly disruptive. COU called on him "to reject [OCUA's] view of the future of higher education in Ontario and to replace it with a vision of autonomous institutions working in close co-operation with each other and with the Provincial government to create and maintain universities of the highest quality, universities which can play a major role in the economic, social and cultural future of Ontario." (Since) "Ontario universities continue to enhance the self-regulatory accountability framework which maintains the locus of accountability within each institution's board of governors," OCUA's recommendations on credit transfer standards and new accountability criteria should be ignored. Its recommendation that OCUA should undertake reviews to determine societal need for academic programs should be rejected because it would "lead to further bureaucratic controls and a high probability of major planning errors."[23]

At a time when Ontario universities and COU were wrestling with the Rae government over OCUA proposals to impose new regulations on the system, events at the federal level were adversely affecting the financial prospects of all Canadian universities. When the Liberals were returned to power in 1993, the federal government undertook a new approach to social issues. The Employment and Immigration Commission and the Department of the Secretariat of State were dissolved and a new Department of Human Resources Development was created with a strong minister, Lloyd Axworthy. Its mandate was to reconstruct the entire array of federal social programs, including post-secondary education. In October 1994, the minister issued a wide-ranging discussion paper that outlined a major reorganization of the programs that fell under his mandate. The paper proposed cancellation of the post-secondary portion of Established Programmes Funding (EPF) and its replacement by a new, expanded federal student loan program. The heart of this new loan program was to be an income contingency loan repayment plan (ICLRP), a proposal that at the time was being vigorously promoted by AUCC and by COU. Loans would be made available to students without a means test and would be repayable after graduation on a formula based on future earnings.

The ICLRP proposal drew immediate criticism from many quarters. Student leaders considered it a thinly disguised device to ramp up tuition fees. Some universities were concerned about its uneven impact on their institutions. Many questions were raised about how the various provincial governments would react. Some economic projections showed that up to a quarter of student users would never earn enough income to repay their loans. The proposal did not remain long on the federal agenda. It was laid to rest in the February 1995 federal budget, when the federal government decided to give highest priority to drawing down the federal debt and reducing its spending. This budget expanded EPF to include the Canada Assistance Program and renamed the program the Canada Health and Social Transfer (CHST). The new program was given wider scope but less money. In tightening its spending belt, the federal government reduced its contributions to the new CHST. As a result, the Ontario government (as well as the governments of the other provinces and territories) were provided with fewer funds to support their programs in health, welfare, and post-secondary education. As part of the same belt-tightening exercise, the federal government also reduced the budgets of its three federal granting councils (MRC, NSERC, and SSHRC).[24]

● A NEW COMMON SENSE GOVERNMENT

COU and its member universities were heartily relieved to see the end of the interventionist NDP government, but concerned (with justification) over what might come next. While in opposition, in 1992 the PC caucus had issued a policy position on post-secondary education, *New Directions II: A Blueprint for Learning in Ontario*. It contained a clear statement that, if elected, the Tories planned to pursue a smaller role for government both in financing and in university affairs. This was part of the broader platform embodied in the party's Common Sense Revolution that promised smaller government, cuts in public spending, and reduced taxes. For the universities, the blueprint proposed "partnership funding," with students and the private sector joining with government in increasing contributions in a balanced way to restore Ontario's universities and colleges to sound financial health. It foresaw higher tuition fees in combination with an expanded government student loan plan, one that involved an income contingency loan repayment scheme, plus enhanced institutional support for students through scholarships and bursaries. The blueprint presumed additional private-sector support for university research and development activities. The universities were to be encouraged to specialize—for example, in research and graduate studies or in undergraduate work. Public accountability would be enhanced by the introduction of "value-for-money" auditing. Restrictions on the operation of private degree-granting institutions would be lifted, provided these institutions offered programs of acceptable quality, were self-supporting, and focused on "areas of emerging need."[25]

Apart from the proposal that universities specialize, which some members of COU already supported in principle, and the proposal that universities be required to undergo "value-for-money" audits, this approach was consistent with what the COU *Recovery Plan* had proposed in the early months of the Rae government. Accordingly, these ideas resonated well with a good number of university leaders; that is, senior administrators and members of governing boards. Faculty and student leaders and their respective associations—OCUFA and OFS—of course, were almost uniformly opposed. COU was already a strong advocate of higher tuition fees, an income contingency loan repayment plan (ICLRP) and a smaller role for government in university affairs. Having persuaded itself that the universities were now overregulated, COU was preaching less regulation. Once again, "collective autonomy" became a slogan promoted in COU publications and press releases. Unlike its earlier use, however, more emphasis was now laid on the noun rather than on the adjective. In the current circumstances of the universities, COU and its member institutions were much more concerned with protecting their autonomy than they were with pursuing collective action in support of the provincial university system. Apart from issuing their *Election Fact Book*, which outlined the plight of the universities, COU stood on the sidelines during the election campaign (though FOU was active in some ridings). After the election, COU and the universities adopted a wait-and-see attitude toward the new Tory government.

They did not have to wait very long. They soon began to see some things they did not like. In September 1995, the Speech from the Throne opening the legislative session laid down the broad outlines of the new government's policies. Based on the Common Sense Revolution, the government committed itself to reducing the size and scope of its involvement in university affairs. Addressing the Council of Board Chairs of Ontario Universities later that fall, the new minister, John Snobelen was more specific. Snobelen, a rookie MPP and a businessman whose formal educational attainments did not extend beyond secondary school, was already seen as a "heavy hitter" in the new Harris cabinet. "Universities [he told the board chairs], like other educational institutions and the government itself, will have to restructure and rationalize to come to grips with the reality that there is less tax money available, and there will continue to be less tax money available for the foreseeable future. So, when I tell you today to plan for significant additional cuts from both the provincial and the federal government, you should understand that I am talking now about cuts on a scale never seen before in our postsecondary sector. That will mean setting priorities and sticking to them. It will mean living within your means. And planning major change, fundamental change in the way you work. It will mean downsizing, rationalizing, even eliminating in some areas."[26]

The OCUA advisory memorandum on Resource Allocation Review for universities (RAR) was delivered on June 27, 1995, to a government that was less than two weeks old. The government made no official response. The term of the OCUA chair had ended just before the spring election. In September, Stefan Dupré, original chair of OCUA when the buffer body had been reorganized in 1974, was named interim chair. However, several vacancies on the advisory body remained unfilled. On November 30, 1995, the new minister responded to the RAR memorandum, politely rejecting the advice it contained. The minister said that this advice was too complex and would be too disruptive to the universities. Then, he announced his intention to initiate yet another review of post-secondary education in Ontario. The decision to make drastic reductions in government funding of universities, although unannounced, had already been made. Now a lame duck, OCUA's days were numbered.

In its Fiscal and Economic Statement issued in November 1995, the government announced the establishment of a Task Force on Agencies, Boards and Commissions to review the continuing need for some two hundred groups. The following spring (1996), the chair of management board tabled in the legislature a list of agencies that were to be abolished to save money and reduce government bureaucracy. OCUA was included on this list. The university community had not been consulted. Abolition of the advisory body seems to have been recommended by ministry staff without much thought of the possible consequences. Still, no voice was raised in opposition. Meeting shortly after the 1995 election, COU executive heads concluded that OCUA should be retained as an intermediary body, but failed to agree on what functions the advisory body should have. An agency that for more than 20 years had played a key role in the planning and development of the Ontario university system passed from the scene almost completely unnoticed, with neither a bang nor a whimper.

The universities, however, were not to be left alone. Rejecting the option that the government should reduce funding substantially and leave it to the universities to manage the results as best they could, the minister announced his intention to establish a three-person advisory group to begin consultations with universities in January 1996. Working from a discussion paper to be prepared within the ministry, this advisory group would "review and update the policy framework within which [the government] currently makes decisions concerning postsecondary education."[27] The minister proved unable to meet his deadline. Delay in appointing the panel, however, did not affect the government's determination to reduce spending on the universities. An initial cut of 1 percent in operating grants for 1995–96 was followed by the announcement that global operating funds for the year 1996–97 would be cut by an unprecedented 15 percent, a reduction amounting to some $280 million. No provision was made to allow the universities any compensating increase in tuition fees. Capital grants were also reduced by almost $50 million. Staggered by the decision, the universities had no option but to accept it. The new government had a clear mandate to reduce public expenditure; the universities had no leverage.

In July 1966, the minister released the promised discussion paper dealing with universities. At the same time, he announced the establishment of a "blue ribbon committee," the Advisory Panel on Future Directions for Postsecondary Education. It was to be made up of six members and chaired by David Smith, principal emeritus of Queen's University and a former chair of COU.[28] The panel was directed to address three key issues: (1) the most appropriate sharing of costs among students, the private sector, and government, and the ways in which this might best be achieved; (2) ways to promote co-operation between colleges and universities, and between them and the secondary schools, to meet the changing needs of students; and (3) ways to meet expected levels of demand for post-secondary education, with reference to existing public institutions and existing or proposed private institutions. Directed to consult with stakeholders and the general public, the panel was provided with a small research staff and secretarial support, and given five months to complete its task.

The Smith Panel met the minister's deadline. Its report, *Excellence, Accessibility, Responsibility: Report of the Advisory Panel on Future Directions for Post-secondary Education*, was released on December 16, 1996.[29] Judging the basic structure of Ontario's post-secondary sector to be sound, the panel saw no need to impose a grand new design. Current public policy on accessibility—a place in an Ontario post-secondary institution for all qualified students desiring to attend—was reaffirmed, as was the binary divide between universities and CAATs. The existing number of institutions was seen as sufficient for the foreseeable future. Adopting the philosophical approach embodied in the new government's "common sense" program, the panel accepted an ad hoc approach to planning and co-ordination, and proposed a less regulated university system. Its recommendations (it stated) were "based on pragmatism not ideology." The overall thrust of the Smith Report emphasized less regulation, more voluntary differentiation among the institutions, greater accountability, and a large commitment on the part of the private sector and individuals to assist in the provision of the necessary financial resources to the institutions and to students facing financial barriers to access. The panel stated that institutional differentiation, program rationalization, and improved interinstitutional articulation would evolve naturally as increased competition among the institutions forced greater specialization in programs and services. Furthermore, deregulation of fees, in combination with enhanced financial assistance for needy students, would force institutions to become more accountable to students, parents, and private donors, both individual and corporate. This was what the government wanted to hear.

On the level of public funding, the Smith Panel judged that government grants should be comparable to the average for other Canadian provinces, and recommended that this "be achieved by arresting reduction in government grants now and building toward this goal over the next several years."[30] At the same time, the panel proposed that the institutions be given greater freedom in setting tuition fees. If set above the limits established by government, 30 percent of the additional institutional revenues derived therefrom should be distributed by the university for student assistance based on need. It also recommended that the government institute an income contingency loan repayment plan (ICLRP).[31] The panel reaffirmed the appropriateness of the current corridor approach to the allocation of operating grants to the universities, and recommended that a similar system be designed for the CAATs. It did, however, recommend that the system be made more flexible to facilitate short-term adjustments in order to prevent "severe financial penalties" that might be caused by program closures or institutions' decisions to lower their corridor limit. Noting that Ontario was in urgent need of a research policy covering both basic and applied research in the public and private sectors, the panel recommended that the Research Overheads/Infrastructure Envelope in the formula be substantially increased to $100 million per year (from the current $23 million). Although charged to provide advice on the entire post-secondary sector, because of the short time frame given it, most of the panel's analysis and the majority of its recommendations were directed toward the university sector, not the CAAT sector. The proposed change in policy on accessibility—that a place would be available in a post-secondary institution, not necessarily in a university—passed largely unnoticed. The government ministers and their officials had been employing this shift for sometime; now it came into common use.

The approach taken by the Smith Panel was entirely congruent with what COU was advocating for the system. In a paper presented at an OECD (Organization for Economic Co-operation and Development) conference in September 1994, the president of COU, Peter George, outlined Ontario universities' preference for a policy framework with less regulation by government and greater institutional self-regulation. It would involve "an enhanced self-regulatory process, which would include, inter alia, graduate program quality appraisals and undergraduate program reviews, annual institutional accountability reports issued by each university's board of governors aimed at measuring success in meeting institutional mission, and a system-wide performance indicators and outcomes measures report prepared under the auspices of COU.... [These reports] would be subjected to periodic audit by a process to be determined by the Minister of Education and Training and acceptable to the Provincial Auditor."[32] COU also favoured the Smith Panel's recommendation that co-operation between the universities and colleges, including credit transfers, should be developed further, but "with government encouragement rather than with government direction." The Smith Panel's proposals on tuition fees and an income contingency loan repayment plan had for several years been a main plank in COU funding policy, as had the need for more research funding and for an increase in operating grants. The proposal that government funding be increased to meet the national average would now become featured in COU advocacy.

The Smith Panel was heard. Within a week of its report's publication, the government announced that there would be no further cuts to transfer payment levels to post-secondary education. Some weeks later, Professor Smith was retained by the ministry to provide additional advice on the development of a policy framework for research consistent with the recommendations of the panel. It would be another four years, however, before substantial amounts of new funding were provided for university operations, and then much of the new funding was tied to a matching formula that required each university to raise a corresponding amount from the private sector. The universities were permitted to increase tuition fees, but were required to allocate a specified portion of the additional revenue to improve student aid. An income contingency loan repayment plan, although often spoken of with favour by ministry officials, however, has remained a distant possibility.

That said, a corner of sorts was turned. The universities would still have to struggle with the ongoing negative effects of the substantial reductions in public funding—25 percent in operating grants between 1993 and 1996—but at least they knew that the haemorrhaging would cease. For the universities, a glimmer of light appeared at the end of the tunnel. In the new, deregulated environment where the emphasis was on privatization, competition, and voluntarism, the universities were to be given more freedom to raise fees, and encouraged to seek more private support and to compete more with one another. The era of excessive government regulation ended; the universities were left more on their own, with fewer controls and regulations. However, they were by no means left to themselves. By exercising its power over the purse, the new government would manipulate the universities into acceptance of policies that promoted its vision of higher education, a vision much different from the more traditional one in which the Ontario university system had evolved. By astute use of the financial carrot, the new government was able to obtain a shift in academic program and research balance toward the practical and the entrepreneurial.

This new environment was also much more "political." In some respects, the universities now found themselves in the worst of two worlds—not as autonomous as they would like, and not able to count on the support of an intermediary body such as OCUA to argue the case for the long-term interests of a public university system for Ontario. COU was in the middle, committed to protecting institutional autonomy while fostering the commonweal of the system. Moreover, in pursuing its objectives, council was limited by the practical requirement to obtain consensus among its members as a precondition to advocating any specific action. And it had to do so in a new, much more competitive environment—one in which the playing field was tilted in favour of those institutions willing and able to expand programs advocated by the government.

The incoming chair of COU, James Downey, president of the University of Waterloo, clearly identified the new environment. A university system that had been established on the basis of a strong social consensus that higher education was a public good deserving to be generously funded was being transformed into one that emphasized private values. The new government considered education primarily a private good, not a public good. Accordingly, it was moving away from a publicly *supported* university system toward a publicly *assisted* one. In the new "common sense" environment, public investment in universities would be based on the ability of the institutions to produce commensurate and measurable public benefits. At the same time, the private costs of university education (namely, fees) could be expected to become more closely linked to the private benefits the students derived from their investment.[33]

In this environment, individual institutions tended to put their own needs and concerns first. There was a corresponding decline in the priority accorded system issues. With sharply increased competition among the universities for funding and for students, the strong institutions would get stronger and the weak weaker. Enthusiasm and support for common action among the universities on behalf of the collectivity would correspondingly decline. Inevitably, the role of COU was affected.

COU took a pragmatic approach and elected to work with the ministry. Given the government's strong majority and little, if any, public support for the policies earlier promoted by the universities, there was no practical alternative. Council faced a formidable task. The government's program to reduce expenditures, already underway, involved massive cuts in public spending in all sectors and a substantial downsizing of the provincial civil service across all ministries. In this exercise, the Ministry of Education and Training would suffer a reduction in staff of 40 percent. To implement the substantial reduction in public funding to the post-secondary sector, the new minister selected a new team willing to take on the task. The new deputy minister came with no previous administrative experience in education at any level. Among the five new assistant deputy ministers, only one had previous experience in the sector. The ministry's principal focus would be on major reform in the elementary and secondary sectors; the post-secondary sector was not accorded high priority.

COU itself was in a weakened position. Facing its own budget difficulties but determined to maintain advocacy as its highest priority, council had reduced its capacity for research. The turnover of senior secretariat staff, including the president, weakened it further. Council now found itself in a largely reactive stance, responding to ministry initiatives as best it could. From the perspective of the universities, some minor successes were registered. When tuition fees for visa students were deregulated, COU proposals on how this should be done were accepted. When the ministry mandated that a portion of additional revenue derived from increased tuition fees be spent to improve student aid, it accepted COU proposals on how to do it. In 1998, COU President Bonnie Patterson reported to council that she and the chair "had worked in a confidential mode with very senior government officials ... [and that] this had proved challenging and time consuming but worthwhile ...." Some members expressed discomfort at this mode of interaction; however, it was generally agreed that such conditions had to be accepted if council was to advance its agenda.[34]

In 1998, a separate ministry was once again established for the post-secondary sector. To emphasize the importance the government placed on the practical, it was called the Ministry of Training, Colleges and

Universities. Diane Cunningham, a former Conservative opposition critic, was named minister. The new ministry became more proactive. In keeping with government policy, its approach was market-oriented and directed to more intervention in academic programming and research in support of government policies. New capital funding was provided in the form of matching grants; the universities were required to find the additional resources needed to qualify for these funds. New operating grants were restricted to program areas that the government viewed as being of high priority; the universities were forced to compete among one another for these funds. The limit on tuition fees was again raised; in certain academic programs (such as business, law, and medicine, whose graduates could expect high career earnings), the ceiling was lifted entirely. In March 2000, the minister announced that, for the first time, a portion of the operating grants to universities would be performance-based. Beginning in the year 2000–2001, some $16.5 million of these grants would be tied to three performance criteria: institutional graduation rates, graduate employment after six months, and graduate employment after three years. Not all institutions would receive a share. There would be winners and losers. Although this sum was small, 1 percent of the global grant, it remains to be seen how this approach will develop. These carrots, to which some unpalatable conditions have been attached, soon showed that the government could work its will without imposing a plethora of regulations like those that had a short time earlier so incensed the university community. In this new environment, COU, limited almost entirely to exercising a reactive role, fulfills an informal, behind-the-scenes, surrogate advisory role. No mention is made of the effect of this approach on university autonomy.

● UNIVERSITY–COLLEGE RELATIONS

When Ontario's colleges of applied arts and technology were established in the mid-'60s, a deliberate decision was taken to constitute them as distinct from the universities. Basic admission requirements involved four years of secondary schooling at the general level. No CAAT was authorized to offer any university-level courses or programs. Unique in Canada, Ontario's universities and colleges were given distinct and separate missions. Universities were autonomous institutions, each with its own charter; CAATs were organized centrally and governed by a Council of Regents. Despite occasional bursts of rhetoric and a few fitful efforts to develop collaborative activities, the two post-secondary systems evolved largely as two solitudes.

By the mid-'80s, recognition began to grow that the Ontario design of post-secondary education and training needed to be modified to meet the demands of an increasingly knowledge-based economy and the importance of life-long learning. The early '80s had seen two major reviews of the universities (Fisher and Bovey). But no serious study of the CAAT system had been undertaken since the Wright Commission had reported in the early '70s. In the late '80s, government attention was directed to this matter. The ministry and the Council of Regents jointly undertook a comprehensive review of the CAATs. The results of this review were published in 1990. The report, *Vision 2000: Quality and Opportunity: A Summary*, made a strong case for much greater collaboration between the college and university sectors. *Vision 2000* envisioned a future in which "in partnership with schools and universities, the colleges are part of an educational system that offers students the widest possible educational horizons." It recommended that colleges and universities enter into formal bilateral agreements regarding credit transfer and joint programming. A new institute without walls was proposed to facilitate combined college-university activities. Should the universities not be prepared to enter into such agreements, it was recommended that the government itself vest degree-granting authority in the proposed institute.[35]

A report issued that same year by the Ontario Premier's Council, *People and Skills in the New Global Economy*, took the same approach. Also emphasizing the desirability of strengthening relations between the colleges and universities, it proposed a co-ordinating council to deal with system issues across the binary divide: admission requirements, program standards, transfer credits, degree requirements, and the like.[36] Two years later, the ministry struck a Task Force on Advanced Training headed by Walter Pitman, former director of the Ontario Institute for Studies in Education and former president of Ryerson Polytechnical Institute. Its report, *No Dead Ends*, published in April 1993, once more stressed the need to eliminate barriers to intersectoral transfer. It recommended an arm's-length body to advise on credit transfer policy between colleges and universities to facilitate fair, equitable, and consistent transfer arrangements. It also recommended that funding arrangements be modified to facilitate university-college transfer agreements and the development of new, advanced training programs.[37] A year later, the ministry announced its intention to promote greater collaboration between the college and university sectors by the establishment of a voluntary consortium to serve as a promotional/brokering agency. Preoccupied with other problems, however, the intention remained unfulfilled and was lost when the Rae government fell.

At the national level, in his 1991 study of Canadian university education sponsored by the Association of Universities and Colleges of

Canada (AUCC), Stuart Smith, a former leader of the Ontario Liberal Party, identified credit transfer problems from the colleges to universities and between universities as one of the most frequently mentioned issues confronting the universities. He recommended the establishment of a National Council on Credit Transfer under the aegis of the Council of Ministers of Education, Canada (CMEC) and the federal Secretary of State.[38]

The Ontario universities were far from keen to see the establishment of any more co-ordinating agencies, however admirable the cause. Still, they recognized that the time had come to become more heavily involved in reaching across the binary divide. In the late '60s (when it was still the Committee of Presidents of the Universities of Ontario), COU had had a committee on university-CAAT relations, but it had long since ceased to be active. Reorganized in 1988 under the chairmanship of Terry Grier, president of Ryerson, this committee established a closer working relationship with the Association of Colleges of Applied Arts and Technology of Ontario (ACAATO) and the colleges it represented. COU and ACAATO then began together to deal with a growing list of issues of common concern, of which credit transfer was one.

In 1996, the two organizations established the College–University Consortium Council (CUCC), whose purpose was to "facilitate and co-ordinate joint education and training ventures that will: aid the transfer of students from sector to sector; facilitate the creation of joint programs between colleges and universities; and further the development of a more seamless continuum of postsecondary education in Ontario."[39] Funded by the ministry, this consortium was initially given a two-year mandate to promote joint ventures involving education and training, to establish an electronic credit-transfer guide covering Ontario universities and CAATs, and to undertake research on post-secondary student mobility. A year later, CUCC launched the Ontario College–University Transfer Guide on the Web. This guide provides information on credit-transfer policies, articulation and credit transfer agreements, and collaborative programs between Ontario colleges and universities. A further enhancement, completed in September 1999, was a template that enables participating institutions to enter data covering their out-of-province agreements. In an agreement signed in April 1999, the Ontario College–University Degree-Completion Accord sets out a series of principles for developing degree-completion arrangements between the CAATs and universities, and provides a matrix to guide its creation. The mandate of CUCC was later extended for a further one to two years.

As part of its increasing involvement in issues across the binary divide, again under external pressure, COU began to look at prior learning assessment (PLA). In the early '90s, stimulated by *Vision 2000* and other reports that emphasized the importance of lifelong learning and the problems facing adult learners wishing to enter post-secondary schools, the Rae government had mandated the CAATs to develop procedures for the evaluation of students' prior learning as part of the standard intake/admissions process. In 1995, the new government signalled that the universities should take similar action. A number of business and industry leaders and student groups with whom COU had contact through its advocacy activities urged the same thing. As a result, COU set up a Working Group on Prior Learning Assessment, chaired by Claude Lajeunesse, president of Ryerson. The group urged an immediate, more proactive approach. It stated bluntly, albeit correctly, that the universities needed to demonstrate a real commitment to students with relevant work experience and training who sought entry to university. Such action, it was noted, would be one way of countering the decline in part-time enrolment now being experienced by a number of universities; it would make them more competitive with U.S. institutions and the CAATs, which already had PLA programs in place. A small grant from the ministry ($165,000) was provided to assist in the funding of pilot projects and other PLA activities. At its October 1998 meeting, COU endorsed PLA in principle and encouraged member institutions to develop institutional policies as appropriate. A year later, COU and the Office for Partnerships for Advanced Skills (OPAS) were among the sponsors of the National Forum on Prior Learning Assessment, organized by the federal government, at which recent advances in PLA at Ontario universities were highlighted. However, the going has been slow. In program areas where universities are interested in developing partnerships with business or industry, or where enrolment in declining, some progress has been made. But in university programs where enrolment is limited and there is a surplus of qualified applicants, as is the case currently in many professional programs, university interest in PLA remains low—to the continuing detriment of potential students who do not fit the traditional mould.

University credit transfer also became an issue in the 1990s. Traditional notions of academic quality mixed with institutional autonomy had long bedevilled the efforts of those seeking to ease the problems of students moving from one university to another or in changing programs within the same institution. Spurred on by the (Stuart) Smith Report, in 1993 the Council of Ministers of Education, Canada (CMEC) decided to examine this issue. Two years later, in 1995, CMEC issued its Pan-Canadian Protocol on the Transferability of University Credits calling on all degree-granting institutions in the country to implement measures that would provide for a Canada-wide transferability of first- and second-year university courses.[40] Although somewhat late into the game, by this time COU was ready. In 1992, it had adopted a report on university credit transfer prepared by the Ontario Council of Academic Vice-

Presidents (OCAV), which recommended greater consistency among the credit-transfer practices of member institutions.[41] Because of this action, COU was in a good position to respond positively to the CMEC initiative. Council accepted the CMEC protocol and it was implemented across the Ontario university system, effective 1996–97. In 1995, when CMEC announced the protocol, its secretariat was asked to report the following year on the feasibility of extending credit transfer arrangements between colleges and universities. The objective was to extend the protocol to the third and fourth years of undergraduate programming. This has proved to be a much tougher sell among the universities, and to date it remains largely unachieved.

●OTHER ADVOCACY ACTIVITIES

As part of its expanding advocacy activities in the early 1990s, COU strengthened relations with leaders in Canadian business and industry. A Task Force on Labour Force Training and Adjustment was struck. Anticipating the move toward greater privatization in this area, in 1992 a senior staff appointment was made to explore opportunities for strengthening relations between Ontario universities and the private sector in the development of training modules to assist those in the private sector in upgrading staff. This led three years later to the establishment within the COU secretariat of the Office for Partnerships for Advanced Skills (OPAS), a partnership involving all Ontario universities and three key sectors in industry: telecommunications, software, and electrical/electronics. Its mandates: to improve access to all the intellectual resources of the universities as a means of fostering continued learning and upgrading of skills for those in the sectors' workforce; and to promote stronger ties between the industry and university communities. With funding from both the federal and provincial governments plus a modest contribution from COU members, OPAS was established initially for a three-year period. Despite the false starts and frustration that marked the initial period, a review of the program in 1998 concluded that tangible progress has been made, including the generation of useful activities valued at more than $800,000. As a result, approval was given for continuation of the program for a second three-year period, to 2001.

Given the renewal of interest in university-based research that accompanied the evolving emphasis on a "knowledge-based" economy, COU and the Ontario universities expanded their efforts to obtain increased funding for university research. These efforts were focused at both the provincial and federal levels. In Canada, a significant proportion of research, both pure and applied, is undertaken in the universities. Typically, some

40 percent of this research is done in Ontario universities. Because of low levels of funding in the early '90s, investment in university research in Ontario declined. So too, did the proportion of research funding awarded by the three federal granting councils (NSERC, MRC, and SSHRC) to Ontario universities.

While government funding for university research was declining in this period, among some Canadian business and industry leaders, such as those associated with the Corporate-Higher Education Forum (an organization backed by the AUCC and COU), opinion was growing that Canada should be increasing support for R & D and strengthening ties between the universities and the corporate sector in the new "knowledge-based" economy. These views were analogous to those that had fuelled university expansion in the 1960s. This time, however, the focus was on research not on student numbers, and the preferred mode of funding was much different.

To strengthen efforts to obtain increased funding for university research, in 1996 a new council, the Ontario Council on University Research (OCUR), was established and became an affiliate of COU. Composed of the senior administrative officers responsible for research in member universities, its mandate is to promote the importance of university research for Canada's socio-economy and to assist in the development of appropriate research programs. In 1996, in a rare show of solidarity the AUCC (supported by COU) and the CAUT, along with a National Consortium of Scientific and Educational Societies, submitted a brief that called on the federal government to make a substantial increase in federal research spending, including start-up grants for new scholars and support for research infrastructure.[42]

These efforts achieved some success. With its budget deficit now in hand, the federal government decided to increase its commitment to the support of research. It confirmed the mandate of the earlier established Networks of Centres of Excellence, granted that agency permanent status, and increased its funding. One hundred million dollars was added to the budgets of the three federal granting agencies, thereby restoring them to 1994–95 levels. A Canada Foundation for Innovation (CFI) was established and provided with an initial endowment of $800 million. The mandate of this new agency was to invest in research structure in universities and research hospitals to carry out "world class research and technology development" by means of programs that would be funded in part by matching grants from the provinces and territories and from the private sector. In 1998, the federal government introduced the Millennium Scholarships program. Actually a "needs-based" bursary program, it was initially provided with a fund of $285 million to be distributed among the provinces and the territories on the basis of population to assist students to attend university.

In 2000, the federal budget added the Canada Research Chairs program. Nine hundred million dollars was made available to hire 2,000 new faculty at Canadian universities over a five-year period.[43]

Concurrently, similar commitments to the research enterprise were being made by the Ontario government. The Ontario Research and Development Challenge Fund (ORDCF) was established to provide grants in support of research partnerships between the private and public sectors. The spring-1998 provincial budget accelerated $135 million of ORDCF funds over a three-year period to match the initial federal CFI awards. In making the announcement, the treasurer publicly acknowledged the efforts of President George of McMaster and Principal Leggett of Queen's in making the case. Two years later, the Ontario R & D challenge fund was doubled in size to $100 million; the Ontario Innovation Trust was expanded by $500 million to total $750 million; and the Ontario Research Performance Fund was created to support the overhead costs of Ontario-sponsored research in universities, colleges and institutes.[44] COU, through OCUR, played a major role in achieving these improvements. As well, it assisted the ministry in the administration of the Premier's Research Excellence Awards and the Graduate Scholarships in Science and Technology program.

In this area, despite their public disagreements over the adequacy of federal support for post-secondary education through the Canada Health and Social Transfer (CHST), both levels of governments were cooperating in efforts to funnel more funds into research. In so doing, they shared both the objectives and the methods. Forty years earlier, the St. Laurent government decided to provide federal operating grants to all Canadian universities on a per capita basis with no strings attached. This time, however, federal research monies were being targeted on research programs calculated to meet government policy objectives and disbursed on a matching grant basis. By focusing the funds on research (and on student support), areas in which the federal government is seen to have a more legitimate role, these initiatives have in large measure avoided the constitutional arguments that have long bedevilled the Canadian federation. This federal approach was very much in line with the views of the Harris government, which also favoured sharper focus on economic objectives and heavier involvement by the private sector. These contributions eased the financial problems of those Canadian universities, including Ontario universities, that were in a position to take advantage of them. They also changed the dynamics of university–government relations in this country, introducing what Robert Pritchard, the president of the University of Toronto and chair of COU, described as a "new paradigm."[45] The full effects of this new federal involvement have yet to be measured. It will certainly provide for greater institutional differentiation. While the rising tide of research funding will likely raise all boats, those universities with a greater commitment to graduate studies and research, as well as the internal resources to support it, will be the major beneficiaries—as perhaps they should be.

In the late 1990s, the Council of Board Chairs of Ontario Universities established a formal relationship with COU by becoming an affiliate. The COU Office of Health Sciences continued in operation. Although the Secondary School Liaison Office was closed, COU remained heavily involved in the ongoing reform of Ontario secondary school education. The year 1999 saw the completion of the Curriculum Validation Project, an exercise involving more than four hundred university faculty and administrative staff. A joint ministry-council working group continued to plan for the "double cohort" of Ontario secondary school graduates, which was to arrive when the fifth year of secondary schooling finally disappeared in 2002.

●GRADUATE STUDIES AND RESEARCH

In the newer, more flexible environment, COU also revisited graduate studies. Pressured by the "research-intensive" universities desirous of being better recognized for their research strengths, in 1998 COU undertook a review of the Ontario Council on Graduate Studies (OCGS), conducted by external examiners. This review committee was chaired by George Connell, a former president of the University of Western Ontario and of the University of Toronto and a former chair of COU, assisted by four out-of-province members. It focused on the graduate program appraisal process in the context of the changed circumstances affecting graduate studies and research. Initially, this process had been established to determine whether a graduate program met the minimum standard of quality required for eligibility for public funding. Some now argued that the process was failing to meet the requirements of a rapidly changing environment in which different universities had significantly different educational missions. This question was raised: should the appraisal process be augmented to include an assessment above the minimum threshold for those universities desirous of making comparisons with "peer" universities outside the province? Those favouring such augmentation were the larger research-oriented universities, led by the University of Toronto. From the beginning, the committee made it clear that, since the appraisals process was not in a state of crisis, it would not be proposing its termination. It would examine carefully the concerns and criticisms of the stakeholders, and formulate recommendations to ensure the continuing dependability and utility of the process.[46]

In its report, the committee made several proposals to strengthen the appraisal process and to clarify the role of OCGS. It recommended that the definition of "good quality" (in an academic program) be strengthened to place much greater emphasis on the academic substance and vitality of the faculty engaged in the program, and on evidence that the students are growing in academic depth and in the acquisition of relevant skills. Noting significant support for the proposal for augmented appraisals from among the executive heads of the larger universities, it recommended that for those universities wishing it, the appraisals process should provide opportunity to put additional questions to the consultants. Acknowledging that other executive heads and deans were apprehensive that the augmented appraisal could lead to province-wide ranking of programs, the committee urged those universities that sought additional evaluation not to use the results for promotional purposes. After both OCGS and COU accepted the Connell Report, OCGS moved immediately to consideration of the operational features of an "augmented" appraisal. Plans have been made to initiate a number of pilot projects by which possible elements of such an appraisal could be clarified and assessed.[47]

● UNIVERSITY ADMISSIONS REVISITED

With the advent of a new, more competitive environment surrounding university admissions, COU revisited this area in 1996. The Task Force on University Admissions Issues was struck under the chairmanship of William Leggett, principal of Queen's University. Its report, presented to council in March 1998, focused on two areas: the admissions cycle and scholarship policy. The task force recommended major changes in COU policy and practice in both areas. More than two decades earlier, the universities had agreed to a common date in June on which all offers of admission to first year would be issued to secondary school matriculants. In the early '90s, this practice was modified to permit early offers of university admission to applicants being offered prestige scholarships. Under the new policy, universities were free to make an offer of admission to all secondary school applicants after the end of the first semester, i.e., in February, provided the applicant had submitted a completed application form. Furthermore, all other admissions-related elements, including scholarships, other forms of financial assistance and incentives, and offers of residence, were considered as part of the offer of admission. Should the applicant not possess the final OAC grade requirements for admission at the time of application, the offer was to be conditional. Applicants would be free to accept an offer once made. However, they were not to be induced or compelled to sign, and they could not be required to make a decision before the agreed-upon common date in June. These new procedures reversed previous practice that prohibited universities from making offers of admission before the agreed-upon common date. On scholarships, the task force concluded that the earlier COU guidelines, which placed limits on the number and value of undergraduate scholarships and bursaries, were out of date and should be abolished. It recommended that institutions be free to allocate funds for scholarships without restriction or control. The task force expressed a strong lack of interest in developing any form of compliance policy covering admissions and scholarship practices. This was said to be inconsistent with the spirit of a more flexible and deregulated admissions environment, and incompatible with the nature of COU as a voluntary advocacy association. It proposed instead that allegations of institutional non-compliance be reported to the president of COU, who would bring them to the meetings of the executive heads for open discussion.[48] Council's adoption of this report marked the end of an effort, one extending back for more than a quarter century, to regulate the admissions procedures of Ontario universities in order to afford all of them, regardless of their ability/willingness to provide financial and other inducements, the same basic opportunity to attract qualified students. In the new, competitive environment, those universities with the financial ability to provide inducements and the interest in doing so were now given an advantage. Whether or not this change was in the best interests of the system seems not to have been directly addressed.

● ANOTHER LOOK AT COU STRUCTURE

Seizing the opportunity provided by the need to find a new president for council, at the suggestion of its Committee on Policy and Planning, in 1998 COU undertook another review of its structure. The committee noted that the intensity of council's advocacy efforts over the preceding two to three years had caused it to leave aside discussion of some fundamental issues that might otherwise have been faced. The committee also saw that the demise of OCUA had left a "forum [sic] vacuum" in which some important non-monetary issues (for example, the structure of the system, institutional differentiation, and tiering) had gone unexamined. The review was "to consider the major purposes, functions and processes of COU and to look for new or modified roles for COU in light of the disappearance of OCUA, changes in public policy, the evolution of a new role for OUAC, new technologies, etc."[49] Brief in duration, this review was conducted in a workshop format at the February 1998 meeting of council. Organized around the issue of whether Ontario universities constitute a system, with two short papers presenting alternative sides of the case, the review involved a debate of the resolution that, "COU can only [*sic*] work effectively and serve the interests of its own members when it advocates on issues where there is consensus and an explicit agreement to co-operate." The debate was followed by small workshop discussions. At the following meeting of council (April 1998), the chair of the committee, President Ross Paul of Windsor, reported that the workshop had been very constructive. A number of useful suggestions for change had been made, as well as points for further consideration. These were to be brought to the attention of the new president. From the record, it appears that no proposals for significant changes in structure emerged from this review, and no significant changes made.

The thrust of continuing major COU activities may be gleaned from the title of a paper presented by the new president, Ian Clark, to the Oxford University Roundtable on Higher Education in the summer of 1999, *Advocacy, Self-Management, Advice to Government: The Evolving Functions of the Council of Ontario Universities.* In it, Dr. Clark describes council as having three primary functions: advocacy (advancing the cause of higher education, to both the public and the provincial government); self-management (providing common services, promoting best practices, undertaking quality appraisals, and occasionally dealing with issues of resource allocation among member institutions); and providing advice to government (often through joint staff committees).[50]

● MORE DEGREE-GRANTING INSTITUTIONS IN ONTARIO

When the major expansion of higher education occurred in the 1960s, with a few minor exceptions all of the institutions involved were secular, publicly funded institutions. In 1963, Premier Robarts announced that Ontario had enough publicly funded universities and that the government would not issue any more charters. Any new institutions seeking public funds would be required to affiliate with one of Ontario's existing institutions. The Robarts Policy (as it came to be known) remained in force for more than thirty years. Some modifications were made, however, to accommodate changed circumstances. When direct federal grants to universities ended in 1967, the provincial government made provisions for those religiously affiliated institutions that already existed in federation or affiliation with a secular university to be funded at 50 percent of the level provided to the secular institutions (the level at which they had been receiving federal grants). Waterloo Lutheran, which had its own charter, was also provided funding at 50 percent. In 1972, it became secularized as Wilfrid Laurier thereby and became eligible for full provincial funding. One tiny institution, Collège Dominicain in Ottawa, was also granted an exemption, which it retains to this day, and receives 50 percent funding. In the early '70s, Ryerson was granted a limited charter.

In the early '80s, the ministry developed a policy for dealing with the growing number of private bible colleges and other theological institutions desirous of obtaining degree-granting status. The ministry did not oppose the granting of an application for incorporation as long as the institution could demonstrate the support of its religious community, provide evidence of financial viability, agree not to seek public funding, and be willing to confine its academic programs to religious or theologically based curricula leading to a degree with a religious connotation. Under these provisions, Redeemer Reformed Christian College, a liberal arts college belonging to the Dutch Reformed Church, was granted a limited charter, as were a number of bible colleges.

Religiously affiliated institutions, however, were not the only ones interested in being granted the right to offer degree-level academic programs in Ontario. In the early '80s, several out-of-province Canadian universities, interested in providing graduate programs in business and education, applied for the right to operate in Ontario. One of these, the Canadian School of Management—affiliated with Northland Open University, incorporated under the federal Corporation Act and registered in Whitehorse, Yukon (where it had a postal address)—applied to offer degree programs in Ontario. Concerned about the academic quality of the programs offered by this institution, COU intervened. Its formal opposition was largely responsible for the application being withdrawn.

Realizing that it had no power beyond that of ministerial suasion to enforce the Robarts Policy, in 1982 the government passed the Degree-Granting Act. Under the provisions of this act, the term "university" was restricted to institutions so designated by the legislature (namely, secular universities), and a means was provided whereby out-of-province degree-granting institutions might offer degree programs in Ontario, subject to regulation. The act did not prohibit the establishment of new degree-granting institutions in the province; it gave the government the authority to decide on whether and under what conditions a degree-granting institution that did not hold a charter from the government of Ontario would be permitted to offer university degree programs.

When the Degree-Granting Act was promulgated, OCUA accepted the task of administering it on behalf of the government. The advisory body undertook to review the applications against the published terms and regulations, and to advise the minister on whether to grant permission. Most applications were from U.S. institutions offering "niche" programs to teachers on a part-time basis, and most were successful. In 1986, the minister asked OCUA to undertake a policy review of this matter, but pressure of other business prevented the review from going forward until 1988. OCUA issued a discussion paper the following year and invited comments from the university community. In its submission to OCUA, COU took the position that it did not object in principle to granting private institutions the right to grant university degrees in the province so long as two basic conditions were met: (1) the programs offered were of satisfactory academic quality as judged by an appropriate accreditation procedure, and (2) the impact of the operations of these private institutions on the existing publicly funded system was measured and judged not to be unduly negative.[51]

In a lengthy advisory memorandum to the minister in the fall of 1990, OCUA came down strongly in favour of the status quo. Only provincially assisted institutions should be granted independent degree-granting authority and given the right to use the designation "university." No new independent, freestanding secular degree-granting institutions should be established in Ontario until it was clear that public need for such services could no longer be met by the existing institutions. Any other institution desirous of achieving degree-granting status should be required to do so through affiliation with one of the existing publicly funded institutions. The government did not respond to this advice. The memorandum was not released for almost five years, when it was published under the Freedom of Information and Protection of Privacy Access Act.[52]

In the policy paper on post-secondary education issued in 1992, the Conservatives had indicated support for the establishment of private degree-granting institutions in the province. The issue was included in the terms of reference of the Smith Panel. One of its members, Bette Stephenson, a former minister of Colleges and Universities in the Davis government, had become a strong proponent of private universities. In its report, the Smith Panel recommended that "Ontario's policy precluding the establishment of new, privately financed universities be amended to permit, under strict conditions, the establishment of privately financed, not-for-profit universities with the authority to grant degrees with a secular name."[53] The panel laid down strict conditions covering four broad areas: institutional mission and governance structures; institutional and academic quality, as determined by nationally or internationally recognized peer review; financial responsibility; and protection of students in the event of institutional failure. It recommended that the proposed new advisory body be given the task of developing and administering these standards. The Smith Panel also recommended that arrangements for credit transfer and for co-operative program planning between Ontario universities and colleges be encouraged, and that the advisory body be given responsibility for stimulating and monitoring the evolution of such linkages. On the question of extending degree-granting powers to the CAATs, the Smith Panel recommended that the right to award university degrees continue to be the responsibility of the universities at this time. However, it did not rule out the future possibility that a college could transform itself into a polytechnic and from there to a university.[54]

Given the Harris government's openness to private universities, it is not surprising that the number of applications from out-of-province institutions for permission to offer degree programs by ministerial consent under the Degree-Granting Act increased. A number of these applications fell outside the category of "niche" programs intended to meet a temporary need for programs not offered by one of the publicly funded universities. Some were proposals from other Canadian universities to offer programs in partnership with a CAAT. Several involved a plan to establish permanent facilities in the province. In short, the scene was rapidly changing. In response to a request from the ministry for advice on a policy framework to deal with these applications, in 1998 COU established a Task Force on Ministerial Consents with Claude Lajeunesse, president of Ryerson, as chair.

The Lajeunesse Report addressed a range of issues, including the application from Redeemer College for an unrestricted charter, and pressure to provide degree-granting status to some CAATs. It proposed a number of principles to govern the process of Ministerial Consents. The Ontario system should be open and competitive in allowing not-for-profit institutions to apply for degree-granting authority in the province. But all degree programs offered in the province should be required to meet an Ontario university standard of quality. Institutional accreditation is not a sufficient determinant of academic quality. Other institutions seeking collaboration in degree programming in Ontario should consider the existing publicly supported Ontario institutions first. All considerations should involve an assessment of duplication. Proposed new graduate programs should be subject to the OCGS appraisal process. (Since some applicants might consider OCGS a protectionist agency biased against non-member institutions, the task force proposed that a representative of the ministry be added to the appraisal committee as an observer.) Proposed undergraduate programs should be submitted to the Undergraduate Program Review Audit. Ministerial consents should be limited to a period of seven years and any renewal application made subject to a quality review.

The Lajeunesse Report went on to recommend that applicant institutions intending to establish a permanent presence in Ontario should not be allowed to do so under a ministerial consent; they should be required to apply for a private university charter. No institution operating under a ministerial consent or granted a private university charter should be eligible for government operating or capital support. Only not-for-profit private institutions should be given consideration for a charter. Students enrolled in programs offered under ministerial consent or by a private institution should be eligible for OSAP under the same rules as apply to deregulated programs offered in the publicly funded institutions.[55]

Judged by a majority of council members to be a good compromise between openness to changing circumstances and the need to protect the universities, the Report of the Task Force on Ministerial Consents was adopted by COU and forwarded to the ministry. Shortly thereafter, the minister granted Redeemer College, which earlier had been granted the right to award degrees designated by a religious qualification, the right to grant degrees without a denominational classification. COU subsequently rejected Redeemer's application to become a member, stating that membership in COU was restricted to Ontario's publicly funded universities.

In the spring of 2000, Minister Cunningham announced a new policy on degree-granting institutions in Ontario. Ontario was now open for business in the degree-granting sector. Ontario CAATs would be permitted to offer university-level programs and degrees in applied fields. Both not-for-profit and for-profit private degree-granting institutions would be permitted to operate in the province. This new policy, it was stated, would expand the range of choices available to students to acquire knowledge and skills. Cognizant of the need to protect program quality and the financial investment of students, the government would establish a Quality Assessment Board to assess new degree programs proposed by CAATs, by out-of-province public universities, and by private institutions seeking to set up degree programs in the province. The new initiative involving CAATs would begin with a series of five pilot programs that the colleges would propose in the fall of 2000 for implementation in September 2001. The response of COU to this announcement, much muted and containing no substantive criticism, received little attention. As of the time of writing, the proposed Quality Assessment Board has yet to be established and no applications have been processed.

Conclusion

THE PRESIDENTS OF ONTARIO's publicly funded universities created the Council of Ontario Universities (COU) to assist their institutions in meeting the challenge of developing a provincial university system. The principal purpose was to serve the people of the province through the expansion of the universities to meet the growing demand for higher education among the young people of the province, while at the same time preserving the autonomy of their institutions. Although determined to maintain this autonomy, these university heads recognized—as did most members of the university community—the need to increase co-operation and co-ordination among their institutions, and between them and the government that was funding a growing proportion of university costs. Both the universities and the government agreed on the fundamental object: to serve the common good by developing a system of higher education of high quality capable of meeting the needs and desires of a growing population.

By the 1960s, the government of Ontario was beginning to provide a substantial sum to the universities within the province. As a consequence, it developed a significant interest in the activities of these important institutions. Public funding is provided to institutions of higher education because the state has determined that universities are an essential element in the economic, social and cultural well-being of the society it represents and has the responsibility of serving. As the custodian of the common good, the state has a vital interest in what universities do and in how well they do it. This is the basic justification for government's involvement in university affairs. In democratic states, where academic freedom is recognized as an essential element of strong and healthy universities, enlightened governments also recognize, as a corollary, that universities operate more effectively when they are left largely alone to manage their own internal affairs. Accordingly, a considerable degree of institutional autonomy is usually provided.

Notes to the Conclusion are on p. 225

Autonomy is one of those frequently used but seldom precisely defined terms, even in the university community, where it is very common coin. Defined broadly, autonomy as it is applied to the institution refers to the power or right of the university to govern and to manage itself without (undue) external interference or control. All concede, however, that university autonomy is relative, not absolute. There are limits. Moreover, the boundaries are not fixed, but moveable. Over time, these boundaries move when new factors and circumstances come into play. In the case of publicly funded universities, which receive a substantial proportion of their revenues from taxpayers (whether juridically they be state or private institutions), the government has a legitimate interest in exercising a degree of control over them sufficient to ensure that they are fulfilling the purposes for which the funding is being provided, and that they are doing so in an efficient and economical manner. In principle, this is a simple matter of accountability, another commonly used but often poorly defined term. As publicly funded institutions, the universities are accountable to the government, and through the government to the citizens. A fundamental responsibility of the universities is accountability for what they do with the public funds they receive. In return, the government has a correlative responsibility to see that it provides the requisite resources for the universities to fulfil their mandate, and that the institutions are given the degree of autonomy necessary to enable them to fulfil their fundamental missions of research and teaching.

In a democratic society, where universities receive a substantial portion of their revenues from the public purse there is broad agreement on these principles. The devil, however, is in the details—in determining how to develop and maintain the delicate balance between institutional/system accountability and autonomy. The issue is not whether there will be government control or not, but rather whether this control by the legitimate authority—government—will be exercised through means that are appropriately sensitive to the nature of universities. By their very nature, the forms of control exercised by government tend to be clumsy and procedurally complex. Often, they are more a hindrance to good institutional management than a necessary safeguard to the public interest. That said, the universities' defence of their autonomy is sometimes insensitive to the legitimate demands of accountability and reflects an unwillingness to adjust to changing circumstances.

The history of university–government relations in any jurisdiction where universities are publicly funded focuses (inevitably) on an account of the ongoing struggle between the universities and government over where the line that balances university autonomy and accountability is drawn, and how this line of demarcation is maintained. The ongoing tension created by the issue of where to draw this line is a major theme in the history of Ontario universities and of COU during the past four decades. It provides a valid and important measure for any judgment determining council's successes and failures.

The definition of university autonomy most commonly referred to by its Ontario proponents is that articulated by Claude Bissell, president of the University of Toronto, at a time when he was chair of the Committee of Presidents of the Universities of Ontario (CPUO). He described university autonomy as involving three basic freedoms: "the freedom to determine who shall be taught, the freedom to determine what shall be taught, and the freedom to determine who shall teach ... [to which he added a fourth] ... implied in the first three: the freedom to distribute its financial resources as it sees fit."[1] The connection between institutional autonomy and academic freedom in this definition is obvious. Academic freedom and university autonomy are closely related, and most scholars defend university autonomy as an important bulwark of academic freedom. At the same time, most recognize that university autonomy and academic freedom are not identical. Members of a university, both faculty and students, can enjoy a very high degree of academic freedom in a institution that possesses limited autonomy. An example would be a publicly funded state institution where all academic staff are civil servants; where decisions on budgets, faculty appointments, and academic programming are made centrally by a state co-ordinating body or by a governmental department or ministry. Equally, a university can enjoy a high degree of autonomy while placing very real limitations on the academic freedom of faculty and students; For example, in an institution that imposes rigid religious tests on faculty and students.

Although scholars disagree on the precise nature and desirable limits of both academic freedom and university autonomy, with few exceptions all agree that universities operate best when faculty and students enjoy a maximum degree of academic freedom and their institutions are free to determine for themselves how they shall be governed and managed.

The views of the university community on what constitutes the essential requirements of institutional autonomy, however, often differ from those of the government. The government may agree in principle with the universities that they should be left alone to determine who should teach (faculty appointments, promotions, and tenure policies); who should be taught (admission and degree requirements); and what should be taught (program and curricular matters). That said, when faced with complaints that the universities are hiring too many non-citizens, government may be inclined to intervene to enforce "politically correct" appointment policies. When faced with complaints that public policy on

accessibility is being thwarted by too-rigid university admission requirements, requirements that prevent or limit admission of students from
racially or socially disadvantaged backgrounds and prevent or limit easy
transfer between institutions; and that universities are not adequately sensitive to the needs of business and industry for more and better-trained
workers, government is also tempted to intervene. And sometimes does.

For their part, universities generally accept that government is the
final arbiter on the overall level of funding to be provided to a publicly
funded university system. However, the judgments of the universities on
the appropriate level of funding often differ from those of the funder,
particularly when government decisions are based on budget constraints
and conflicting priorities. Moreover, universities prefer to receive public funds in the form of a block grant, since this gives them maximum
flexibility in internal allocation. In principle, they are opposed to targeted
or matching grants, which they see as limiting their autonomy.
Universities are also very sensitive to any efforts by government to determine what academic programs should be expanded or reduced.

Proper respect for academic freedom plus a high degree of institutional autonomy are necessary conditions for a high-quality system of
higher education, but they are not sufficient for the development and
maintenance of a good state university system that includes a large number of separate institutions—as is the case in Ontario. When Ontario
universities faced the unprecedented task of moving from elite to mass
higher education, all parties realized that an unplanned, unco-ordi-
nated development of a system with a number of universities would
likely result in undesirable gaps and overlaps in academic programming.
This would involve less than optimal use of scarce resources, something
clearly not in the public interest. The university president founders of
CPUO clearly recognized the need for better planning. They also recognized, as perhaps their political masters did not at the time, that co-
ordination is not the same as governance. While prepared to do their part
in developing a provincial university system to serve the citizens of the
province, the presidents were determined to maintain as much freedom of action as possible—a maximum degree of autonomy and a minimum of external control—with institutional co-operation and
co-ordination undertaken largely on a voluntary basis. The presidents
envisaged their own voluntary association (CPUO) as the agency to promote the development of a provincial university system through the
exercise of "collective autonomy." The provincial university system would
expand and grow strong as the institutions themselves expanded and
grew strong, with a maximum of institutional freedom to make their
own planning decisions and a minimum of government control and
regulation. Never explicitly articulated, this concept implied that the

good of the system would be the result of the sum of the goods of its individual institutional members.

Although cognizant of the need for improved system planning, the government of Ontario had no clear or fixed notion of how best to go about the task. It was content to have the universities take on the job. Stated in its simplest terms, the Ontario university system has developed on the basis of an informal social contract between the universities and the government. There would be a place in an Ontario university for every citizen of the province who was qualified for admission and who wanted to attend. The universities would provide the places; the government, the financial resources. Despite the problems this policy has presented, some of them major and still unresolved, the system has worked reasonably well.

Despite its heavy involvement in the financing of the system, apart from maintaining ultimate control over the global amount of public funding provided, with some few exceptions the Ontario government has never shown any sustained interest in taking control of this significant public sector. This approach has been described by one thoughtful analyst as "managerialism at the margins."[2] Laws and regulations aimed at improving the institutions' accountability excepted, most interventions by government have taken the form of financial incentives and disincentives ("carrots and sticks"), mainly involving targeted funding in support of specific provincial policy objectives. Government control over the system has been exercised almost exclusively through its use of the power of the purse. No clear public policy statement on the role of universities has ever been articulated. No master plan was developed; none was ever seriously contemplated.

In Ontario, the system planning that has been done has been undertaken by the universities themselves, under the leadership of CPUO/COU, acting in concert with the advisory body (CUA/OCUA) and under the watchful (but seldom very focused) eye of the ministry. The role of government has been largely reactive. Its actions have usually been ad hoc, based on short-term political considerations. For good or ill, the Ontario university system is largely the creation of the universities themselves, managed by CPUO/COU. The universities, through CPUO/COU, provided the engine; the advisory body (CUA/OCUA) assisted with steering; the government provided the fuel and sometimes the brake. When a shortage of fuel developed, more frequent use was made of the brake. Occasionally, more fuel was provided in the form of targeted grants to encourage the universities to move in certain directions.

In the early days, when funds were flowing freely, this approach worked well. The universities, led by CPUO, exercised successful leadership. Important system planning results were achieved. Results, however, were mixed. The government rejected the presidents' initial proposal that all new institutions be affiliated with existing universities. Instead, it established a number of new universities, each with its own charter. While a limit on the number of new institutions was set early, with few exceptions (Erindale and Scarborough colleges, affiliated with the University of Toronto, and Algoma and Nipissing colleges, affiliated with Laurentian University) all of these new institutions were granted charters as "full" universities. No limitations were placed on their degree-granting privileges; each of these universities was given, in law, the "right" to offer the academic programs it chose. In the early '70s when funding was more limited, the smaller universities—Brock, Trent, Lakehead, Laurentian and Wilfrid Laurier—were effectively denied doctoral programs by a decision of government not to provide funding to doctoral programs at these institutions. Moreover, when Ryerson was granted a university charter, it was initially limited to certain academic fields. These limitations, however, are exceptions.

This decision to create all Ontario universities "equal" in terms of their charter rights—one not recommended by CPUO—has had significant consequences. It would serve to preclude any practical possibility of creating a "tiered" university system, such as the ones that developed in many U.S. state jurisdictions. Once created as (full) universities, it would prove very difficult to curb institutional academic ambitions. Moreover, given Ontario's area-based legislature, once a community obtained a local or regional university, political realities would make it very difficult to reduce the scope of any institution's activity, much less to close it. When, as a result of reduced public funding, the planning focus shifted to the need for institutional role differentiation, it would also prove difficult to dissuade institutions from insisting on their right to be a "full-service" university. This early policy decision by government has given Ontario a university system of uniformly high quality, but it has proved costly in financial terms. When comparisons are made with other jurisdictions that chose a tiered university system, there is no clear evidence that "the Ontario way" has led to any readily identifiable greater academic benefits.

Another early proposal of the presidents, one accepted by government, would have an equally far-reaching effect on the provincial system of post-secondary education. Following the advice of CPUO, the government rejected the option of creating in the province a network of junior colleges based on the U.S. model. Instead, it established a new form of post-secondary institution, the college of applied arts and technology (CAAT), one with lesser admission requirements and, as a consequence, no university-level academic programs. This decision, unique among the provincial jurisdictions in Canada, created a binary divide with two separate post-secondary tracks: a university track and a college track. An accompanying decision to establish a centralized governance structure for the new CAATs, with no provision made for bridges to be built between the colleges and the universities, produced a vacuum that more than thirty years later continues to create difficulties. Maintaining this separate college track has disadvantaged several generations of college students who have experienced problems in moving easily across this binary divide.

Other early proposals from the presidents produced more positive results. Despite the furor caused by the recommendation from the Spinks Commission that a graduate University of Ontario be established—an issue that would continue to haunt the corridors of COU—many of the commission's proposals were accepted by both universities and the government. With strong leadership from CPUO and strong support from CUA, the government provided substantial new funding for the expansion of graduate studies and for the development of university library holdings. An operating grants formula was developed jointly and implemented. A centralized admissions process, operated by the universities themselves, was designed and put in place. So too was a protocol covering requirements for enrolment counting and financial reporting. For almost two decades, this agreement constituted the essential accountability requirements for Ontario universities to receive government operating and capital grants. At the provincial level, a tripartite co-ordination structure involving the ministry, CPUO, and the intermediate body (CUA), described as an advanced model of university-government relations, was likewise put in place. The 1960s, which saw strong leadership by CPUO, was marked by many important successes, most of which endured. The pattern of success, however, proved short-lived. With the decrease in public financial support for universities that began in the '70s, the early successes would not be repeated. Neither the degree of universities' leadership nor the level of success in system planning would be achieved again.

As long as voluntary co-operation and co-ordination were taking place within an expansionary environment in which the universities were receiving generous funding, the ambiguities of the government's public policy and the inherent weaknesses of the structure developed for its implementation went largely unnoticed. When the expansionary period ended, however, defects began to emerge. The first effort at system academic-discipline planning, in engineering, proved difficult for COU to handle. The problems encountered by council indicated to both CUA and the government the inherent weaknesses of having system planning undertaken by a voluntary association of autonomous universities. The early and undoubted success of the OCGS graduate program appraisal process was a major COU success story. Its lustre, however, was dimmed by council's inability to develop an acceptable discipline-assessment process and a companion system-planning tool, and later by its abandonment of the effort to do so.

When in the 1970s economic conditions changed and higher education became a lower spending priority for government, new factors came into play. At the same time, the projected continuing expansion of university enrolment failed to materialize. New challenges then faced the system. Realization of the fundamental structural weakness, however, grew slowly. When the draft report of the Wright Commission, issued as a discussion document, was published in 1970, in addition to proposing that a new University Co-ordinating Board be given authority to determine the total size of provincial grants to universities and determine their distribution, the commission proposed that this body be given the power to authorize new university faculties and academic programs, and to discontinue others. COU's response to this proposal was almost apoplectic. Council stated that, if implemented, this would remove from Ontario universities all of the freedoms essential to the idea of the university. The final report of the commission contained a much-modified recommendation on proposed powers for the co-ordinating body.

When the colder economic climate of the 1970s dictated a tighter control on government spending, the focus on co-operation and co-ordination shifted. The need for system stabilization became a major objective. Institutional ambitions now needed to be curbed for the sake of the collectivity. At this point, voluntary planning through the exercise of collective autonomy began to be recognized as inadequate. Pressures developed first in the area of graduate studies. The discipline assessment process developed by CPUO/COU and intended to provide for rational planning in this important (and expensive) area of university activity had only just begun. Alerted by the advisory body (CUA) about impending "overproduction" of doctorates in some areas of the humanities and social sciences, and of the scarcity of Canadians qualified for admission to graduate programs in the hard sciences and engineering, the government imposed an embargo on funding for new graduate programs. Vigorous protests from COU succeeded in having the terms of the embargo relaxed. This signal from the buffer body that perhaps the universities were being unrealistically ambitious in their program planning went largely unnoticed in the universities. The inherent weakness in a voluntary association composed of institutions each with its own vested interests, being asked to make system-level policy decisions was on display. However, it would be some time yet before the full implications of this weakness became clear.

In the mid-'70s, a revitalized advisory body (OCUA) undertook two major tasks. In support of the claims of COU that the government was providing inadequate funding to enable them to fulfil their mandate, OCUA undertook the task of putting a price tag on public policy affecting accessibility to university education. At the same time, the intermediary body began a careful analysis of graduate programming in Ontario. The results of this analysis led OCUA to develop a set of criteria for the funding of new graduate programs, one that included non-academic considerations. Did the proposed program meet a current need? Was this need sufficient to warrant these programs being funded when global funding was constrained? Was the university proposing the new program a suitable institution for such a program? These questions were addressed to COU. Council found them exceedingly difficult to answer, since the answers involved making judgments about its member institutions. After review and debate, COU decided that such non-academic issues were inappropriate for a voluntary association of member universities to address. This led to the decision that COU should vacate the field of graduate planning, except for academic program appraisal, and leave this responsibility to OCUA. A little later, COU ceded analogous responsibility for undergraduate program planning to OCUA, but only after failing to support proposals from its own Committee on Long-Range Planning (the [Percy] Smith Committee), which had recommended putting some teeth in the undergraduate program planning process.

During this period, from the late '70s through the early '80s (the era of the Fisher Committee and the Bovey Commission), both COU and OCUA acknowledged the need for greater co-ordination and co-operation to improve system program planning. However, in Gaston-and-Alfonse fashion, each proposed that the other take on greater responsibility for the task. In the end, COU withdrew and left the task to OCUA. When this occurred, it became increasingly clear that the advisory body too lacked the requisite strength to succeed.

No effort was made by government to change a system structure that many now conceded was inadequate to the task. Given the financial circumstances, fewer new academic programs were being put forward by the universities for funding approval. At this juncture, what was needed was consolidation and retrenchment—a focus on employing steadily diminishing funding to maintain academic programs of high quality and to expand interuniversity co-ordination and co-operation to do so. However, little interinstitutional co-ordination took place, and no serious effort was made by any university to close any programs that were academically weak or for which there was insufficient enrolment to support the program on the operating grants formula. At the undergraduate level, institutions remained entirely free to make programming decisions. Obvious programming duplication and gaps remained. No system of academic quality control was introduced.

In its presentation to the government that led to the decision to strike the Fisher Committee, COU argued that the operating grants formula presented a major problem in dealing with system issues; but, unable to agree on how the formula should be amended, council offered no constructive proposals. Council argued strongly that inadequate public funding had begun to jeopardize academic program quality. The argument proved not to be credible with either the government or the public, in part because no agreed-upon measures of quality were in place. Despite claims of deteriorating quality, without providing any persuasive evidence in support of this claim, it was apparent to any knowledgeable observer that the universities were continuing to enrol more students and to expand their academic programming. In the eyes of the government, faced with many claims on public funds, as long as students were finding a place, its accessibility policy remained viable. By the mid-'80s, the little system planning that was being done was undertaken by OCUA. The advisory body, however, lacked the required resources or sufficient clout with either the government or the universities to be effective. The result was a continuing lack of any real effort to pursue system program planning. During this period, COU continued to be active in other areas—such as applications for admission to university, instructional development, athletics, and health sciences—where interuniversity co-operation was strengthened and expanded to the benefit of both the institutions and the system. Here, council continued to lead. For the most part, however, these were second-order issues.

When the new Liberal government was elected in 1985, COU sought to regain the initiative on long-range planning and on formula revision. Unable yet again to obtain member agreement on how to proceed, council quickly abandoned the exercise. A reality check undertaken by external consultants revealed how little support the universities enjoyed among the power brokers in the government or with the public. This provided a jolt to COU. The main result, however, was a decision to devote more resources to advocacy. This had a positive short-term effect. Funding was increased. To the annoyance of the universities, however, most of the new money was targeted to identified government priorities, and OCUA became the manager of the distribution of these targeted funds. By the end of the '80s, as a result of a combination of circumstances and factors, many of which were outside its control, COU found itself in a largely responsive, defensive mode. No longer was it seen as the proactive leader of Ontario universities.

The environment worsened during the Rae government years. The agenda of this new, populist government was soon forcing the universities once more to do more with less. At the same time, a host of new government regulations was seen as impinging further on university autonomy. Another major review of the university sector, this one directed by OCUA, was begun. Pressures from government to improve accessibility and accountability collided with the requirements of autonomy. COU now found itself very much on the defensive, advocating vigorously for greater freedom on fees to offset the inadequate level of government grants, while protesting vigorously against the wave of new regulations that inhibited the universities' freedom to manage their own affairs. For example, government decisions on the composition of university governing boards, which in the '60s had been successfully opposed by CPUO as an unacceptable violation of university autonomy, in the early '90s were accepted without a murmur. In the rising din, rhetoric aside, neither party paid much attention to system planning or to declining academic quality.

In the mid-'90s, the advent of the common sense revolution, with its promise of fewer regulations, greater institutional freedom, and more competition, was regarded favourably by most members of COU, including the leadership. Despite the evidence, some members around the council table harboured the hope that things might improve. After assuming power, one of the first decisions of the Harris government affecting the universities was to set aside the recently received OCUA recommendations for a more centrally controlled and regulated university system. This decision was welcomed by COU. Much less welcome was the decision that came soon thereafter to reduce operating grants to universities by 15 percent. The universities were to be given more freedom, at least ostensibly; but they were now much poorer.

Following the recommendations of the Smith Panel, supported by COU, the new minister once again spoke of system planning to be undertaken on a largely voluntary basis, led by the universities themselves. This was mostly rhetoric. Financial resources were in short supply; the government was preoccupied with issues in elementary and secondary education and in the health care sector. Neither the ministry nor COU possessed the staff resources required for planning. Moreover, with the abolition of OCUA, a key element in the planning structure was removed, leaving the universities directly facing the government.

Facing up to these considerably changed circumstances, COU undertook to establish a closer relationship with the ministry in order to assist in managing the system, a role it had long criticized OCUA for accepting. There was little choice. Were COU not involved on behalf of the universities, it was feared that an insensitive government with little knowledge of or respect for the system would be left alone to work its will. Council, however, remained in a mainly reactive mode. Few, if any, of the current policy issues were being driven by COU. Of necessity, its role was limited: advocacy, provision of common services, promoting best practices, providing advice to government, and occasionally dealing with issues of resource management among member institutions. At the same time, while consensus among member institutions was always sought and frequently achieved, within council the older, larger, and stronger institutions—those in a better position to "go it alone"—tended to dominate the debates. With competition among the universities now a major factor, in a group that had long struggled to provide equal opportunity among its members, the stronger became "more equal" than the rest. Around the council table, there was little discussion about the negative implications on autonomy, institutional and collective, of the growing use by governments of matching grants and their inevitable steering effects on management decisions.

As the 1990s came to a close, COU once again found itself in the midst of system planning for the anticipated massive expansion in Ontario university enrolment. In a report published in March 1999, *Ontario Students, Ontario's Future,* a synthesis based on research undertaken by Pricewaterhouse Coopers, an independent consultant, council projected an increase of some 90,000 students over the first decade of the twenty-first century.[3] The projected increase would be fuelled by the combined impact of three factors: (1) a double cohort of secondary school graduates, produced by the result of a decision made two decades earlier, but only now being implemented, to abolish the fifth year of Ontario secondary schooling; (2) an increase in the size of the 18- to 24-year-old cohort, caused by the "baby boom echo"; and (3) a continuing rise in the university participation rate, already one of the highest in the world. Together, they were projected to produce an overall increase in university enrolment of some 40 percent.

The problems posed by such an increase are similar to those faced by the university system in the early '60s. Given the current aging faculty profile and anticipated retirements, handling the increased volume was projected to require some 13,500 new academic staff, a number greater than the current total faculty complement. The stock of aging physical plant would require renovation and new equipment; additional physical facilities would have to be built and equipped. For this, substantial additional revenues would be needed. Significant amounts were being provided under the Ontario Super Build Program (a matching grant program) to fund capital renewal, and some modest increases in base operating grants have been made. But much more was needed. COU has estimated a need for an additional $455 million in government operating support during the five-year period 2000 to 2005. And this did not include additional funding in support of university research.

In this new environment, COU continued to play an important role. The changed circumstance are aptly illustrated by two working groups, one on university capacity, the other on university research, each of which was given major responsibility for developing system plans. The president of COU was named co-chair of each. For the university capacity group, the group dealing with the issues surrounding the double cohort, the other co-chair was the assistant deputy minister of Training, Colleges and Universities. For the university research group, it was the deputy minister of Engineering, Science and Technology. The universities, through COU, are certainly directly involved in these important system planning exercises.[4] However, the university–government relationship here is not one of equal partners. Nor does there seem to be much discussion about the adverse effects on university autonomy that may result.

In their willingness to accept the funding that they need in order to expand enrolment and research activities, the universities have implicitly accepted the current definitions of accountability used by governments to justify their economic focus and their use of targeted funding to achieve their objectives. This has moved the institutional autonomy yardsticks well beyond what would have been accepted by the universities and COU at an earlier time. The new concept of the "entrepreneurial university" is transforming Ontario universities from "public utilities" into institutions essentially committed to the promotion of private goods as defined by governments in the interest of promoting economic well-being. In this much more competitive environment, with much less emphasis on interinstitutional co-operation, the research-intensive universities, with their large graduate schools and generous support for research, enjoy a competitive advantage over the smaller, largely undergraduate sister institutions.

Nor is COU in as strong a position as was its predecessor, CPUO, in the early '60s. The prospects for a voluntary association of universities leading a successful campaign to strengthen the university system are not nearly as good now. When higher education is no longer considered by government to be a public good, but essentially a private one, factors promoting a strong system are not regarded as important as those calculated to maximize institutional strengths. As the twenty-first century opened, public investment in Ontario universities had become calculated on the basis of the universities' ability to produce measurable benefits, the most important of which are economic ones. Council's estimate of the amount of the additional required provincial government funding was now based on a projected revenue mix of 55 percent from government grants, 35 percent from tuition fee revenue, and 10 percent from other university resources. This is roughly the same revenue mix obtained in the immediate post-World War II period, prior to the expansion in the '60s. For the government, the expanded system that has been projected will not be a public one, generously funded because of a strong consensus that higher education is an important public good. It will be one that largely ignores the traditional role of universities in research and teaching, and in developing the intellectual, social, and cultural capital of the people. While COU continues to maintain its efforts to develop an academically sound and socially responsive provincial university system, the association lacks the strength it had in former times. Yet despite its present weaknesses, with strong leadership council may succeed in meeting and overcoming these formidable challenges. The next chapter of the history of the Council of Ontario Universities will record the results.

 Notes

INTRODUCTION

1 For an account of the early history of Ontario's universities, see W.G. Fleming, *Ontario's Educative Society IV: Post-secondary and Adult Education* (Toronto: University of Toronto Press, 1971). See also Robin Harris, *A History of Higher Education in Canada 1663-1960* (Toronto: University of Toronto Press, 1976).

  For an account of the role of government in the evolution of Ontario universities prior to the period covered here, see Edward E. Stewart, "The Role of the Provincial Government in the Development of the Universities of Ontario, 1791-1964" (unpublished doctoral thesis, University of Toronto, 1970).

  For a good account of the "political economy of higher education" in Ontario in the period following World War II, see Paul Axelrod, *Scholars and Dollars: Politics, Economics and the Universities of Ontario, 1945-1980* (Toronto: University of Toronto Press, 1982).

2 For a description of the U.S. scene at the time, see Robert O. Berdahl, *Statewide Coordination of Higher Education* (Washington, DC: American Council on Education, 1971).

  For a full and penetrating account of the role played by the University Grants Committee in the management of British universities, see Michael Shattock, *The UCG and the Management of British Universities* (Buckingham: Society for Research into Higher Education and Open University Press, 1994).

  For an excellent, comprehensive account of how the provinces handled university–government relations in Canada, see David Cameron, *More Than an Academic Question: Universities, Government, and Public Policy* in Canada (Halifax: The Institute for Research on Public Policy, 1991.)

1
ESTABLISHING A FIRM FOUNDATION

1 *From the Sixties to the Seventies* (Toronto: Committee of Presidents of the Universities of Ontario, 1966), 16.

2 Ontario, Legislative Assembly, Debates (February 25, 1959), 611 (J.N. Allen).

3 Ontario Department of Education, news release, November 18, 1960, in *Scholars and Dollars*, by Paul Axelrod, 92.

4 *Post-Secondary Education in Ontario, 1962-1970*: Report of the Committee of Presidents of the Universities of Ontario to the Advisory Committee on University Affairs (Toronto: May 1962, revised January 1963, 4-5.

213

5 Ibid., 6.

6 Ibid., 20–21.

7 Minutes of the Committee of Presidents of the Provincially-Assisted Universities of Ontario, July 3, 1962, 1–2. For more details, see 30ff.

8 *The Structure of Post-Secondary Education in Ontario*, Supplementary Report No.1. (Toronto: Committee of Presidents of Provincially-Assisted Universities and Colleges of Ontario, June 1963), 19.

9 Minutes of the Meeting of November 25,1963. Committee of Presidents of the Provincially–Assisted Universities of Ontario, Appendix A.

10 William G. Davis, "The Government of Ontario and the Universities of the Province," in *Governments and the University* (Toronto: York University Press, 1966), 33.

11 Ibid.

12 *Variations on a Theme*: Fourth Annual Review, 1969–70 (Toronto: Committee of Presidents of the Universities of Ontario, 1970), 6.

13 *The Learning Society*: Report of the Commission on Post-Secondary Education in Ontario (Toronto: Queen's Printer, 1972), Terms of Reference, iii.

14 *Post-Secondary Education in Ontario 1962–1970*: Report of the Committee of Presidents of the Universities of Ontario to the Advisory Committee on University Affairs (Toronto, May 1962, revised January 1963), 20.

15 *Development of Graduate Programmes in Ontario Universities*: Report of the Commission of the Provincially–Assisted Universities of Ontario to the Committee on University Affairs and the Committee of Presidents (Toronto: 1966), iii.

16 Ibid., 77.

17 Minutes of the Meeting to Study the Development of Graduate Programmes in Ontario Universities, Committee of Presidents of the Provincially-Assisted Universities of Ontario, September 29, 1966, #11, 9.

18 *The First Three Years of Appraisal of Graduate Programmes* (Toronto: Committee of Presidents of the Universities of Ontario, 1970), 9–10.

19 *Ontario Council on University Affairs Thirteenth Annual Report 1986–87*. Report to the Ontario Council on University Affairs on an Assessment of the Appraisals Process, Advisory Memorandum 86–III, 82.

20 *Review of the Ontario Council on Graduate Studies*: Report of the Review Committee (Toronto: April 5, 1999), 3.

21 *Collective Autonomy*: Second Annual Review 1967–1968 of the Committee of Presidents of the Universities of Ontario (Toronto: 1968), Appendix D, 62.

22 Robin Mathews and James Steele, eds., *The Struggle for Canadian Universities* (Toronto: New Press, 1969.)

See also Robin Mathews and James Steele, "The Universities and the Takeover of the Mind," in *Close the 49th Parallel*, ed. I. Lumsden (Toronto: University of Toronto Press, 1970), Robin Mathews, Brief to CUA, "The Graduate Department of English, University of Toronto: A Study in Cringing Colonialism." Archives of Ontario, CUA files, RG–32; and Ontario, Legislative Assembly, *Debates* (November 25, 1969), (Stephen Lewis).

23 *Variations on a Theme*, 52–53.

This was not the first time a government in Canada expressed the view that universities in this country should be staffed by Canadians. In 1936, President Cody of the University of Toronto wrote the federal Ministry of Immigration and Colonization requesting that a British national be admitted to Canada in order to take up a faculty position in the Department of Mathematics of the university. While granting the request, the deputy minister made it clear that the ministry expected that "it will not be necessary to use in the future any but Canadian-born instructors in the Department of Mathematics." J. Magladery, deputy minister of Immigration and Colonization, to President Cody of the University of Toronto, July 10 1936, in *Henry John Cody: An Outstanding Life*, by D.C. Masters (Toronto: Dundurn Press, 1995), 212.

24 *Financing Higher Education in Canada*: Report of a Commission to the Association of Universities and Colleges of Canada (Toronto: University of Toronto Press, 1965).

25 William G. Davis, minister of University Affairs, statement in the Ontario legislature when presenting "Estimates of the Department of University Affairs" (mimeograph, June 6, 1967), 13.

26 *The Learning Society*, 141–42, Recommendation 110, 201.

27 For a comprehensive account of the development of the operating grants formula, see Paul Stenton, "The Ontario University Operating Grants Formula: Its Development to 1986" (unpublished doctoral thesis, University of Toronto, 1992).

   See also Edward J. Monahan, "The Allocation of Financial Support by Formula: The Experience of Ontario," *Minerva* 27, 3 (1988): 347–66.

28 *System Emerging*: First Annual Review (1966–67) of the Committee of Presidents of the Universities of Ontario (Toronto: 1967), Appendix B, 46.

29 Minutes of the Committee of Presidents of the Provincially-Assisted Universities of Ontario; June 16–17, 1966, # 6 b) I), 6.

30 James Duff, and R.O. Berdahl, *University Government in Canada*. Report of the Commission sponsored by the Canadian Association of University Teachers and the Association of Universities and Colleges of Canada (Toronto: University of Toronto Press, 1966).

31 *Student Participation in University Government*: Study Paper prepared for the Committee of Presidents of the Universities of Ontario by its Sub-Committee on Research and Planning (Toronto: 1968).

   In his memoirs, Robin Ross, registrar of the University of Toronto and a member of the committee, writes: "It [the Duff-Berdahl report] achieved almost the same lack of respect among our [U of T] students as did the report of the Ontario Universities' Sub-Committee on Research called *Student Participation in University Government*. I admit to writing part of that report, which rapidly became known as the 'Grey Flannel Report.' I had thought that we expressed almost perilously advanced views in our study!" (Robin Ross, *The Short Road Down: A University Changes* (Toronto: University of Toronto Press, 1984), 35.

32 Minutes of the Committee of Presidents of the Provincially-Assisted Universities of Ontario, January 3–4, 1968, #2.1, 3.

33 *Proposal for Establishing a Council of Universities of Ontario:* Campus and Forum Third Annual Review, 1968–69 (Toronto: Committee of Presidents of the Universities of Ontario, 1969), Appendix E, 64–73.

   When the report was presented, the association was called a "confederation." During the course of the debate, this was changed to "council." (See Minutes of February 7, 1969, # 3.)

34 *University Television:* Supplementary Report No. 3 (Toronto: Committee of Presidents of Provincially Assisted Universities and Colleges of Ontario, 1965).

35 *Variations on a Theme:* Fourth Annual Review, 1969–70 (Toronto: Committee of Presidents of Universities of Ontario, 1970), 24–29.

36 A.P. Gordon, "Ontario Universities' Application Centre." A proposal for the establishment of a central clearinghouse for applications for admission to the universities of Ontario (Toronto: 1965.)

37 *Living and Learning*: Report of the Provincial Commission on the Aims and Objectives of Education in the Schools of Ontario (Toronto, 1968).

38 *Report of the Minister's Committee on the Training of Elementary School Teachers* (Chair: C.R. MacLeod) (Toronto: Ontario Department of Education, 1966).

39 *Financing University Programs in Education*: Report on the Special Study of Requirements of the Formula Financing of Education Programs in Ontario Universities (Toronto: CUA/COU Joint Subcommittee on Finance/Operating Grants, released December 1970, revised for publication March 1971).

2
THE WINDS SHIFT: DARK CLOUDS BEGIN TO FORM

1 *Variations on a Theme*: Fourth Annual Review (1969–70) of the Committee of Presidents of the Universities of Ontario (Toronto: 1970), 5–6.

2 Ontario, Legislative Assembly, Budget Speech, March 12, 1968, 11.

3 Ontario, Legislative Assembly, *Debates* (November 25, 1969), 8859.

4 David Dodge, *Returns to Investment in University Training: The Case of Accountants, Engineers and Scientists* (Kingston: Queen's University Press, 1971). See also David Dodge and David Stager, "Economic Returns to Graduate Study in Science, Engineering and Business," *Canadian Journal of Economics* 2 (May 1972): 195–98.

5 William G. Davis to Charles MacNaughton, January 8, 1970. In *Scholars and Dollars*, by Paul Axelrod, 159–60.

6 *Stimulus and Response:* Sixth Annual Review (1971–72). (Toronto: Council of Ontario Universities, 1972), 4–5.

7 CPUO and the Council of Ontario Deans of Engineering, *Ring of Iron: A Study of Engineering Education in Ontario* (Toronto: Ontario Department of University Affairs, 1970).

8 Ibid., 61.

9 Ibid., 66.

10 Minutes of the Committee of Presidents of the Universities of Ontario, April 16 1971, #4, 6.

11 CPUO Committee on Research and Planning, *Towards 2000: The Future of Post-Secondary Education in Ontario* (Toronto: McClelland and Stewart, 1971).

12 *Participatory Planning:* Fifth Annual Review (1970–71) (Toronto: Council of Ontario Universities, 1971), 10–11.

13 Minutes of the Council of Ontario Universities, June 11, 1971, #4, 5–6.

14 Minutes of the Council of Ontario Universities, January 7, 1972, #12.1, 10.

15 *Draft Report of the Commission on Post-Secondary Education in Ontario.* (Toronto: Queen's Printer, 1971).

16 *Stimulus and Response*, 8.

17 Ibid., 12.

18 Ibid.

19 *The Learning Society*: Report of the Commission on Post-Secondary Education in Ontario (Toronto: Queen's Printer, 1972).

20 Ibid., 107. This judgment likely reflects the firmly held view of Dr. Wright, based on his experience as chair of CUA when confronting the position of Treasury Board on global funding in the early 1970s.

21 Ibid., 111–112.

22 *New Structure, New Environment*: Review of 1972–73 to 1974–75. (Toronto: Council of Ontario Universities, 1976), 3.

23 William G. Davis, interview by Diana Royce, April 16, 1997: "there was a recognition that we were really developing a system that would become somewhat centralized, and there, the committee, if it had executive powers, would … run into the possibility of encroaching on institutional and academic freedom. I think there was sufficient understanding on the part of universities, that without doing this bit of legislation, we could build greater discipline in by paying more attention to advice of the committee …. I think … that, in many respects, that happened … the decision was made very simply in a recognition that once you went down the path of giving executive responsibility … knowing how these creatures take on a life of their own, that would have become a very dominant institution, and I think, might have impacted in a negative sense, not economically, but in terms of the functioning of the institutions, I look back and I don't second guess that decision."

   In Diana M. Royce, *University System Co-ordination and Planning in Ontario 1945 to 1996* (unpublished doctoral thesis, Ontario Institute for Studies in Education of the University of Toronto, 1998), 138.

24 See Benson A. Wilson, "UAD and URB: An idiosyncratic set of recollections and observations about the activities the University Affairs Division and the University Relations Branch, 1974–84" (mimeograph, n.d.), 5–6.

   "There had been a number of discussions and meetings about the information needs of the Ministry in order to fulfil its accountability to the House and the public at large. The universities felt quite strongly that the government had no business prescribing information to be provided to it. Such a requirement would be an intrusion on academic freedom and autonomy; the discussions broke down. When the legislation authorizing the establishment of the Ontario Council on University Affairs was introduced, it contained a clause requiring the universities to provide certain statistical information upon request of the government. This power actually existed under the Statistics Act, but its inclusion in the OCUA legislation seemed to confirm the further intrusion of the government in university autonomy and triggered university-induced opposition to this clause in the house."

25 *An Uncertain Future*: Review of 1975–76 to 1977–78 (Toronto: Council of Ontario Universities, 1978), 10.

26 Minutes of the Council of Ontario Universities, July 19, 1973, #4.2, 21.

27 Minutes of the Council of Ontario Universities, October 5–6, 1973, #4.2, 21.

28 In December 1972, Jim Parr, chair of OCUA, had written the executive director of COU expressing concern that the universities were failing to implement COU resolutions, remarking that this was a test of university self-discipline and "a valuable barometer." (See Minutes of the Council of Ontario Universities, December 1, 1972, #8.3, 9.) During this same period, Douglas Wright, former chair of OCUA and then chair of the Commission on Post-Secondary Education in Ontario, responded to COU criticisms about the suggestion in the Commission's recently issued *Draft Report* that the university buffer body be

given extensive executive authority: "Multi-lateral decision-making [by the universities] does not reveal attractive results *except* under duress. Alex Corry convened all university department heads to make the case for voluntary co-operation years ago. Nothing much happened until the University Affairs Committee dropped the [funding] embargo. I can only conclude that some external influence is required for excellence." Douglas Wright to COU, March 10, 1972.

29 *Ontario Council on University Affairs Second Annual Report, 1975–76.* Advisory Memorandum 75–IV, 31.

30 Ibid.

31 James A.C. Auld, minister of Colleges and Universities, to the Ontario Council on University Affairs, July 22, 1975, 2–4.

32 Ibid.

33 *Ontario Council on University Affairs Second Annual Report, 1975–76.* Advisory Memorandum 75–V, 36.

34 Harold B. Stewart, *The Development of Graduate Studies in Ontario Universities between 1960 and 1985* (Toronto: Council of Ontario Universities, 1988), 33.

35 *Ontario Council on University Affairs Fourth Annual Report, 1977–78.* Advisory Memorandum 77–VII, 56.

36 Bette Stephenson to the university presidents, in *Squeezing the Triangle*: Review of 1978–79 to 1981–82 (Toronto: Council of Ontario Universities, 1982), 14.

37 *The Learning Society*, 141–142.

38 Minutes of the Council of Ontario Universities, March 1, 1974, #4.3, 6.

Earlier, in 1972, at his first meeting with COU, the new minister, Jack McNie (himself a former advertising executive), "raised his concern that universities may become overly competitive in the coming year, and place too great an emphasis on advertising and public relations. The universities must be very responsible in this; internecine warfare could result in public backlash against the universities." Minutes of the Council of Ontario Universities, November 3, 1972, #3, 4.

39 See Paul Axelrod, *Scholars and Dollars*, 160–161.

40 *An Uncertain Future*: Review of 1975–76 to 1977–78, (Toronto: Council of Ontario Universities 1978).

41 *Ontario Council on University Affairs Second Annual Report, 1975–76.* Advisory Memorandum 76–VII, 51.

42 This is an excellent example illustrating the point that enrolment projecting is a far from scientific exercise. In 1975, the chief projectionist at Statistics Canada wrote, "18-to-24 year-olds constitute about 80% of full-time post-secondary enrolment, and the enrolment rate is about 20%. That rate is not expected to rise until the end of the century." Demographic projections indicated that the size of this cohort would increase slightly, to peak in 1982, slightly above 1975 levels, then drop until 1991 (to reach the 1964 level) before again increasing. See Zoltan Zsigmond, *Population and Enrolment Trends 1961–2001: The Canadian Case* (Ottawa: Statistics Canada, 1975), 31.

The COU Research Division agreed. Enrolment in Ontario universities followed this track for several years, until a sharp increase in the participation rate of females and post-25 year olds confounded the experts. Only a small minority of demographers, of whom David Foote was one, disagreed. See David Foote. "A Troubled Future? University Enrolments in Canada and the Provinces," in

Financing Canadian Universities: For Whom and By Whom?, ed. David M. Nowlan and Richard Bellaire (Toronto: OISE Press, 1981), 37–63.

43 *The Ten O'Clock Scholar: What a Professor Does for His Pay* (Toronto: Council of Ontario Universities, 1972).

Joint COU–OCUFA Study of Early Retirement Options: interim report. Minutes of the Council of Ontario Universities, March 1, 1974, 8.

Joint COU–OCUFA Committee on Academic Career Development Report. *The Ivory Tower and the Crystal Ball* (Toronto: Council of Ontario Universities, 1976). Minutes of September 6, 1976, #3, 4, Appendix 3.

44 For the report from the COU Executive Committee on the work of the Joint Committee on Two-tier Bargaining, see minutes of the Council of Ontario Universities, January 30, 1976, #13, 10. See also, David Cameron, *More Than an Academic Question*, 351–353.

45 Minutes of the Council of Ontario Universities, 17 February, 1978, #4.5, 4.

46 *An Uncertain Future*, 19.

47 *Variations on a Theme*: Fourth Annual Review (1969–70) (Toronto: Committee of Presidents of the Universities of Ontario, 1970), 28.

48 Minutes of the Council of Ontario Universities, May 5, 1972, Appendix 5.12.

49 A beneficial by-product for COU of the construction of the Robarts Library was that the secretariat became located there. During construction, costs exceeded the original estimates twice. On both occasions, the university went back to the government requesting an increase in the capital grant allocated for the project. The ministry agreed. However, the second time, arguing that the building was intended to serve as a provincial resource, a portion of the total floor space (18,000 square feet) was designated provincial space, and the capital allocations of the other universities were discounted pro rata. A portion of this space was then provided to COU to house the secretariat. This arrangement, which some considered to have been agreed to in perpetuity, lasted until 1988, when the University of Toronto required the space to expand the library.

50 "A Proposal for the Establishment of a Co-operative Library System for the Ontario Universities," (working paper, 1973). See also *New Structure, New Environment*: Review of 1972–73 to 1974–75 (Toronto: Council of Ontario Universities, 1976), 24–29.

51 Bernard Trotter, *Television and Technology in University Teaching* (Toronto: Committee of Presidents of the Universities of Ontario, 1970).

52 *New Structure, New Environment*, 36.

53 In his memoirs, the then executive director of COU, John B. Macdonald, records his experience when, with the chair of council, President Carl Williams of UWO, they appeared before the committee. "Our presentation did not satisfy the committee. Some were out for blood. The question was put: will you provide the committee with a breakdown of data by university and by department? ... My reply was, 'No Sir. I was unable to release such data.' The room was briefly silent and I was uncertain how the committee would react. Quiet grumbling followed and the meeting drew to a close without further incident." John B. Macdonald, *Chances and Choices: A Memoir* (Vancouver: University of British Columbia and the Alumni Association of UBC, 2001), 34.

54 *An Uncertain Future*, 34.

55 Thomas H.B. Symons and James E. Page, *Some Questions of Balance: Human Resources, Higher Education and Canadian Studies*, Vol. 3 (Ottawa: Association of

Universities and Colleges of Canada, 1984). See review by Edward J. Monahan in *University Affairs* (March 1984).

56 Minutes of the Council of Ontario Universities, January 30, 1976, # 6.3, 5.

57 *Squeezing the Triangle*: Review of 1978–79 to 1981–82, (Toronto: Council of Ontario Universities, 1982), 21.

58 *The Present State of the Ontario University System.* Minutes of the Council of Ontario Universities, April 21, 1978, Appendix 2.A.

59 Minutes of the Council of Ontario Universities, September 22, 1978, #3.3, 3. Minutes of the Council of Ontario Universities, November 3, 1978, #4.3, 3. Minutes of the Council of Ontario Universities, March 14, 1980, # 4, 5–6, Appendix 4. Minutes of the Council of Ontario Universities, January 29, 1982, #6.1, 6–7.

60 *Stabilization of the Ontario University System.* Minutes of the Council of Ontario Universities, April 21, 1978, Appendix 2.B.

61 Minutes of the Council of Ontario Universities, September 22, 1978, Appendix 2.A.

62 Minutes of the Council of Ontario Universities, November 3, 1978, #3.2 and 3.3, 4–6.

63 *The Ontario University System: A Statement of Issues.* Ontario Council on University Affairs Fifth Annual Report, 1978–79, 9–53.

64 Minutes of the Council of Ontario Universities, March 9, 1979, #2.2, 3.

65 *Squeezing the Triangle*, 23, 25.

3
THE WEATHER WORSENS

1 *Squeezing the Triangle*, Review of 1978–79 to 1981–82, Council of Ontario Universities (Toronto: 1982).

2 *System on the Brink: A Financial Analysis of the Ontario University System 1979*: Ontario Council on University Affairs Sixth Annual Report, 1979–80, 9–41. *System Rationalization: A Responsibility and An Opportunity.* Ontario Council on University Affairs Seventh Annual Report, 1980–81, 43–106.

3 *Report of the Special Committee on Provincial Support for University Research.* Minutes of the Council of Ontario Universities, March 14, 1980, Appendix 5.

4 Committee on Long-Range Planning of the Council of Ontario Universities, *Challenge of Substance: A Report on Undergraduate Programmes in Ontario Universities* (Toronto: Council of Ontario Universities, 1980), 26.

5 Ibid. See *Report from the Special Committee to Assess University Policies and Plans* (Toronto: Council of Ontario Universities, 1976).

6 *The First Essential:* A Report on Faculty by the Committee on Long-Range Planning, 8. Minutes of the Council of Ontario Universities, September 19, 1980, Appendix 5.

7 Ontario Council on University Affairs' Letter to Executive Heads concerning 1978 Briefs to OCUA, October 7, 1977. Fourth Annual Report 1977–78, 13.

8 *System on the Brink*, Introduction, 9.

9 *System Rationalization: A Responsibility and an Opportunity.* Ontario Council on University Affairs Seventh Annual Report, 1980–81, 45.

10 Minutes of the Council of Ontario Universities, September 13, 1980. #6, 7–8.

11 *Ontario Council on University Affairs Ninth Annual Report, 1982–83.* Advisory Memorandum 82-VII, 102.

12 Minutes of the Council of Ontario Universities, March 13, 1981, Appendix 8 *Final Report of the Special Committee to Review Graduate Planning.*
  See also Minutes of the Council of Ontario Universities, June 17, 1981, # 2.1, 2.2, 3.
  See also COU Circuletter 3000, June 26, 1981, Appendix 2.1. D.
13 *Ontario Council on University Affairs Thirteenth Annual Report, 1986–87.* Advisory Memorandum 86–III. *Report to the Ontario Council on University Affairs on an Assessment of the* OCGS *Appraisals Process,* 82.
14 David Cameron, *More Than an Academic Question,* 23.
15 Harold B. Stewart, *The Development of Graduate Studies in Ontario Universities between 1960 and 1985* (Toronto: Council of Ontario Universities, 1988) 45.
16 Minutes of the Council of Ontario Universities, March 13, 1981, # 2, 3, and Appendix 2.
17 Minutes of the Council of Ontario Universities, December 19, 1980, *The Situation of the Ontario Universities,* Appendix 2.
18 Ibid., 16–17.
19 Ibid., 26.
20 Ontario, Legislative Assembly, *Hansard* (November 18, 1980).
  In addition to the chair, Harry Fisher, the other members of the committee were R.J. Butler, G.E. Connell, J.S. Dupré, M.L.Hamilton, G.A. Harrower, A.R. Marchment, M.S. Paikin, M.L. Pilkington, R.P. Riggin, R.L. Watts, B.A. Wilson and W.C. Winegard. R.L. Cummins (MCU) served as secretary and E.J. Monahan (COU) as a resource person. Connell, Harrower, and Watts were members of COU; Hamilton, Paikin, Pilkington, Riggin, and Winegard were members of OCUA. Dupré was a former chair of OCUA; Marchment, a university board chair; Butler, the secretary of Management Board; and Wilson, assistant deputy minister at MCU. Given the broadly representative character of the Committee, the minister always referred to it by its formal name and objected to it being called the Fisher Committee.
21 "Brief to the Committee on the Future Role of Universities in Ontario" (Toronto: Council of Ontario Universities, 1980), 41–42.
22 *Report of the Committee on the Future Role of Universities in Ontario* (Toronto: Ministry of Colleges and Universities, July 1981).
33 Ibid., 43–44.
24 Diana M. Royce, "University System Coordination and Planning in Ontario 1945 to 1996," 163–164.
25 *Once More, with Feeling:* COU Brief to OCUA (Toronto: Spring 1982), 19.
26 *Federal–Provincial Relations and Support for Universities* (Toronto: Council of Ontario Universities, February 1982).
27 "When a provincial government is criticized for inadequate support, it responds that the federal government reduced the money for post-secondary education through the 1982, 1984 and 1986 amendments to the legislation. When the federal government is criticized for reducing the money, it replies that the provinces are not spending it on education anyway." Canada, Senate, Standing Committee on National Finance, *Federal Policy on Post-Secondary Education* (Ottawa: Ministry of Supply and Services, 1987), 32–33.
28 Minutes of the Council of Ontario Universities, December 18, 1981, # 6, 7.
29 *Bottoming Out:* Review of 1982–83 to 1985–86 (Toronto: Council of Ontario Universities, 1986), 2.

30 Ibid., 3.

31 Minutes of the Council of Ontario Universities, December 18, 1981, Appendix 5.2.

32 *Ontario Universities: Options and Futures,* The Commission on the Future Development of the Universities of Ontario (Toronto: Ministry of Colleges and Universities, December 1984), Terms of Reference.

33 Ibid., 14.

34 Minutes of the Council of Ontario Universities, May 21, 1985, #2.1, 3.

35 See *Status of Women in Provincially-Assisted Ontario Universities and Related Institutions, 1986–87 to 1995–96* (Toronto: Council of Ontario Universities, 1998).

36 Minutes of the Council of Ontario Universities, April 19, 1985, #2.1, 3.

37 Minutes of the Council of Ontario Universities, December 6, 1985, #3.2, 9–10.

38 Minutes of the Council of Ontario Universities, September 27, 1985, #3, 6.

39 Minutes of the Council of Ontario Universities, December 6, 1985, PAM *Interim Report to the Council of Ontario Universities,* Appendix 3.3.

40 Michael L. Skolnik, and Norman S. Rowen, *"Please, sir, I want some more": Canadian Universities and Financial Restraint* (Toronto: OISE Press, The Ontario Institute for Studies in Education, 1984), 143. See also 87.

Michael L. Skolnik, "If the cuts are so deep, where is the blood?" *The Review of Higher Education* 9, 4 (Summer 1986): 435–55.

41 Ontario, Legislative Assembly, *Debates and Proceedings,* April 22 1986, 4.

42 Minutes of the Council of Ontario Universities, May 28, 1986, Appendix 2.6.

43 Minutes of the Council of Ontario Universities, January 19–20, 1986, #1, 3–4.

44 Minutes of the Council of Ontario Universities, October 20, 1987, #3.1, 3–4.

45 Minutes of the Council of Ontario Universities, October 6, 1989, #4, 6–7.

46 *Report of the Committee to Review the Role and Structure of the Council of Ontario Universities.* Minutes of the Council of Ontario Universities, May 23, 1990, Appendix 3.B.

47 Ibid., 5.

48 Minutes of the Council of Ontario Universities, February 26, 1988, #4.2.

49 John O. Stubbs, *The Report of the External Advisor to the Minister of Colleges and Universities on the Future Role and Function of the Ontario Council on University Affairs and Its Academic Advisory Committee* (Toronto: Ministry of Colleges and Universities, 1988), passim, 17–18.

50 Minutes of the Council of Ontario Universities, December 12, 1986, #2.2.

51 Minutes of the Council of Ontario Universities, February 8, 1991, Appendix 9.A.

4
COMES THE DELUGE

1 Minutes of the Council of Ontario Universities, November 26, 1990, 5.

2 Minutes of the Council of Ontario Universities, May 21, 1991, #2.1, 3.

3 Minutes of the Council of Ontario Universities, December 9, 1988, #3, 4.

4 Minutes of the Council of Ontario Universities, February 9, 1996, 8.

5 Minutes of the Council of Ontario Universities, May 19, 1992, Appendix 4.2A.

6 Minutes of the Council of Ontario Universities, April 9, 1999, Appendix 10.B.

7 Minutes of the Council of Ontario Universities, May 19, 1994, #5, 6.

8 Minutes of the Council of Ontario Universities, April 5, 1991, #2.2, 3.

9 Besides the chair, the Task Force was composed of individuals nominated by COU (four), the Council of Board Chairs of Ontario Universities (two), OCUFA

(one), OCUA (one), the Council of Ontario University Staff Associations (one), the Ontario Federation of Students (one), the Ontario Graduate Association (one) and the ministry. The review was limited to individual universities. See *University Accountability: A Strengthened Framework*: Report of the Task Force on University Accountability (Toronto: May 1993), 16.

"Given the broad mandate, initially there was some question about whether the Task Force should focus on the accountability of individual universities (institutional accountability) or on 'system' accountability. This matter was clarified by the Minister in an early meeting with the Task Force at which he emphasized that the group should focus on accountability at the institutional level. Following this meeting the mandate of the Task Force, as clarified, was described in a letter from the Chair to the Minister, a copy of which is included in Appendix B."

10 Minutes of the Council of Ontario Universities, December 6, 1991, #4.1, 4.

11 Open letter to the members of the Ontario University Community and other interested persons (October 30, 1992), 1.

12 *University Accountability: A Strengthened Framework*: Report of the Task Force on University Accountability (Toronto: May 1993), 6.2, 74.

13 *Ontario Council on University Affairs Twentieth Annual Report, 1993–94*. Advisory Memorandum 93–VI, Academic Quality Reviews (Toronto: December 1994), 246.

14 *University Accountability*: Report of the Task Force of the Council of Senior Administrative Officers, Universities of Ontario (Toronto: Council of Ontario Universities, November 29, 1988).

15 For a critique of the task force recommendation that a new agency be established to monitor university accountability, see Michael Skolnik, "University Accountability in the Nineties: Is There a Role for a Provincial Agency?" *Ontario Journal of Higher Education* (1994): 108–27.

See also, Stefan Dupré, "When Does Accountability Become Accountabilitis?" Address to the Queen's University Board of Trustees, mimeograph, November 11, 1994.

16 Memorandum from Dave Cooke, minister of Education and Training, to executive heads and chairs of the governing boards/councils of the provincially assisted universities, Ontario College of Art, and Ontario Institute for Studies in Education. Re: Creation of an Education Quality and Accountability Office (February 17, 1995).

17 *Higher Education in Ontario: The Face of Leadership*: Annual Review, 1994 (Toronto: Council of Ontario Universities, 1994), 11–12.

18 Dave Cooke, minister of Education and Training, to Prof. Joy Cohnstaedt, chair of the Ontario Council on University Affairs (November 24, 1993).

19 *Sustaining Quality in Changing Times Funding: Ontario Universities*. Ontario Council on University Affairs 21st Annual Report, 1994–95 (Toronto: 1995), 71–119.

20 *Higher Education in Ontario: The Face of Leadership*. Council of Ontario Universities Annual Review, 1994 (Toronto: Council of Ontario Universities, 1995), 3.

For a more extended account of the debate, see the analysis by Michael Skolnik, "Upsetting the Balance: The Debate on Proposals for Radically Altering the Relationship Between Universities and Government in Ontario," *Ontario Journal of Higher Education*, 1995: 2–14.

21 *Ontario Council on University Affairs 22nd Annual Report 1995–96.* Advisory Memorandum 95–III, Resource Allocation for Ontario Universities (June 1995), 23.

22 Ibid., p. 24.

23 Bonnie Patterson, president, Council of Ontario Universities, to John Snobelen, minister of Education and Training (September 20, 1995), Attachment: "Submission to the Minister of Education and Training on the OCUA" Advisory Memorandum 95–III, 1.

24 See David M. Cameron, "The Federal Perspective," in *Higher Education in Canada: Different Systems, Different Perspectives,* ed. Glenn A. Jones (New York: Garland, 1997), 9–29.

25 *New Directions Volume Two: A Blueprint for Learning in Ontario,* Ontario Progressive Conservative Caucus, October 1992, 24.

26 Remarks by the Hon. John Snobelen, minister of Education and Training, Ontario, to the board chairs of Ontario universities (November 8, 1995).

27 Ibid.

28 In addition to the chair, David Smith, the Advisory Panel included Bette Stephenson, a former minister of Colleges and Universities in the Davis government; Fred W. Gorbet, senior vice-president of Manulife Financial and a former federal deputy minister of Finance; Catherine Henderson, president of Centennial College; and David Cameron, chair of the Department of Political Science, Dalhousie University, Halifax, and a member of both the Nova Scotia Council on Higher Education and the Maritimes Higher Education Commission.

29 *Excellence, Accessibility, Responsibility:* Report of the Advisory Panel on Future Directions for Post-secondary Education (Toronto: Queen's Printer, 1996).

30 Ibid., Recommendation 2, 27.

31 Ibid., Recommendations 6 and 7, 34.

32 Peter J. George and James A. McAllister, *The Expanding Role of the State in Canadian Universities: Can University Autonomy and Accountability Be Reconciled?* Discussion Series, Issue 3 (Toronto: Council of Ontario Universities, September 1994), 14.

33 *Responding to the Challenges of Change, 1995–1996 Review* (Toronto: Council of Ontario Universities, 1996), 4.

34 Minutes of the Council of Ontario Universities, February 1, 1998, #2, 3.

35 *Vision 2000: Quality and Opportunity: A Summary* (Toronto: Ministry of Colleges and Universities, 1990), 21.

36 *People and Skills in the New Global Economy,* Premier's Council of Ontario (Toronto: Queen's Printer, 1990), 80.

37 *No Dead Ends:* Report of the Task Force on Advanced Training to the Minister of Education and Training (Toronto: Ministry of Education and Training, April 30, 1993), 3–4.

38 Stuart L. Smith, *Report of the Commission of Inquiry on Canadian University Education* (Ottawa: Association of Universities and Colleges of Canada, September 1991), 7.

39 *Statement of Agreement/Mission Statement.* College–University Consortium Council 1996, 3.

40 *Pan-Canadian Protocol on the Transferability of University Credits,* Council of Ministers of Education, Canada (February 7, 1995), 1.

41 Donald Baker, *Transfer of Undergraduate Course Credits among Ontario Universities: Report and Recommendations* (Toronto: Council of Ontario Universities, 1992).

42 "Putting Knowledge to Work: Sustaining Canada as an Innovative Society—An Action Agenda." Brief by the Association of Universities and Colleges of Canada, the Canadian Association of University Teachers, and the National Consortium of Scientific and Educational Societies (Ottawa: AUCC, October 18, 1996).

43 See the *Canada Foundation for Innovation* Web site, www.innovation.ca; the *Millennium Scholarships* Web site, www.millenniumscholarships.ca; and Canada Research Chairs, *Program Guide* (Ottawa: Canada Research Chairs, 2001).

44 *Council of Ontario Universities Biennial Report 1996-1998.* (Toronto: Council of Ontario Universities, 1998), 11-13. *Council of Ontario Universities Biennial Report,* 1998-2000 (Toronto: Council of Ontario Universities, 2000), 15, 18.

45 J. Robert S. Pritchard, "Federal Support for Higher Education and Research in Canada: The New Paradigm." 2000 Killam Lecture, Toronto, 2000.

46 *Review of the Ontario Council on Graduate Studies:* Report of the Review Committee (Toronto: Council of Ontario Universities, April 5 1999), 3.

47 Minutes of the Council of Ontario Universities, May 28, 1999, Appendix 12.

48 Minutes of the Council of Ontario Universities, April 24, 1998, Appendix 6. Final Report of the COU Task Force on Admissions Issues.

49 Minutes of the Council of Ontario Universities, February 20, 1998, Appendix 5.

50 Ian D. Clark, *Advocacy, Self-Management, Advice to Government: The Evolving Functions of the Council of Ontario Universities* (Toronto: Council of Ontario Universities, 1999, revised November 30, 1999).

51 Minutes of the Council of Ontario Universities, May 24, 1989, Report of the Special Committee on Degree Granting Institutions in Ontario, Appendix 4.C.

52 *Ontario Council on University Affairs 22nd Annual Report, 1995-96.* Advisory Memorandum 90–VI: A Policy Recommendation on Freestanding, Secular Degree-Granting Institutions in Ontario (Toronto: 1996), 243-273.

53 *Excellence, Accessibility, Responsibility.* Recommendation 18, 60.

54 Ibid.

55 Minutes of the Council of Ontario Universities, October 23, 1998, Appendix 8.

CONCLUSION

1 Claude T. Bissell, "The Independence of Universities," in *The Strength of the University* (Toronto: University of Toronto Press, 1968), 236.

For an excellent overview of the policy issues involved in working out the complex interrelationships between academic freedom, autonomy, and accountability, one that includes a select bibliography, see Task Force on Resource Allocation, *Some Perspectives on Academic Freedom, Autonomy and Accountability* (background paper) (Toronto: Ontario Council on University Affairs, 1995).

2 Glenn A. Jones, "Higher Education Policy in Ontario," in *Higher Education Policy: An International Comparative Perspective,* ed. L. Geodebuure et al. (Oxford: Pergamon Press, 1994), 234.

3 *Ontario's Students, Ontario's Future* (Toronto: Council of Ontario Universities, 1999).

4 *Biennial Review 1998-2000* (Toronto: Council of Ontario Universities, 2001), 8-21 and 29-30.

# Select Bibliography

Advisory Panel on Future Directions for Postsecondary Education. *Excellence, Accessibility, Responsibility*. Report of the Advisory Panel on Future Directions for Postsecondary Education. Toronto: Queen's Printer, 1996. (David Smith Report).

Allen, Richard. Open Letter (from the Minister) to the Members of the Ontario University Community and Other Interested Persons. October 30, 1991. Ministry of Colleges and Universities, Toronto.

Association of Universities and Colleges of Canada. *Financing Higher Education in Canada*. Report of a commission to the Association of Universities and Colleges of Canada. Toronto: University of Toronto Press, 1965. (Bladen Report).

Axelrod, Paul. *Scholars and Dollars: Politics, Economics and the Universities of Ontario 1945-1980*. Toronto: University of Toronto Press, 1982.

Baker, Donald. *Transfer of Undergraduate Course Credits among Ontario Universities: Report and Recommendations*. Toronto: Council of Ontario Universities, 1992.

Beard, Patrick. *The Ontario Council on University Affairs*. Toronto: Ontario Council on University Affairs, 1983.

Berdahl, Robert O. *Statewide Coordination of Higher Education*. Washington DC: American Council on Education, 1971.

———. "System-Wide Decision-Making." In *Critical Issues Facing Ontario Universities*. Toronto: Higher Education Group, Ontario Institute for Studies in Education, 1980.

Bissell, Claude T. *The Strength of the University*. Toronto: University of Toronto Press, 1968.

Cameron, David. *More Than an Academic Question: Universities, Government, and Public Policy in Canada*. Halifax: The Institute for Research in Public Policy, 1991.

———. "The Federal Perspective." In *Higher Education in Canada: Different Systems, Different Perspectives*. Ed. Glenn A. Jones. New York: Garland, 1997.

Clark, Burton. *Creating Entrepreneurial Universities: Organizational Pathways of Transformation*. Oxford: Pergamon Press, for the International Association of Universities, 1998.

Clark, Ian D. *Advocacy, Self-Management, Advice to Government: The Evolving Functions of the Council of Ontario Universities.* Toronto: Council of Ontario Universities, 1999.

Commission on Post-Secondary Education in Ontario. *Draft Report.* Toronto: Queen's Printer, 1971. (Wright Report).

———. *The Learning Society: Report of the Commission on Post-Secondary Education in Ontario.* Toronto: Queen's Printer, 1972. (Wright-Davis Report).

Committee of Presidents of Provincially-Assisted Universities of Ontario. *Post-Secondary Education in Ontario, 1962–1970.* Report of the Presidents of the Universities of Ontario to the Advisory Committee on University Affairs. Toronto: May 1962, revised January 1963. (Deutsch Report).

———. *The Structure of Post-Secondary Education in Ontario.* Supplementary Report No. 1 of the Committee of Presidents of Provincially-Assisted Universities and Colleges of Ontario. Toronto: June 1963.

———. *The City College.* Supplementary Report No. 2 of the Committee of Presidents of Provincially-Assisted Universities and Colleges of Ontario. Toronto: February 1965.

———. *University Television.* Supplementary Report No. 3 of the Committee of Presidents of Provincially-Assisted Universities and Colleges of Ontario. Toronto: June 1965.

———. *Development of Graduate Programmes in Ontario Universities.* Report of a Commission to the Committee on University Affairs and the Committee of Presidents of Provincially-Assisted Universities of Ontario. Toronto, 1966. (Spinks Report).

Committee of Presidents of the Universities of Ontario. *From the Sixties to the Seventies.* An Appraisal of Higher Education in Ontario by the Research Committee of the Committee of Presidents of the Universities of Ontario. Toronto: June 1966.

———. *System Emerging.* First Annual Review (1966–67) of the Committee of Presidents of the Universities of Ontario. Toronto: 1967.

———. *Collective Autonomy.* Second Annual Review (1967–68) of the Committee of Presidents of the Universities of Ontario. Toronto: 1968.

———. *Student Participation in University Government.* Study paper prepared for the Committee of Presidents of the Universities of Ontario by its Sub-Committee on Research and Planning. Toronto: 1968.

———. *Campus and Forum.* Third Annual Review (1968–69) of the Committee of Presidents of Universities of Ontario. Toronto: 1969.

———. *Variations on a Theme.* Fourth Annual Review (1969–70) of the Committee of Presidents of the Universities of Ontario. Toronto: 1970.

———. *The First Three Years of Appraisal of Graduate Programmes.* Toronto: Committee of Presidents of the Universities of Ontario, 1970.

———. *Ring of Iron: A Study of Engineering Education in Ontario.* Toronto: Committee of Presidents of the Universities of Ontario, 1970.

———. *Towards 2000: The Future of Post-Secondary Education in Ontario.* Report prepared for the Committee of Presidents of the Universities of Ontario by its Sub-Committee on Research and Planning. Toronto: McClelland and Stewart, 1971.

Committee on the Future Role of Universities in Ontario. *The Challenge of the '80s: Preliminary Report of the Committee on the Future Role of Ontario Universities.* Toronto: Ministry of Colleges and Universities, February 1981.

————. *The Report of the Committee on the Future Role of Ontario Universities.* Toronto: Ministry of Colleges and Universities, July 1981. (Fisher Report).

Committee on University Affairs. *Report of the Committee on University Affairs, 1967.* Toronto: Queen's Printer, 1967.

————. *Biennial Report of the Committee on University Affairs.* Toronto: Queen's Printer, 1972.

————. *Report of the Committee on University Affairs of Ontario, 1972-73, 1973-74.* Toronto: Ministry of Colleges and Universities, 1974.

Cook, Dave. Open Letter (from the minister) to the Members of the Ontario University Community and Other Interested Persons. November 24, 1993. Toronto: Ministry of Colleges and Universities.

Corry, J.A. *Farewell the Ivory Tower.* Montreal: McGill-Queen's University Press, 1967.

Council of Ontario Universities. *Financing University Programs in Education.* Report on the Special Study of Requirements for Formula Funding of Education in Ontario Universities. CUA/COU Joint Sub-committee on Finance/Operating Grants. Toronto: released December 1970, revised for publication March 1971.

————. *Participatory Planning.* Fifth Annual Review, 1970-71. Toronto: Council of Ontario Universities, 1971.

————. *The Ten O'Clock Scholar: What a Professor Does for His Pay.* Toronto: Council of Ontario Universities, 1972.

————. *Stimulus and Response.* Sixth Annual Review, 1971-72. Toronto: Council of Ontario Universities, 1972.

————. *New Structure, New Environment.* Review, 1972-73 to 1974-75. Toronto: Council of Ontario Universities, 1975.

————. *The Ivory Tower and the Crystal Ball.* Report of the Joint COU–OCUFA Committee on the Study of Academic Career Development. Toronto: Council of Ontario Universities, 1976.

————. *Report of the Special Committee to Assess University Policies and Plans.* Toronto: Council of Ontario Universities, 1976. (Guindon Report).

————. *An Uncertain Future.* Review, 1975-76 to 1977-78. Toronto: Council of Ontario Universities, 1978.

————. *Brief to the Committee on the Future Role of Universities in Ontario.* Toronto: Council of Ontario Universities, 1980.

————. *Challenge of Substance: A Report on Undergraduate Programmes in Ontario Universities.* By the Committee on Long-Range Planning of the Council of Ontario Universities. Toronto: 1980. (Percy Smith Report).

————. *Numbers in the Clouds: A Discussion of Enrolment Problems for the 1980s.* By the Committee on Long-Range Planning of the Council of Ontario Universities. Toronto: Council of Ontario Universities, 1980.

————. *Report of the Special Committee on Provincial Support for University Research.* Toronto: Council of Ontario Universities, 1980. (Ham Report).

————. *Report of the Special Committee to Review Graduate Planning.* Toronto: Council of Ontario Universities, 1981. (Forster Report).

————. *Federal-Provincial Relations and Support for Universities.* Toronto: Council of Ontario Universities, 1982.

————. *Once More, with Feeling.* Brief to the Ontario Council on University Affairs. Toronto: Council of Ontario Universities, 1982.

————. *Squeezing the Triangle.* Review, 1978-79 to 1981-82. Toronto: Council of Ontario Universities, 1982.

————. *Response to the Report of the Bovey Commission—Ontario Universities: Options and Futures.* Toronto: Council of Ontario Universities, 1985.

————. *Bottoming Out.* Review, 1982-83 to 1985-86. Toronto: Council of Ontario Universities, 1986.

————. *Report of the Special Committee on Degree-Granting Institutions in Ontario.* Toronto: Council of Ontario Universities, 1989. (Lee Report).

————. *University Accountability.* Report of the Task Force of the Council of Senior Administrative Officers—Universities of Ontario. Toronto: Council of Ontario Universities, 1988.

————. *Higher Education in Ontario: The Face of Leadership.* COU Annual Review, 1994. Toronto: Council of Ontario Universities, 1995.

————. *Submission to the Minister of Education and Training on OCUA Advisory Memorandum 95-III.* Toronto: Council of Ontario Universities, 1995.

————. *Responding to the Challenges of Change, 1995-1996 Review.* Toronto: Council of Ontario Universities, 1996.

————. *Ontario's Students, Ontario's Future.* Toronto: Council of Ontario Universities, 1999.

————. *Report of the Review Committee: Review of the Ontario Council on Graduate Studies.* Toronto: Council of Ontario Universities, 1999. (Connell Report).

————. *Biennial Review, 1998-2000.* Toronto: Council of Ontario Universities, 2001.

Darling, A.L., M.D. England, D.W. Lang, and R. Lopers-Sweetman, "Autonomy and Control: A University Funding Formula as an Instrument of Public Policy." *Higher Education* 18, 5 (1989): 559-83.

Davis, William G. "The Government of Ontario and the Universities of the Province." In *Governments and the University.* Toronto: York University Press, 1966.

Dodge, David. *Returns to Investment in University Training: The Case of Accountants, Engineers and Scientists.* Kingston: Queen's University Press, 1971.

Dodge, David, and David Stager. "Economic Returns to Graduate Study in Science, Engineering and Business." *Canadian Journal of Economics* 2 (May 1972): 195-98.

Duff, James, and Robert O. Berdahl. *University Government in Canada.* Report of a commission sponsored by the Canadian Association of University Teachers and the Association of Universities and Colleges of Canada. Toronto: University of Toronto Press, 1966.

Dupré, Stefan J. "When Does Accountability Become Accountabilitis?" An Address to the Queen's University Board of Trustees. November 11, 1994.

Fisher, Donald, and Kjell Rubinson. "The Changing Political Economy: The Private and Public Lives of Canadian Universities." In *Universities and Globalization: Critical Perspectives*. Ed. J. Currie and J. Newson. Thousand Oaks, CA: Sage, 1998.

Foote, David K. "A Troubled Future? University Enrolments in Canada and the Provinces." In *Financing Canadian Universities: For Whom and By Whom?* Ed. M. David and Richard Bellaire. Toronto: OISE Press, 1981.

George, Peter J., and James A. McAllister. *The Expanding Role of the State in Canadian Universities: Can University Autonomy and Accountability be Reconciled?* Council of Ontario Universities, Discussion Series, Issue 3. Toronto: Council of Ontario Universities, 1994.

Gordon, A.P. "Ontario Universities' Application Centre." Proposal for the establishment of a central clearing house for applications for admission to the universities of Ontario. Toronto: 1965.

Harris, Robin. *A History of Higher Education in Canada, 1663-1960*. Toronto: University of Toronto Press, 1976.

Jones, Glenn A., ed. *Higher Education in Canada: Different Systems, Different Perspectives*. New York and London: Garland, 1995.

Jones, Glenn A. "Higher Education Policy in Ontario." In *Higher Education Policy: An International Comparative Perspective*. Ed. A.L. Geodebuure, F. Kaiser, P. Maasen, L. Meek, F. van Vught, and E. de Weert. Published for the IAU Press by Pergamon Press: Oxford, 1994.

Macdonald, John B. *Chances and Choices: A Memoir*. Vancouver: Alumni Association UBC, 2000.

Masters, D.C. *Henry John Cody: An Outstanding Life*. Toronto: Dundurn Press, 1995.

Monahan, Edward J. Review of Symons and Page, *Some Questions of Balance*. In *University Affairs*, March 1984.

———. "The Allocation of Financial Support by Formula: The Experience of Ontario." *Minerva* 27, 3 (1988): 370-91.

———. "University-Government Relations in Ontario: The History of a Buffer Body, 1958-1996." *Minerva* 36, 3 (1996): 347-66.

Ontario Ministry of Colleges and Universities. *Options and Futures*. The Commission on the Future Development of the Universities of Ontario. Toronto: Ministry of Colleges and Universities, 1984. (Bovey Report).

———. *Report of the External Advisor to the Minister of Colleges and Universities on the Future Role and Function of the Ontario Council on University Affairs and its Academic Advisory Committee*. Toronto: Ministry of Colleges and Universities, 1988. (Stubbs Report).

———. *Vision 2000: Quality and Opportunity* Toronto: Ministry of Colleges and Universities, 1991.

Ontario Ministry of Education and Training. *No Dead Ends*. Report of the Task Force on Advanced Training to the Minister of Education and Training. Toronto: Ministry of Education and Training, 1993. (Pitman Report).

———. *University Accountability: A Strengthened Framework*. Report of the Task Force on Accountability. Toronto: Ministry of Education and Training, 1993. (Broadhurst Report).

Ontario Council on Graduate Studies. *Graduate Planning in Ontario Universities.* Toronto: Council of Ontario Universities, 1976.

———. *The Appraisals Process in Ontario.* Toronto: Council of Ontario Universities, 1996.

Ontario Council on University Affairs. *First Annual Report, 1974–75.* Toronto: Ministry of Colleges and Universities, 1975.

———. *Second Annual Report, 1975–76.* Toronto: Ministry of Colleges and Universities, 1976.

———. *Third Annual Report, 1976–77.* Toronto: Ministry of Colleges and Universities, 1977.

———. *Fourth Annual Report, 1977–78.* Toronto: Ministry of Colleges and Universities, 1978.

———. *Sixth Annual Report, 1979–80.* Toronto: Ministry of Colleges and Universities, 1980.

———. *Seventh Annual Report, 1980–81.* Toronto: Ministry of Colleges and Universities, 1981.

———. *Report to the Ontario Council on University Affairs on an Assessment of the Appraisals Process.* Toronto: 1986. (Dupré Report).

———. *Thirteenth Annual Report, 1986–87.* Toronto: Ministry of Colleges and Universities, 1987.

———. *Twentieth Annual Report, 1993–94.* Toronto: Ministry of Education and Training, 1994.

———. *Twenty-first Annual Report, 1994–95.* Toronto: Ministry of Education and Training, 1995.

———. *Twenty-second Annual Report, 1995–96.* Toronto: Ministry of Education and Training, 1996.

Ontario Progressive Conservative Party Caucus. *New Directions, Volume Two: A Blueprint for Learning in Ontario.* Toronto: 1992.

Ontario Committee on the Training of Elementary School Teachers. *Report to the Minister.* Toronto: 1966. (MacLeod Report).

Perkins, James A., ed. *Higher Education: From Autonomy to Systems.* New York: International Council for Educational Development, 1972.

Premier's Council of Ontario. *People and Skills in the New Global Economy.* Toronto: Queen's Printer, 1990.

Pritchard, J. Robert S. "Federal Support for Higher Education and Research in Canada: The New Paradigm." 2000 Killam Lecture. Toronto: Killam Foundation, 2000.

Provincial Commission on the Aims and Objectives of Education in the Schools of Ontario. *Living and Learning.* Report. Toronto: 1968. (Hall-Dennis Report).

Ross, Robin. *The Short Road Down: A University Changes.* Toronto: University of Toronto Press, 1984.

Royce, Diana. "University System Co-ordination and Planning in Ontario, 1945 to 1996." Doctor of Education thesis, Ontario Institute for Studies in Education, University of Toronto, 1998.

Skolnik, Michael. "If the cuts are so deep, where is the blood?" *The Review of Higher Education* 9, no. 4 (Summer 1986): 435–55.

———. "University Accountability in the Nineties: Is There a Role for a Provincial Agency?" *Ontario Journal of Higher Education,* (1994): 108-27.

———. "Upsetting the Balance: The Debate on Proposals for Radically Altering the Relationship between Universities and Government in Ontario" *Ontario Journal of Higher Education* (1995): 2-14.

Skolnik, Michael, and Norman S. Rowen. *"Please sir, I want some more": Canadian Universities and Financial Restraint.* Toronto: OISE Press, 1984.

Smith, Stuart L. *Report of the Commission of Inquiry on Canadian University Education.* Ottawa: Association of Universities and Colleges of Canada, 1991. (Stuart Smith Report).

Stenton, Paul. *"The Ontario Operating Grants Formula: Its Development to 1986."* Doctor of Education thesis, University of Toronto, 1992.

Stewart, Edward E. *"The Role of the Provincial Government in the Development of the Universities of Ontario, 1791-1964."* Doctor of Education thesis, University of Toronto, 1970.

Stewart, Harold B. *The Development of Graduate Studies in Ontario Universities between 1960 and 1985.* Toronto: Council of Ontario Universities, 1988.

Stubbs, John O. *The Report of the External Advisor to the Minister of Colleges and Universities on the Future Role and Function of the Ontario Council on University Affairs and its Academic Advisory Committee.* Toronto: Ministry of Colleges and Universities, 1988. (Stubbs Report).

Symons, Thomas H.B., and James E. Page. *Some Questions of Balance: Human Resources, Higher Education and Canadian Studies.* Vol. 3. Ottawa: Association of Universities and Colleges of Canada, 1984.

Trotter, Bernard. *Television and Technology in University Teaching.* Toronto: Committee of Presidents of the Universities of Ontario, 1970.

Watt, L. A.K. *"Graduate Studies and Planning in Ontario: The Role of OCGS 1967-1987."* Unpublished.

Wilson, Benson A. *"UAD and URB: An idiosyncratic set of recollections and observations about the activities of the University Affairs Division and the University Relations Branch, 1974-84."* mimeograph, n.d., 5-6.

Zsigmund, Zoltan. *Population and Enrolment Trends 1961-2001: The Canadian Case.* Ottawa: Statistics Canada, 1975.

In addition:

Minutes of the Meetings of the Committee of Presidents of the Universities of Ontario and of the Council of Ontario Universities. Numbers 1-250, dated March 1962–December 2000.

Index of Names

Subject Index